GETTING SCIENCE

Science is rightly a fundamental part of primary school education, but that doesn't make it easy to teach, especially for teachers without a science background. This straight-talking book from an experienced science writer and communicator looks at how to make the most of science and give primary school children a good grounding in the topic. It shows how to turn a difficult subject into a fun one, and encourages teachers to make the most of the available resources that can make science enjoyable for the children and for the teacher.

There's plenty of help already on curriculum contents, lesson plans and the practical aspects of teaching science, but it's hard to get enthused about a subject that seems alien or, frankly, dull. *Getting Science* sets out to bring the sense of wonder into science. The science in this book is not for the children, but for the adults who have to explain science. Starting with a whirlwind tour of the great milestones of modern science, *Getting Science* goes on to take each of the main curriculum topics and give it a new twist. It provides the information needed to understand the key science topics better and be able to put them across with enthusiasm and energy.

The book is there to help teachers to get children excited by science, to 'get' science rather than just answer science questions. *Getting Science* makes science fun, approachable and comprehensible to those who just don't get it.

Brian Clegg has masters' degrees from Cambridge (Natural Sciences) and Lancaster (Operational Research), and is a fellow of the RSA. He now specializes in writing popular science books and regularly speaks at venues from schools to science festivals.

GETTING SCIENCE

The teacher's guide to exciting and painless primary school science

Brian Clegg

Routledge
Taylor & Francis Group

LONDON AND NEW YORK

First published 2007
by Routledge
2 Park Square, Milton Park, Abingdon, Oxon OX14 4RN

Simultaneously published in the USA and Canada
by Routledge
270 Madison Ave, New York, NY 10016

Routledge is an imprint of the Taylor & Francis Group, an informa business

Typeset in Times New Roman and Gill Sans by
Florence Production Ltd, Stoodleigh, Devon
Printed and bound in Great Britain by
MPG Books Ltd, Bodmin

British Library Cataloguing in Publication Data
A catalogue record for this book is available from
the British Library

Library of Congress Cataloging in Publication Data
Clegg, Brian
    Getting Science: the teacher's guide to exciting and painless primary
    school science/Brian Clegg
        p. cm
    Includes index
    1. Science–Study and teaching (Elementary)   I. Title.
    LB1585.C46 2007
    372.3'5–dc22   2006035125

ISBN10: 0–415–42199–3 (pbk)
ISBN10: 0–203–96185–4 (ebk)

ISBN13: 978–0–415–42199–7 (pbk)
ISBN13: 978–0–203–96185–8 (ebk)

To my wife Gillian
and the teachers of
Wanborough Primary School

CONTENTS

ACKNOWLEDGEMENTS

Thanks to Philip Mudd at Taylor & Francis for making writing this book fun. Thanks also to a number of primary school teachers who I can't name, but who have been very helpful in telling me what's right and wrong with primary school science.

The following items are reproduced with permission:

- Screenshot of Popular Science website by permission of Creativity Unleashed Limited
- Screenshot of New Scientist website by permission of New Scientist

A NOTE ON TERMINOLOGY

I have kept equations and such to a minimum – they are rarely necessary to understand what is going on, and often get in the way.

All measurements are given in the 'scientific' SI (System International) metric units. Temperatures are shown in degrees Celsius (identical with degrees Centigrade).

INTRODUCTION

At the end of the day, what really matters in schools is having excellent science teaching.

Lord Adonis, UK Schools Minister in a talk in 2005

I am not a primary school teacher, which may make you wonder what gives me the right to tell you how to teach. I wouldn't dream of doing so. Of course, I have experienced primary schools, as a pupil (many years ago) and as a parent, but that gives me no real insight into the difficulties of the job. Instead, the content of this book is based on my experience as a writer of popular science books, on what I've learned from being a speaker giving talks on science to children in schools, and on the outcome of speaking to many teachers.

A good number of those I've spoken to did not themselves have a science background, and they describe a situation that can be quite uncomfortable. It can be (and I stress that this remark came from a teacher, not from me) like the blind leading the blind. It's not that the teachers can't do the science. They tell me that they know the curriculum and have appropriate strategies and all those good things in place. But something more is required. Science seems an alien, unfriendly topic. They don't have a good feel for what it's all *about*. Specifically, they find science uninspiring. And that makes it difficult to communicate to the class with any enthusiasm.

My day job is writing popular science books. These are books designed for the general reader, to make science approachable and interesting. And that's the skill I want to pass on to you. Not to tell you how to teach, or to tell you what's in the curriculum – there are plenty of sources for finding that out – but to show you why I believe that science is so fascinating, and how to make it more exciting.

My hope is that, with *Getting Science*, the fundamentals of science will begin to make sense – and that the opportunities to make science come alive will help transform your science teaching.

CHAPTER I

WONDER, ADVENTURE AND HOPE

A common fallacy in much of the adverse criticism to which science is subjected today is that it claims certainty, infallibility and complete emotional objectivity. It would be more nearly true to say that it is based on wonder, adventure and hope.

Cyril Hinshelwood, chemical reaction specialist who laid the groundwork for the discovery of the structure of DNA, quoted in E. J. Bowen's obituary of Hinshelwood, *Chemistry in Britain*

'A sense of wonder.' It's a phrase that is used a lot when describing the golden age of science fiction, back in the 1930s to 1950s, but it's equally applicable to science itself. Science ought to inspire a sense of wonder. It ought to be *thrilling*.

So why doesn't science send a tingle down your spine? I hope you will agree by the end of this book that it should do, whatever your initial views. But it's certainly true that plenty of people, when asked about science, will not come up with words like thrilling, wonderful and adventure. All too often you will hear dull, boring, inaccessible, cold and clinical. For many people – certainly for many adults – it's enough to shrug the shoulders and say 'I don't get science. It doesn't interest me.'

Where did science get this bad press? It starts with the way science is presented in secondary school. At its best, this can indeed be inspiring, but much secondary school science is average and, yes, dull. Because of the shortage of subject teachers, science subjects are often taught by non-specialists who may lack the inspirational drive of someone who truly loves their field. And there is too much focus on the mechanical churning out of formulae and rote-learned facts, with insufficient context both in terms of where the ideas came from and how the science is applied in the world. To make matters worse, the expense of lab equipment coupled with concern about the risk involved in undertaking experiments has reduced the opportunity for hands-on secondary school science. Watching is rarely as engaging as doing.

Though secondary schools are partly responsible, a fair amount of the blame has to be laid at the feet of scientists themselves. A small percentage of scientists are good at communicating with the general public, but it's only fair to say that most of them aren't. In fact, most of them are terrible at it. Despite increased effort being put into science communication, including Famelab, an X-Factor-style competition for science communicators, science isn't put across well by the people who are active in the field. Even a scientist who is good at communicating like Richard Dawkins can often suffer from what seems like arrogance when he shows his very obvious disdain for any views he regards as unscientific. You don't have to be religious, for instance, to find his attacks on belief irritating.

Perhaps the ultimate example of scientists' painful inability to communicate well is the scientific paper. These practical documents are designed to get the point across to other scientists, but too many authors of papers confuse objectivity with dullness. All too often the wording of papers is stilted and confusing, not helped by the convention of writing everything in a detached form ('it was observed that the cationic reaction . . .'). There really is no reason for this. Newton was quite happy to write 'I did this', or 'we did that'. But the convention is there, and it isn't going to change overnight.

Of course, the impenetrable nature of scientists' attempts to communicate isn't helped by the jargon. Scientists use it very heavily, and that's fine in the workplace. But they seem to find it particularly hard to remember that these mystifying words aren't conventional English when they speak to a general audience. I cringe whenever I hear a scientist on the radio, or see one on TV, and they persist in using jargon and unnecessarily overcomplicated language. 'It's the tactile kinaesthetic that is significant to over three standard deviations' is sadly more common than 'it's touch that matters'.

The final nail in the coffin of science's reputation is the approach taken by the media. Despite some improvements in recent years, scientists in films are still more likely to be presented as a caricature than anything approximating to a real person. We might have moved from Colin Clive's agonized *Frankenstein* or Peter Sellers' mad ex-Nazi in *Doctor Strangelove*, but today's movie scientists are little different from the 1960s stereotype suggested by Cyril Hinshelwood's quote at the start of this chapter – claiming certainty, infallibility (though always proved wrong) and complete emotional objectivity.

TV is always telling us how difficult science is. There may be some flashy high-budget science shows like *Horizon*, but they make sure they tell us it's all difficult stuff, or it would be if they hadn't seriously dumbed it down. And though there's a lot to be said for the more recent, lightweight science programmes like *Brainiac* that take a fun, laddish approach to science, they too perpetuate the image of white-coated boffins who aren't of this world.

The good news, though, is that while most adults think that science is dull, this isn't the case for children (at least, not for primary school children). They have no problem with engaging that childlike sense of wonder. It comes naturally to them until we socialize and educate it out of them. They are prepared to be awed by the wonders of the universe. They don't worry about science being too hard. For them, done the right way, science is an adventure.

What we need to do is to transplant that sense of wonder into all of us, an operation that I spend a fair amount of my time attempting to perform. When I'm not writing books like this, I write popular science. This leads to an amusing if frustrating exchange when I first meet people. They will ask what I do, and I say I'm an author. Their eyes light up: authors are interesting. Okay, things go a little downhill when I say it's non-fiction – after all, novels are much more glamorous – but when I then say I write popular science, their eyes glaze over. The assumption is that science books are hard and boring. Textbooks. A necessary evil. But a good popular science book is quite different.

One or two such books have come into the general public eye, though oddly the two best known titles are not ideal examples. Stephen Hawking's *A Brief History of Time* was certainly a hugely popular buy, but an awful lot of people, when pressed, will admit to having left it on a shelf unread, or only getting as far as the first few chapters. It isn't great as a popular science book, because Hawking doesn't always understand what is difficult to grasp. The other example is Bill Bryson's *A Short History of Everything*. The main problem here is that it is anything but short. Although it's a very readable book (if not as good as Bryson's superb travel books), it gives the impression that science books have to be weighty tomes that you need a wheelbarrow to carry around.

In fact there are many popular science books out there now that really do the job very well. Something I would strongly urge is reading a few of them to get a feel for the way science is put across, and also for some of the excitement that science can generate. I will point out a few specific books along the way, but the best thing is to take a look at the *www.popularscience.co.uk* website, which reviews these books. Take a dip into the five-star-rated 'best' section for some inspiration.

What we haven't identified yet is why a sense of wonder is appropriate for science, and how to get that across. A lot of this will come out in the rest of the book, but I want to be clear upfront what the driving forces are.

Why a sense of wonder? It doesn't take a huge amount of imagination to see that this is an entirely appropriate response. We're talking about how the universe works, where it comes from, how it got here and where it's going. We're looking at how we, ourselves, work. We're exploring incredible phenomena such as light or gravity or what it means to be alive. Some have accused science of taking the joy and beauty out of nature. Keats famously accused Newton of 'unweaving the rainbow' in his poem 'Lamia':

Do not all charms fly
At the mere touch of cold philosophy?
There was an awful rainbow once in heaven:
We know her woof, her texture; she is given
In the dull catalogue of common things.
Philosophy will clip an Angel's wings,
Conquer all the mysteries by rule and line,
Empty the haunted air, and gnomèd mine
Unweave a rainbow.

When Keats mentions philosophy, he means what we would now call science. But the poet misses the point. To know, for instance, the immense and delicate complexity and the wondrous mechanisms in the human body doesn't make people more dull and common. Instead we realize just how amazing a human being – or even a housefly or a virus – is. Light isn't made less exciting by knowing more about it. Instead something that is easy to take for granted becomes much more wonderful.

In looking at how to put this across we can learn a lot from the popular science writer. Although such books are largely aimed at adults, the techniques apply to all ages, and there are also examples of popular science books (as opposed to textbooks, reference books and picture books) aimed at children, such as the highly successful *Horrid Science* series. Top tips that the popular science perspective of such books gives us are:

- put the science into context
- sprinkle it with amazing facts
- find it in real life
- make it hands-on
- make it fun.

Of course a lot of this is meat and drink to the teacher, particularly at the primary school level. But the popular science perspective can give a rather different flavour to a well-known fact, so let's consider each of those points in a little more detail.

PUTTING THE SCIENCE INTO CONTEXT

One problem that presenting science can have is that it is sometimes dry and detached. It can help to add context. How did this particular scientific fact or theory come about? What other theories (the stranger the better) were around at the time? Who came up with the theory, and what bizarre things happened in their lives?

Bringing in people overcomes one of the big resistance factors – that science is impersonal. I went all through the school system and through a natural science degree specializing in physics without ever finding out much about the key characters behind the formulae and the theories that were being drummed into me. But we all like people. We're all interested in people – just look at the popularity of soap operas and reality TV shows. If you can bring a touch of the soap to science – tell a little about the individual, and his or her quirks and adventures – the subject already has more appeal.

Alternative theories from the past, ideas that your audience is unlikely to have come across, are great for putting science into context. Not only can you see what environment the theory was developed in, but you can help the children get a better idea of the scientific method by giving them the alternative theory and asking them which sounds better, and how they would tell the difference.

For example, it used to be thought that creatures like maggots were spontaneously generated – they simply sprang into being from nothing. This resulted in some pretty strange ideas, which could amuse a class. At the same time, they could look at how you would test to see if maggots truly appeared spontaneously from rotting meat, as was honestly believed by intelligent people. (It doesn't hurt that there's a touch of the disgusting in the example – grossness always goes down well.) How could you test to see if maggots really did appear from nowhere on rotting meat? What would you do to make sure they weren't coming from somewhere else? There are lots of opportunities arising out of context.

SPRINKLING IT WITH AMAZING FACTS

When I write a popular science book, I first have to persuade a publisher that it's worth spending money on. (Sadly, they have a strong urge to spend as little money as possible.) This involves writing a proposal which has to sell the idea to a group of people who are mostly arts graduates with very little knowledge of (and in some cases, little interest in) science. A colleague once said that the best way to set the level of a proposal is to imagine it being read by Bridget Jones. Selling the idea to this group of people is a little like making a concept attractive to children. One of the essential tricks of the trade in a good science proposal is to sprinkle it with amazing facts. These should be little snippets of information that surprise the reader – and it's just as valuable a technique for making science interesting to children.

Take light as an example. As far as I'm concerned, this is an inherently exciting subject. Light is something so insubstantial that billions upon billions of photons are constantly being destroyed in your eye to make your vision work. Yet a photon can cross space for millions of years undisturbed. For many people, though, light is just a commonplace. When I was selling a book on light to a publisher I came up with a string of little 'wow!' facts. For example:

- There are a lot of photons out there – *a 100 watt light bulb produces around 100,000,000,000 photons every billionth of a second.*

- Slow glass could give us windows that see anywhere in the world – *scientists have managed to slow down the passage of light to a crawl through special materials. If this could be taken to the extreme of taking several months to pass through, you could imagine glass manufactured in slow glass farms, looking out on beautiful views which would then be placed in buildings, where you would have a real view out onto the scenery.*

- We are creatures of light – *the only thing that holds atoms together is a constant stream of invisible light passing between the electrons and the nucleus. Every single atom in our bodies is glued together with light. Like everything else in the universe, we are filled with light.*

- You can't run away from a laser – *sometimes light behaves in totally unexpected ways. If you were to travel at 99 per cent of the speed of light away from someone shooting you with a laser, the light would still come towards you at the full 300,000,000 metres per second. Unlike anything else, however fast you move away from or towards light, it still comes at you at the same speed.*

- The human eye can see a candle flame ten miles away – *your eye is remarkably sensitive, needing only five or six of the individual photons that make up a light beam to trigger a response. Because of this, in clear conditions you can see a candle flame over ten miles away. Sadly, thanks to pollution, there's hardly anywhere in the world now that has such truly clear conditions.*

- Astronomers use galaxies as vast lenses – *Einstein's general relativity predicts that gravity should bend light. Astronomers use the immense gravitational pull of distant galaxies to focus light from objects that are incredibly far away. The tiny quantities of light heading off in different directions are bent inwards so that they arrive together at the Earth, making a visible image. Strangely, this means that the distant objects that can be seen best are those that are hidden behind galaxies – the light gets bent around the outside of the galaxy.*

- The night sky shouldn't be black – *look in any direction and there should be stars, adding up to a background glow, so for years it was a mystery (now solved) why there is blackness between the stars.*

- Algae rules – *more light energy from the sun is absorbed in photosynthesis by tiny algae in the sea than by all the plants on the land.*

- Our eyes are incredibly flexible – *light on a sunny day is 100 times brighter than a typical office, but our eyes balance out the difference. Full moonlight, which we can see quite well by, is around 300,000 times weaker than sunlight.*

- Death rays date back 2,000 years – *the invention of the laser made it easy to produce a killing beam of light, but back in 287 BC, Archimedes devised giant focusing mirrors that concentrated the sun's light on the Roman fleet and set some of them alight. Unfortunately for Archimedes, the Romans still got through and killed him.*

- Light dwarfs the weather – *we're all used to seeing TV shows about the awesome forces of nature, the unparalleled power of the storm, etc. All wind and storm is generated by sunlight, so light is the power behind that awesome force. What's more, the whole Earth's weather uses up only 2 per cent of the light energy reaching us from the sun.*

Convinced? Normally, of course, you wouldn't get such a concentrated dose of amazing facts, but by dusting them through a book (or a lesson), it gives a subject more appeal. The facts above were largely chosen to appeal to adults. Sometimes the same ones will work for children, but you can pick out facts that seem quite ordinary to us, but still amaze a younger audience. Of course, you need to make sure the facts themselves are understandable, and it never hurts to throw in a few 'gross' or 'disgusting' facts if you can come up with them.

FINDING IT IN REAL LIFE

Science can seem very detached from reality. Popular science often uses the favourite trick of TV news, relating the topic to the everyday life of the audience. Just as the news team, when presenting budget results, will inevitably have a go at saying 'what does it mean for you' and giving real life examples of Mr and Mrs Smith who will feel these effects from the budgetary changes, so popular science – particularly children's popular science – will relate scientific facts to things we all know.

There are three strands to this. In part it's a matter of applications. Although science can be purely theoretical with no concept of being useful, we naturally look for ways to introduce what the science means for the world – to find out what will be different as a result of it. When I wrote my book *The God Effect*, on the obscure-sounding topic of quantum entanglement – in fact a truly fascinating physical phenomenon which we will revisit later – I dedicated around three-quarters of the book to the applications of the science. What can it do for us? And what might be possible using it in the future? In this particular case, there's a rich seam already under development – unbreakable encryption, quantum computers and teleportation, to give the headline examples – which makes this an easy choice. But even if the applications are more mundane (look at the sort of thing Adam Hart-Davis does), looking for the real life uses of the science is essential.

Secondly, it's possible to make use of the natural occurrences of the science. Not 'what can we do with it?' but 'where in our everyday world can we see it in action?' Practically every scientific theory of any significance, from relativity and quantum theory to evolution, has direct implications for the everyday items and living things that surround us in the classroom, and in the world immediately outside the window.

The third opportunity to make science real is to look for the slightly less direct, but still significant, implication of the science. This can often produce a double whammy – because it might not be expected by the audience, and it can throw in a 'fascinating facts' element. Take the apparently simple question of what we humans are made of. Let's home in specifically on the carbon atoms that are essential for all types of life, forming the structural backbone of the DNA, proteins and other complex molecules that make life possible. Short of a nuclear reaction, those carbon atoms that the classroom is packed with are pretty well indestructible. So where did the components of your hand, or your eye come from?

At a first level you can look at the way existing carbon atoms are consumed and built into the new structures, but that's just a form of recycling. Eventually you still have to find where those atoms came from originally. The answer, a surprise to many people and a fascinating image, is that our carbon atoms were forged in exploding stars, billions of years ago. As the old sixties song has it, we are stardust. The carbon atoms that make up our bodies were formed from smaller atoms in the inferno of supernovae, massive exploding suns. A fact like this manages both to tie the science into the everyday – carbon is not exactly a rarity – and to provide the wonderful in the image of these atoms being formed in a distant star.

MAKING IT HANDS-ON

Getting hands-on experience is a tenet of school science at all levels, but laboratories are expensive, and experiments often have a degree of risk (even if this is carefully controlled and calculated), so a lot of secondary schools have cut back on the hands-on in favour of more demonstrations by the teacher.

This is a terrible shame, and must not be allowed to filter through to primary schools. Most primary school experiments are safe and low-cost. The challenge is to build on them and help the children make useful observations.

One essential here is a degree of flexibility, and that means having a good understanding of the process being experimented on. If a particular experiment does not generate the required results, it isn't good science to say 'that's not what we expected, so we'll ignore it. *This* is what really should have happened.' Instead it's essential to say 'I didn't expect that. Let's find out just what happened', and look into the way the experiment was undertaken and how that produced the result that was seen.

Even 'proper' scientists regularly produce unexpected results. Sometimes it is because the theory they were testing was, in fact, wrong. At other times they will have made a mistake in the way they carried out the experiment or interpreted the results. Make sure the children know to look for all possibilities.

In this particular category, the school has a huge advantage over the popular science writer. There is very little opportunity to make things hands-on in a book. Even if it's the sort of book where you can include little exercises (say a maths book), plenty of people won't do them. Children's popular science books often contain experiments to try out. These are most successful when they can be done with very little preparation, and without too much adult help. But when they are done, they will make it easier to bring the point home. Both my children, throughout primary school, were more likely to tell me about a science lesson when they came home if they did something during it.

Where hands-on isn't practical, or is too dangerous, it is increasingly possible to give a virtual hands-on experience. A program, DVD or website that has interactive features will never be quite the same as handling something for real. (Try comparing in your mind the experience of interacting with a snake online and holding one in the classroom.) But it's a lot better than no interactivity at all.

MAKING IT FUN

Well, of course, you make everything fun, as much as possible, don't you? But in putting the 'popular' into popular science, we have to give a fact-based subject the appeal of a good story. A great popular science book is just as much a page-turner as a good novel. A lot of this will come from the other aspects above, but it also has to be about the way you tell it. If you haven't had a look at one recently, pick up a children's popular science book such as one of the *Horrid Science* series and see how it makes the content fun.

There's an element of grossology – as we've already mentioned, there's something very appealing about examples that involve something yucky or otherwise unpleasant (hence the 'Horrid' in *Horrid Science*). There's the use of cartoons and jokes (not always very good jokes, it's true, but jokes nonetheless). And underneath it all is just a sense that the whole thing really is fun.

This is an important factor, but perhaps the hardest to deliver. If you are not comfortable with the science you are teaching – for whatever reason – it is very difficult to make it fun. It will come across as something you are nervous about, rather than enjoying. The only way to succeed is to become truly comfortable with science, whatever your educational background and personal experience.

Popular science writers have it easy in this respect. We're (mostly) in this business because we love science and want to communicate the subject. It's not possible to artificially generate that enthusiasm, but what you can do is expose yourself as much as possible to popular science books and TV shows. Find the bits you can be enthusiastic about, and use those to model a sense of excitement. Anyone's sense of wonder can be dented by a cynic. Make sure that yours gives the appearance of being intact. The more you practise giving the impression of enthusiasm, the easier it will become to really mean it.

WONDER, ADVENTURE AND HOPE – ESSENTIALS

Let's have a quick reminder of what has been covered.

- Remember that sense of wonder.
- Use the popular science tricks of the trade:

  - put the science into context
  - sprinkle it with amazing facts
  - find it in real life
  - make it hands-on
  - make it fun.

CHAPTER 2

SCIENCE AROUND US AND THE EXPERIMENT

You look at science (or at least talk of it) as some sort of demoralising invention of man, something apart from real life, and which must be cautiously guarded and kept separate from everyday existence. But science and everyday life cannot and should not be separated.

Rosalind Franklin, a key player in the discovery of the structure of DNA, in an undated letter to her father, Ellis Franklin

IT'S NOT ALL LABS AND WHITE COATS

The laboratory still plays a huge role in scientific research, but the picture most of us have of scientific work is not very accurate. Mention science and you are likely to conjure up for most people a picture of a group of men (almost always men) wearing glasses, clustered about workbenches in white coats, playing with test tubes.

It's hard to know where to start with what's wrong with this picture. Some people do still wear lab coats, it's true. And we shouldn't try to re-write history on the balance between men and women in science over the years. Until the twentieth century, practically every major scientist was male. Marie Curie was the first very visible female scientist. Since that time, things have gradually become more balanced. But it is a slow process. In my final-year Cambridge physics course photograph that hangs on the wall by my desk, of 103 students, I think eight are female (this is a little vague, as the hair preferences of the 1970s make it difficult to be sure). The proportions are better now, but you will still see more men than women in the field.

That doesn't make that mental picture right, though. The image most people have is of a school chemistry lab, rather than the real thing. But the yawn-making stereotype is less important than the fact that this image misses the point of science. The lab is a valuable tool in the process of scientific investigation, but what's interesting is not the lab, it's the discovery itself. What matters is the knowledge that comes out of the lab work and how that is going to enable us to have a better understanding of the world all around us. Science is, fundamentally, a way to look at aspects of our universe through different eyes. To be able to understand more – and to enjoy more.

The great thing about this is that everything becomes an opportunity to expand scientific knowledge. Just observing everyday life. Why and how does the sun wake us up in the morning? Why and how does eating our breakfast stop us feeling hungry? Or taking a look around us. How does the fly manage to walk up a smooth wall? Why when we look through a window do we see both the world outside and a reflection of the room inside? Not only does science help answer these questions, it reflects our sense of wonder.

Real labs can be disappointingly high-tech these days. One of the reasons I personally did not opt for a career in science was because of the way practically everything in physics, even by the 1970s, had come down to interpreting numbers that appeared on the outside of black boxes, or usually now on computers. Admittedly you had to assemble the innards of your black box – but it wasn't exactly hands-on. Vast pieces of commercial machinery, from electron microscopes to mass spectrometers, often loom large in the lab. A modern laboratory is as different from school science as a huge industrial food factory is from making chocolate-coated rice crispies in the classroom.

SCIENCE ACROSS THE DANUBE

That's not to say that science has to be boring, or locked up in the confines of a gloomy room with breezeblock walls. Take one example of real science at work, in the study of quantum entanglement, a subject we'll meet in the next chapter.

Researchers in Vienna wanted to set up a link across the river Danube. This was partly for publicity reasons (science needs money, and publicity never hurts when you are looking for funding), but also because they needed to demonstrate that their idea would work in normal conditions, rather than the rarefied atmosphere of the lab.

The experiment had to be run at night, as they were using light beams, and didn't want them to be overwhelmed by daylight. It was already freezing cold when they set up their hand-built instruments by the river. They managed to get some shelter by putting one of their stations in an old freight container, but this was hardly the nicest of environments as they tried to take readings without their chattering teeth disrupting the equipment. To make matters worse, they needed to route a cable between the two stations either side of the river, so had to resort to the sewers to set up this link.

They were much luckier with the next stage of their experiment, which was to send their beam across two legs of around 7 and 8 kilometres across the city. This wasn't an arbitrary distance. It turns out that sending a light beam through around 6 kilometres of air at ground level is very similar to sending a beam up to an overhead satellite. They wanted to see how practical it would be to route their special beam up to a satellite station. Even though the satellite might be 35,000 kilometres above the Earth's surface, the air thins so quickly that 6 kilometres at ground level has about the same tendency to scatter the beam.

For this second stage, the researchers were loaned offices in two skyscrapers. The transmitting station was on top of a small astronomical observatory that nestles in the hills above Vienna, with receivers in two of Vienna's skyscrapers to enable a clear line of sight across the ancient city. After the experience of trying to set up delicate equipment in the freezing cold Vienna night, the decision was made to put at least some of this experiment inside the buildings, though this attempt to work in comfort nearly wrecked the whole exercise.

Like many modern glazed structures, the Vienna Twin Towers, one of the two office buildings in the experiment, had special window panels that reduce the transmission of infrared. This has the double bonus of cutting down on heat losses from the building, and stopping the office from turning into a greenhouse on sunny days. Unfortunately that same coating totally blocked the photons for the experiment. Nothing was getting through. It was lucky for the team that the enlightened owners of the building were prepared to replace the window in the office housing the experiment with conventional glass to enable the transmission to go ahead without further risk of frostbite.

WHAT'S THE POINT OF EXPERIMENTS?

Whether in the lab, in the field, or in your classroom, experiments remain at the heart of science. The importance of understanding the experimental method is emphasized in the curriculum, but all too often the real nature of a scientific experiment is misunderstood. To see what it's all about, it helps to take a quick look back to the time before the modern scientific method was established.

Go far enough back, to the Ancient Greeks, and science did not exist. In fact this was doubly true. The term itself didn't exist. 'Science' would later be derived from the Latin word scientia, but that just means knowledge. The closest thing the Greeks had was natural philosophy. To make matters worse, the scientific method was entirely alien to the way the Greeks thought. Seen from today, the approach they took fits somewhere between puzzling and laughable. It was armchair science at the extreme. A philosopher would come up with a theory – say that the planets were supported on clear, glass-like spheres. Another philosopher would come up with another theory – perhaps that the planets weren't solid, but small holes in a dark sphere that let the cosmic light through. Then the points of view would be debated. Whoever won the argument now held the accepted theory.

There was no thought of testing the theory against reality. It was right because it had won the debate. Remarkably, the ideas that won the debates back then, once established, held for over 1,500 years. (If the approach of deciding the truth based on who can argue best seems crazy to you, it's sobering to think that we still rely on this approach in courts of law.)

It was only in the medieval period in the West, as the full panoply of Greek thinking was fed back to Europe through the enhancing filter of Arab translators and commentators, that received wisdom began to be questioned – and even then such questioners were in a minority. When Roger Bacon, the thirteenth-century English friar and early scientist, said 'He therefore who wishes to rejoice without doubt in regard to the truths underlying phenomena must know how to devote himself to experiment', he was an oddity amongst his university colleagues who thought it was enough to know what the ancient philosophers said.

Even so, by medieval times, there was a move from debating pure theory to include some learning from practice. Sometimes this was, crudely, what we would call experiment, but all too often what was used as fact was only experience. Looking back it can be difficult to distinguish, as in Latin (which was used for pretty well all scientific writing up to Newton's time) there wasn't a true distinction. Bacon (not to be confused with the later Elizabethan Francis Bacon, who was one of the first to formalize the scientific method) describes clear experiments in the modern sense, but is equally likely to report how best to handle a basilisk, based on stories he had heard – on the doubtful basis (in a scientific sense) of experience.

EXPERIMENT VERSUS EXPERIENCE

As human beings, we are programmed to learn from experience. It's the original basis of story telling – passing on experiences (true or imagined) to help others. This is a powerful tool for survival. If one person has a near-death experience with a wild boar, then passing that on can be the factor that helps others survive a meeting with one of these dangerous animals. But there's a problem with experience when it comes to science. Experience is based on individual observations, often uncorroborated, and is frequently passed on from person to person, the details changing along the way. Experience does not offer anything approximating to truth. It relies on our very flawed ability to casually observe something happening and report back accurately what was seen.

Unfortunately, flawed though experience is, our natural inclination to learn from it means we find it very difficult to ignore. We still rely on witness evidence in court, even though it has been proved that under certain circumstances human beings are disastrously bad at accurately recalling what they have seen. This is made horribly obvious in a video produced by the Visual Cognition Laboratory at the University of Illinois.

The video features a group of people playing a game with two basketballs in a corridor. The audience watching the video is asked to count how many times the balls are bounced. They concentrate hard – the action is moving quite fast, and inevitably the audience members come up with a range of numbers at the end of the exercise. Then they are asked if they saw anything unusual in the video. The vast majority will say no, nothing unusual happened. I have tried this several times and I have always got the same result from most of the audience. No, nothing out of the ordinary happened. Some people played basketball, that's all.

Imagine, for a moment, the members of this audience were witnesses to a crime. They are telling us nothing happened. But they are wrong. Part way through the video, someone dressed in a gorilla costume strolls across the field of view. The gorilla stops in the middle of the players, beats its chest, then strolls off again in an unhurried fashion. Yet most people do not see it. In fact many won't even believe it happened, even if they are shown the video again – they insist it was a different video that they first saw. (You can see the video at viscog.beckman.uiuc.edu/ grafs/demos/15.html. You are likely to see the gorilla because you know it's there, but try it on some people who don't know what to expect. Tell them it's an experiment on counting skills – they have to count how many times the balls hit the ground. And then ask them what they saw.)

We think of sight as operating like a video camera, but it's not like that at all. The brain doesn't simply register what's projected onto the retina at the back of the eye as a series of images. (It's just as well, since that image is upside down. One of the lesser contributions of the brain is to turn that image over. If you wear glasses that make everything upside down, your brain will eventually correct this and stop inverting the image.) Instead of taking in a whole picture, the brain uses different components of the light hitting the eye to separately analyse movement, outlines and other aspects of the contents of your field of view. The actual 'view' you get of the world is an artificial reconstruction.

It has to be. For instance, our eyes don't stay steadily focused on what we're looking at, they jump around in extremely fast little movements called saccades – but the brain smoothes it all out so we appear to see a steady view. Similarly the brain paints out the blind spot on your retina where there is no image picked up because that's where the 'wiring' that links the eye to the brain is connected. To see proof of this complex ability of the brain to turn jerky and disconnected images into a steady picture, all you need do is watch your TV, or take a trip down to the local multiplex.

If you look up cinema in a textbook or on the web, many of the sources you find will tell you that the illusion of moving pictures works by persistence of vision

– unfortunately this is a scientific myth. Persistence of vision was dreamed up in Victorian times to try to explain why we saw a sequence of still pictures as smooth movement, but it doesn't work as an explanation. If we experienced persistence of vision at the cinema, we would see a series of images superimposed on top of each other, not a moving picture. (And in fact the after-image effect in the eye is too slow to cope with the frame speed of film, so such a mechanism couldn't work.) Instead it is the systems in our brain that are used to filter out unwanted information and produce our normal picture of the world that manage to do the same with the broken-up information projected from a cine film.

What's good for the movies is less helpful when it comes to accurate reporting. That same facility to assemble an apparently complete picture from parts of the information means that when we focus on certain aspects of the view we can totally miss others. Hence the inability to see the gorilla in the basketball game. But this also means that witness evidence in court should be treated with a strong degree of suspicion; and that we need to suppress our natural inclination to accept related experience as true if we are to conduct real science.

To heap even more confusion onto the process, science often involves taking a statistical or probabilistic approach – and we simply don't have a built-in understanding of probability and statistics: they are unnatural to most people. That's why casinos make so much money. Statistically we know that smoking is horribly dangerous, but that doesn't stop interviews being shown with old people who say 'I've smoked forty a day for fifty years and it hasn't harmed me.' This tells us nothing. We already know that there will be some people who get away with it. Their existence doesn't change the facts, yet we tend to give undue weight to the stories that people tell us.

So experience is a dangerous phenomenon to trust when trying to be scientific. Robert Park makes a wonderful point in his book *Voodoo Science*: 'Data is not the plural of anecdote.' However much we are inclined to think 'there's no smoke without fire', a few stories about something that may or may not have happened under uncontrolled circumstances give absolutely no indication of scientific fact.

THE SCIENTIFIC METHOD

So what is the difference between an anecdotal experience and a scientific experiment? Let's take the example of homeopathy. Anecdotal evidence might say 'I took a homeopathic remedy and I got better.' I have plenty of friends who say this, and we've all come across people like Prince Charles who are very enthusiastic about homeopathic cures. What we tend to forget is that there are many other explanations for what happened, none of which are tested by experience. We just assume that it was the medicine that made a difference. Yet the person who was cured might have got better anyway. Or it could be that belief in the medicine resulted in the cure –

there is good evidence that the placebo effect, the body's ability to self-heal given the belief that a treatment is working, is real. Equally an anecdotal failure doesn't disprove homeopathy. If someone took a homeopathic remedy and said it did nothing for them, they might have taken the wrong prescription, or upset the workings of it in some way.

Science takes two approaches to understanding homeopathy. The first is to look for a mechanism. This is a fundamental approach in science, but relatively new to medicine, which until recently was more a collection of experience than a science. Various remedies were tried, and if they worked anecdotally, the remedies were assumed to be good. Only in the last fifty years have we started to understand the mechanisms behind the medicine. Knowing what a drug is made up of, and how it will interact with the body, is now usually possible, but that's a very new thing. So science wants to know what is in a homeopathic remedy and how it works.

There is a problem with this approach, though, as far as homeopathy is concerned, because it's hard to find just what the remedy is. The technique used in homeopathy is to take a poison that can produce similar symptoms to the illness being treated, and dilute it. This is a wholly unscientific concept – there is no reason whatsoever to assume a poison producing similar symptoms will have any relationship with a disease – but that's what was thought when homeopathy was first dreamed up. The assumption has to be, if homeopathy *does* work, that the original reasoning is wrong, and homeopathy operates in a different way.

This is perfectly possible. It has been common in history to assume something works for one reason, and to find out later that it works in a totally different way. But the trouble is, homeopathic remedies are diluted so much that there is not a single molecule of the active ingredient left. A homeopathic remedy is pure water (or a sugar pill with a drop of pure water on it). So if there is an effect from the homeopathic remedy itself, rather than the placebo effect, it has to be down to something we don't yet understand, like water somehow remembering the missing ingredient.

So that's one bit of bad news for homeopathy, but it doesn't disprove its existence – it just disproves the original theory of how homeopathy works, and makes it rather less likely that homeopathy has any value, because we struggle to find an explanation.

The second approach scientists can take is to try out homeopathic remedies under controlled conditions. This means first of all having a large sample of tests. There is no point just taking a few examples, because this is not much better than an anecdote. We need enough information to have a good chance of a cure not being a random occurrence. Maths gives us useful tools to establish how likely it is that something happens randomly, or whether there is a cause behind it.

We also need to compare the result of using the remedy against doing nothing. Some people will get better without treatment – is there a difference? And we need to compare the remedy with a placebo. Is the homeopathic remedy any better than an apparently identical sugar pill that hasn't had anything added to it? If it isn't, then the remedy isn't doing anything, even though the patient gets better. It's the person's own body doing the curing.

Ideally, the experiment should be in controlled circumstances. The more outside influences can affect the subjects (what they eat, for instance, or where they go), the less effective the control, which is why scientists like to confine experiments to the laboratory as much as possible. And then there's the matter of who knows what. Where the experiment involves people who are conscious of what is going on, it's essential that the subjects don't know whether they are taking the homeopathic medicine or the placebo. That knowledge will change how they react. More surprisingly, perhaps, we can't let the researcher know either.

In a fascinating piece of psychological research, a group of students were asked to do some tests on rats. Half the students were told that their rats were super rats, highly intelligent, capable of doing almost anything. The other students were told that they had the dregs. The rats they were using were stupid and a waste of space. Not surprisingly, the super rats did significantly better in the test than the stupid rats. At least, not surprisingly until it was revealed they were all identical rats. What made the difference was the experimenters' unconscious expectations. The super rats were more carefully handled, and the experimenters tended to be more generous in their recording of what happened. The stupid rats weren't treated as well, and the experimenters were very hard on their results, never giving them the benefit of the doubt.

For this reason, medical testing uses double-blind testing. Neither the people taking part in the test, nor the researchers, know which remedy has been used, until the test is over. Homeopathy has so far largely proved pretty well identical to a placebo in proper tests. This doesn't mean that homeopathic medicine isn't worth taking if you believe in it, as that belief can make it work. But the mechanism behind it is likely to be the body fixing itself in the belief that the medicine will make it better.

WHICH CAME FIRST, THE CHICKEN OR THE EGG?

Before leaving the exploration of the experiment itself, it's worth taking a look at one of the biggest problems in getting a scientific experiment right – establishing causality. This problem is highlighted in the homeopathic trials, but needs bringing out into the open. Consider this statement:

> The FTSE 100 was down 50 points today on concerns over a possible increase in interest rates.

That's typical of the sort of remark you'll hear on the news, and it is totally unscientific.

IS ECONOMICS A SCIENCE?

It's interesting that economics is treated as a science when it is so dependent on ideas that can't be tested. It's true that economics uses the same mathematical tools as many of the sciences, but it is less clear that much of it has any scientific validity. A good indicator is the way that the theories that have won many economists Nobel prizes have been discarded within decades of the prize being awarded. The theories behind Nobel prizes in the sciences have certainly been built on and extended over the years, but very few of them have been discarded. It's arguable that economic science is still in the classical age, in my classification of scientific eras (see page 29), and hasn't even reached the clockwork.

There are millions of different reasons why shares can move in price, and there's so much interaction and feedback between the various elements that it's pretty well impossible to say why anything actually happens. What the pundits really meant was 'The FTSE 100 was down 50 points today, and there were also fears of a possible increase in interest rates. It's possible that these worries influenced the stock prices' – but that's admittedly a bit clumsy.

The trouble is, as so often when trying to be scientific, that our brains are wired to make best guesses, and to classify things in nice, clear-cut boxes, so that we can spot a possible danger ahead and take action. Let's revisit that old saying 'there's no smoke without fire'. It's patently not true. There are plenty of ways of producing smoke with no fire attached – but when we see clouds of smoke we immediately tend to think 'fire', just in case. The same thing happens with the way the phrase is used in real life – many of the conclusions drawn this way are based on something that's just not true.

Why do we find it so difficult to deal with these false conclusions? Because we aren't designed to handle probability and statistics, and we are very strongly oriented to finding patterns. If two things happen together, they could be connected – causal (one causes the other) – or unconnected – coincidental. Even though statistics tell us coincidences should happen all the time (or things would be very strange), when a coincidence does occur we are amazed. We assume there has to be some sort of linkage.

Shortly after the Second World War, for several years, the birth rate in the UK almost exactly followed the number of bananas being imported into the country. Plot the two on a graph, and they seem very obviously connected. But there was no causal link. The bananas did not result in pregnancies. In scientific speak, the two numbers were correlated – they matched – but were not causal – there was no link, it was just coincidence, or driven by another common factor.

Every now and then, if you toss a coin, you will get a series where the same face comes up repeatedly. Let's say you get head, head, head, head, head and head. Now you toss the coin again. Science will tell you that the coin has no memory. It has no idea what came before. So there's still a 50:50 chance of the next toss coming up with a head. But our love of patterns, and deep-seated desire to see causality, makes us think 'Surely it's time for a tail; it's more likely to be a tail this time.'

Take another example – the National Lottery. In the main lottery draw, six balls are drawn from a total of 49. Let's not bother about the bonus ball. The last draw before I wrote was 04, 21, 25, 37, 45, 46. Nobody comments on this. No one is amazed. There is nothing special about it. Yet if the balls that were drawn were 01, 02, 03, 04, 05, 06 there would probably be a national outcry. 'There's something wrong with the machine', people would splutter. 'They weren't shuffled up properly.' But that combination is *exactly* as likely to come up as 04, 21, 25, 37, 45, 46. There is no difference in chances at all. But when we see a pattern, we expect there to be a cause. (Incidentally, to get a feel for your chances of winning the lottery, remember that they are the same as 01, 02, 03, 04, 05, 06 coming up.)

So, to get away from false expectations, an experiment should have controls, which in scientific terms are just ways of limiting the causes of what's happening. If you can fix everything else and just vary one thing, it's much clearer what's going on. Experimenters have to try to eliminate all the things that are changing to follow the result of a single variable. This is often a lot more possible in the laboratory than it is in the real world.

For example, if you had an experiment where temperature and pressure both varied, it wouldn't be obvious which was involved, so you could fix the pressure (say). It might be that you need to remove the air altogether, to eliminate the impact of air molecules. It might be that you need to isolate the experiment from the ground, to avoid vibrations, perhaps from passing traffic, from interfering with the results. Scientists don't always get it right. It is very difficult to always be aware of what else can be having an effect on your experiment, so you can't always eliminate everything, but experimenters expect to have a good try.

Out in the real world, it's much harder to eliminate extra factors. You have to find ways to cheat the system. For example, in studying how personality is developed, how do you know whether a particular personality trait was formed by the impact of the environment or as a result of inheritance? You can't take the same person and run them through two lives, one totally isolated from the world, the other without a genetic background. But you can look for opportunities where a factor can be eliminated. For instance, identical twins are genetically the same, so that makes them a good control, enabling you to ignore genetic variations. (One of the discoverers of

DNA, Francis Crick, proving that some scientists really are like the stereotype, thought that parents of twins ought to be encouraged to give one away so that experiments could be undertaken on twins in different environments.)

At other times, researchers have to resort to complex maths, which they hope pushes unwanted influences out of the way, but such results are considerably more prone to error than those from a fully controlled experiment.

LIES, DAMNED LIES, AND STATISTICS

We've already seen how probability and statistics can be the cause of confusion when dealing with coin tosses or the lottery. It's worth spending a little longer on this subject, because it is often behind the inaccuracy of experience.

'Statistics' and 'probability' are terms that are frequently used with more enthusiasm than accuracy. Victorian Prime Minister Benjamin Disraeli (later quoted by Mark Twain, who now often gets the credit) said 'There are three kinds of lies: lies, damned lies and statistics.' This contempt for statistics dates back to the original use of the word where it was a political statement of facts about a country or community (the 'stat' part of the word statistics is as in 'state'). The origin of Disraeli's complaint is the way statistics can be used to support almost any political argument – but political distaste should not be allowed to conceal the value that the statistical method has for science. Statistics give us an overview of a large body of items that we couldn't possibly hope to monitor individually – for example, almost any measurement on a gas in the real world (pressure, for instance) is statistical, because it combines the effects of all the many billions of gas molecules present.

Probability, on the other hand, is about chance. It usually describes something that may or may not happen. In any particular case there will be a single actual outcome, but we can give that outcome a probability. So when the weather forecast tells us there's a 50 per cent probability of rain, in practice it will either rain or it won't. We just know that the chances of it happening are pretty evenly balanced.

Let's look at probability and statistics applying to the specific example we've already seen – tossing a coin. Imagine you have a coin, and toss it a hundred times in a row. Each time you toss the coin you note down the result. Probability says that each time you throw the coin you have a 50:50 chance of getting a head or a tail. So probability predicts that on average, after a hundred throws, you will get fifty heads and fifty tails. If you actually count heads and tails you might end up with forty-eight heads and fifty-two tails. These statistics tell us what happened. Probability is the likeliness of what will happen, while statistics describe the actual outcome. Probability tells us which combinations are more or less likely; statistics open up reality. If we continued to throw the coin, the statistical outcome would lead us towards deducing the 50:50 probability. The two are connected, but are only the same for certain if we have an infinitely large statistical sample, something that doesn't exist in the real world.

Let's look a little further into probability using dice. Throwing a die produces a random selection from the six numbers it carries, so we say that there's a one in six chance of getting a particular throw. Let's say I throw a three, then throw the die again. Here's where common sense goes out of the window. As we've seen with my sequence of heads, it seems natural to assume there is less chance of getting a three this time. In fact, though, dice have no memory. Once again there is exactly a one in six chance of getting any particular throw.

So doesn't this mean I could throw three after three after three – say ten times over? Yes it does. But it is very unlikely. There are thousands of different combinations of those ten dice. Each individual combination has exactly the same chance of occurring – but all but one will not produce a three for each throw. Because of this low chance of getting ten sequential threes, it seems particularly unlikely that the final throw will come up three if we've already got a three for each of the last nine throws. But with no memory, the die still has a one in six chance of coming up three.

On average, over time, assuming I haven't got loaded dice, there will be the same number of ones, twos, threes, fours, fives and sixes thrown – but it can take a long time for things to even out.

The other thing that it's important to understand is the way probabilities add together. If there is a one in six chance of getting a three when you throw one die, what is the chance of getting a three in either of two dice? This is important because in the real world we are often dealing with the probabilities of several things happening at once, not just a single, isolated incident.

It would be simple if we could just add the probabilities together. There is a one in six chance on the first die and a one in six chance on the second, so could the chance of getting a three on either of the dice be one plus one, i.e. two in six? Unfortunately it isn't that simple. Otherwise you could guarantee to get a three by throwing six dice, or a single die six times. Real life doesn't work that way.

Mathematicians have come up with a method of combining probabilities, though. The reasoning is slightly obscure, but the result is quite simple. If there is a one in six chance of getting a three, that means there is a five in six chance of not getting a three. To combine a pair of five in six chances of not getting threes, they are multiplied together, saying that there is a 25 in 36 chance of not getting a three from either of two dice. That leaves an 11 in 36 chance that you *will* get a three with the two dice. Note that this is slightly less than the 12 in 36 (two in six) chance we would have got by adding the probabilities together. This slight reduction ensures that, though it gets more and more likely that we will get a three as we throw many times, it is never certain.

GOATS AND FERRARIS

This is a probability game that a few years ago baffled readers of *The Times* so much that indignant letters were written by professors, denying the truth of the outcome.

Imagine you are taking part in a game show. You have won through to the last round, which is a game of chance. There are three doors – all you have to do is to choose which door you want to open – Door 1, Door 2 or Door 3. Behind one door is a Ferrari. Behind each of the other two is a goat. Let's assume that you are normal enough to want a Ferrari.

After a moment's indecision you plump for a door – let's say it's Door 2. The game show host nods, knowingly. 'Okay,' he says, 'I'm going to give you a final chance to change your mind. And I'm even going to help you.' He opens Door 3 and shows you there's a goat behind it. 'Now,' says the host, 'do you want to stick with the door you chose, or do you want to change to another door?'

The question I ask you is subtly different. Should you stick with the door you chose, should you change (to Door 1), or doesn't it matter in probability terms whether you stick or change?

Think about it a little while before reading on. *Don't cheat, think about it.*

Most people reckon it doesn't matter, and their logic – very sensible it is too – goes something like this. The game show host eliminated one door with a goat. So there are two doors left, one with a goat behind it, one with a Ferrari. There's a 50:50 chance that you've picked the right door. So it doesn't matter if you change or not.

If that's what you thought, you are in the majority. And you are wrong. Go back to the start. What was the chance you had the right door? One in three. In two cases out of three you would have picked a goat. In these two out of three cases, the Ferrari was behind a door you didn't choose. Then the host helps you out by showing you which of the other doors *not* to choose. So, in two out of three cases, by moving to the door that the host didn't open, you will hit the Ferrari. In the remaining one case out of the three you would have been better off staying with the first door you chose – but would you prefer a one in three chance of winning to a two in three chance? No. You should always change your choice to the other door that wasn't opened – Door 1 in the example above. It's not just a 50:50 chance, because the game show host has injected some extra information.

WHY EXPERIMENT AT ALL?

Enough on causality, probability and statistics – let's get back to our experiment. Once an experimental result is produced, it is pored over by experts in the field, looking for flaws. And if the experiment is interesting, other people will try to reproduce the result elsewhere. To be an effective experiment it has to be reproducible – to produce the same results reliably. Otherwise the original results could have been a fluke.

By now we can clearly see the difference between experiment and experience ('something that happened to someone I know'). With the experience, we have no way of knowing what other factors were involved, what the causality was, or even, thanks to human weakness of observation, exactly what took place. And if it hasn't been reproduced it could well be a one-off error. This is why scientists are usually very cautious about reporting initial breakthroughs. Until the experiment has been checked, repeated and verified, it could be absolute rubbish.

So we have seen what an experiment is, and what differentiates an experiment from experience, but what is an experiment *for*? Sometimes it is simply an open attempt to see what will happen, but usually it is designed to check a hypothesis. Someone has an idea about what is happening. An experiment is then designed that could disprove that hypothesis. If it does, then the hypothesis is discarded. If it's a good experiment and it can't disprove the hypothesis, then the hypothesis is strengthened and will, with sufficient testing, become a theory.

This sounds rather feeble and negative. How does a theory get proved? Where do scientific laws come from? To be honest, theories don't get proved, while the 'law' word in this context is dated and has little real value. It is pretty well impossible to definitively prove anything in science – all you can do is show that a theory explains all observations . . . until a new and unexplained one comes along. Newton's laws of motion are great practical tools, but they are, in practice, incorrect. We now know they are only approximations to the better theory that emerges from Einstein's relativity.

It's much easier to disprove something than to prove it. One good negative destroys a theory. Funnily, this is what's meant by that confusing saying, 'the exception proves the rule'. It doesn't mean, as it sounds, that having an exception makes the rule true. 'Prove' is being used here in the sense of a proving ground. It means the exception *tests* the rule – and finds it wanting. A lot of positives make a theory more likely, but they can never absolutely prove it.

Take the fact that the Earth moves around the Sun. This is something most of us have to take on faith – experience says it's the other way round. We can see that the Earth stands still and the Sun moves through the sky. In reality, either is an acceptable view, because of relativity (this isn't Einstein's stuff, but the original version that Galileo dreamed up – we'll come back to relativity later). You can say that the Earth orbits the Sun. Equally you could say that the Sun and the whole of the rest of the universe orbit an unmoving Earth. Each is a description that fits the facts. But having the Earth move makes everything else a lot simpler – so given the total indifference of relativity to which view we take, it is more practical to say that it's the Earth that moves.

Scientific theory, then, is a best guess. Like Sherlock Holmes, scientists say 'when you have eliminated the impossible, whatever remains, *however improbable*, must be the truth'. Or more accurately, 'whatever remains, *however improbable*, is the best theory we have until we find out more'.

BIG PICTURES AND SMALL DETAILS

Modern science spends a lot of time with its nose pressed close against the glass of a very small area of study. This results in lots of detail, but sometimes it fails to provide the big picture. Often, the person who makes a huge breakthrough like Newton or Einstein is not the detailed specialist, but someone who can take a wider view. Even if a breakthrough does come from within a discipline, it can take someone from the outside to give a little nudge and to combine knowledge from two different fields.

Most science you will need for primary schools is at the big picture level – but still it doesn't do any harm to be aware of how a detailed, single discipline approach can sometimes be a disadvantage.

Take an example from a book on primary school science topics I've come across. In it, the author suggests that one way to illustrate to a class the way science should be systematic is to imagine two people searching a field for a bracelet. One wanders around at random, the other makes a series of tight sweeps, cutting off one small amount of the field at a time and systematically working from one end to the other. The author asks his readers to ask their class what is wrong with the first approach, and why the second approach is better.

The assumption that the second approach is better depends on there being unlimited time for the exercise. But let's assume that the time available was used up at the point in time when the author drew a couple of diagrams to illustrate the different search patterns. At this point, the systematic person had swept just over one-eighth of the field. The chances are seven to one against this person having found the lost bracelet. The random wanderer had covered well over half the field. If the bracelet were a nice glittery one, then although she might not have passed right over it, she would have seen it. In that limited time, the random walk was more effective than the systematic sweep. Why? Because it gave an overview, rather than focusing tightly on a small area of the field.

We can't go back to having generalists who know everything there is to know about every possible aspect of science – there's just too much to cover. But this does emphasize how much need there is for cross-disciplinary work. Big picture science has a place too – and what's more it tends to be more enjoyable. Popular science books are sometimes criticized for giving too much of the big picture, because real science is often boring, repetitive and very tightly focused on a tiny piece of the action. It's true we shouldn't over-glamorize the life of a scientist (not that many people associate scientists with glamour), but there's no reason why we shouldn't get that impressive big picture too.

SCIENCE AROUND US AND THE EXPERIMENT – ESSENTIALS

Labs are important, but they aren't what science is about, they are just a tool. What's essential is the experiment. Differentiating between experience (especially second- or third-hand experience) and experiment is an essential beginning. And the scientific method adds in a number of tools, from double-blind testing to statistical analysis, to improve on what is possible with an experiment.

Some experiments are simply open 'let's see what will happen' processes, but many are designed to try to see if a hypothesis is false. It's much easier to disprove something than it is to prove it. All our scientific laws and theories are really best guesses that have yet to be disproved (but some of them have been tested so thoroughly that it's very unlikely ever to happen).

CHAPTER 3

THE BASICS

> Once basic knowledge is acquired, any attempt at preventing its fruition would be as futile as hoping to stop the earth from revolving around the sun.
> Enrico Fermi, developer of the first atomic reactor in *Atomic Energy for Power*, from *Collected Papers 1939–45*

The three chapters following this one look at the specific science topics covered in primary school teaching. Here I want to be a little freer to zip through all of science, picking out some of the most remarkable bits. This can't be comprehensive, and that doesn't really matter – what is important is to see beyond the curriculum to the real fundamentals, even when these include topics like quantum theory and relativity that are often thought of as difficult.

There's nothing in this chapter that you can't cope with, but if you find any of it confusing, don't let it put you off – skim over it and think about reading a more detailed book on that bit later on. Don't expect it all to make sense immediately. I need to quote the great Richard Feynman, one of the greatest physicists ever. If you've never heard Feynman speak, imagine Tony Curtis reading these words:

> [Do] you think I'm going to explain it to you so you can understand it? No, you're not going to be able to understand it. . . . It is my task to convince you not to turn away because you don't understand it. You see, my physics students don't understand it either. That is because *I* don't understand it. No one does. . . . The theory describes Nature as absurd from the point of view of common sense. And it fully agrees with experiment. So I hope you can accept Nature as She is – absurd.

WHERE IT ALL STARTED

Before plunging in, it's worth thinking quickly about the historical context (don't worry – no heavy-duty history of science here). Science in the Western world has gone through three broad periods, which I'm going to call classical, clockwork and counter-intuitive. The classical period, lasting from around 500 BC to the 1500s, largely based its science on the Greek approach we've already met of developing a winning theory by argument and this becoming the received wisdom. Almost everything from this period, with some noble exceptions like basic optics, was wrong, often in a dramatic way. What is frightening is that chunks of this 'ancient wisdom' – based, remember, purely on unsubstantiated theorizing – keep recurring as pseudo-science all the way up to the present day. Two obvious examples are astrology and the idea that everything is made of four 'elements', earth, air, fire and water, which has a habit of turning up in New Age thinking.

Occasionally they got it right, though. One of the better known examples of ancient scientific error is fictional propaganda. We are often told that those funny medieval folk thought that the world was flat, and that anyone daring to sail to the far reaches would fall off the edge. This simply isn't true. Ever since the Ancient Greeks it was realized that the world was ball-shaped – anyone who had travelled on a ship knew how places became visible over the horizon, and were seen first from the crow's nest before they could be seen from the deck, a sure sign of curvature. The flat Earth business is partly a misunderstanding of medieval maps, which were often symbolic rather than a projection like a modern map, and partly made up by a Victorian atheist group hoping to show how the Christian hierarchy held back science.

So that's my classical period, brought to an end by the likes of Galileo and Newton who were prepared to challenge received wisdom, basing their theories instead on experiment and observation. This second period (confusingly often referred to as classical science) I would describe as clockwork science. Newton particularly had a vision of the universe as a great machine, obeying universal laws. It was only a matter of discovering those laws and it would be possible to see how it all worked – to predict what would happen, given a set of starting points. Turn the handle, the clockwork whirrs and out comes the exact, predicted result.

The great success of the clockwork period was in being able to reduce much of science to predictable, repeatable numbers. These numbers let us work out the path that a planet would take travelling around the Sun under the influence of gravity, and helped us to describe how a stone accelerates as it falls to Earth. What no one could work out was the mechanism behind the clockwork. Why an object does fall to Earth – how gravity works – would never be answered by clockwork science.

Finally, with the turn of the twentieth century, came our current period, the counter-intuitive. The great thing about the clockwork age was that everything pretty much worked the way you expected it to. The Victorian natural historian Thomas

Huxley, an enthusiastic champion of Darwin, described science as 'nothing but trained and organized common sense'. But in the twentieth century we were to discover that common sense was a very poor guide when it came to science.

The blossoming of the counter-intuitive period was a different sort of revolution from the change from classical to clockwork. At that first boundary, most of the old classical ideas had to be thrown away. The new shift was more subtle. Now most of the clockwork ideas were found to be simplifications that would work to some extent, but needed modifying to get closer to reality. And the counter-intuitive age proved to be one where science moved from description to more fundamental opportunities to answer the question why? Nowhere was this more obvious than in biology, which historically had been a purely descriptive and cataloguing science, but could now hold up its head with a fundamental theory of its own – evolution. We'll return to that later in the chapter.

MOST PEOPLE'S IDEAS OF SCIENCE ARE VICTORIAN

Most of us were brought up on science from the clockwork era. Counter-intuitive science tends only to be lightly touched on below university level. But it's important to go beyond Victorian ideas to really appreciate what's happening in science, and to have a decent grasp of how the universe works. You wouldn't expect even a beginner in literature to be taught the Victorian idea of literary criticism – but that's exactly what happens in science.

Between them, quantum theory and relativity replace much of the science of the clockwork era. You might not be teaching this to primary school children (though it's arguable you should be), but it is important for you to get a broad understanding of what it's about.

We'll start with one of the twin planks of modern physics, quantum theory. This is the science of the very small. A quantum is a small packet of something (and a quantum leap is a very small jump, despite the popular phrase). Once you get down to the nano scale (a billionth of a metre or less), objects go mad. Quantum particles are totally weird – and totally fascinating. Quantum physics explains the behaviour of the building blocks of everything. Your body. The chair you sit in. The earth and the air around it. The sunlight that gives us warmth, the ability to see and breathable air (via photosynthesis). The electricity that powers your lights and your computer. All these are made up of quantum particles.

The strangest aspect of tiny particles like atoms, electrons and photons of light is that they are very difficult to pin down. In Newton's clockwork universe, if you set a particle moving, knowing the speed and direction you set it off with, and if nothing interfered with it, you could come back as long as you liked later, and predict

UNTANGLING UNITS

Science usually makes use of units of measurement that are very handy for the purpose, but don't necessarily have a lot of relevance in everyday life. Generally speaking, scientists stick to the MKS system (that's metres, kilograms and seconds). Many physical values can be expressed using just these, though usually there's a secondary unit to avoid writing out messily long descriptions. For instance, force could be measured as kilograms times metres per second per second, but that's a bit fiddly so there's a unit called a newton (small N) that is just used to replace 'kilograms times metres per second per second'.

You will find all sorts of weird and wonderful prefixes to tack on to the basic measures. We're used to kilo- for 1,000 (e.g. kilograms), and thanks to computers we're also familiar with mega-, giga- and quite possibly tera-. Down at the small end we've milli- for a thousandth, micro- for a millionth and so on. On the whole, the extreme versions aren't used, except by people setting pub quiz questions. There is such a thing, for instance, as a yoctosecond, which is a trillionth of a trillionth of a second – but frankly, who cares? Long before getting to such terms, scientists adopt a more flexible notation, based on powers of ten.

Instead of writing 9,123,456, a scientist might write 9.123456×10^6 – this doesn't seem much of an advantage, but it rapidly becomes one as the numbers get bigger. Instead of writing 10,000,000,000,000,000 it makes a lot of sense to write 10^{16}. The little number after the 10 says how many times to multiply 10 by itself. 10^2 is ten squared, or 100, 10^3 is ten cubed, 1,000, and so on. This is very convenient because the little number is just the number of zeros that come after the 1.

When dealing with small numbers, you'll see, for example, 5×10^{-7} – the 10^{-7} is like dividing by 10^7 (10,000,000), so 2×10^{-3} seconds is two-thousandths of a second, or 2 milliseconds. These little numbers can also be used with units. Instead of saying newtons are kilograms times metres per second per second, it's easier to write $kg\ m\ s^{-2}$.

exactly where that particle will be. In the quantum world, we can only say to a certain degree of probability where something is. Instead of being in a fixed place, a quantum particle has a range of probabilities as to whether it's where Newton would expect it, in your pocket, or on the other side of the world.

It was this dependence on probability that made Einstein dislike quantum theory, even though he was largely responsible for it being taken seriously. This is the source of his famous quote, 'I, at any rate, am convinced that [the Old One] is not playing at dice', usually rendered as 'God doesn't play dice.' Even better was a remark he made in a letter to fellow physicist Max Born, '[If quantum theory were true] I would rather be a cobbler, or even an employee in a gaming house, than a physicist.'

FIRST CATCH YOUR ATOM

Quantum theory evolved from an attempt to explain what atoms are like. The concept of atoms goes all the way back to the Ancient Greeks. One group of Greek philosophers believed that everything was made up of very small, indivisible units – atoms. By the start of the twentieth century, it was not only known that atoms exist, but that they weren't indivisible at all, and contained a collection of positively charged protons (later known to live alongside neutrally charged neutrons) and much smaller, negatively charged electrons. It was originally assumed that the positive charge made up the body of an atom, with the electrons scattered through it like fruit in a plum pudding. But the protons and neutrons were found to be isolated in a tiny lump in the middle of the atom. (To give an idea of relative scale, the nucleus inside the atom has been compared to a fly in a cathedral.)

Where did that leave the negative electrons, ejected from their plum pudding? The picture most of us have is of them flying around the heavy nucleus, just like the planets fly around the sun. This idea, dreamed up by Danish physicist Niels Bohr, was so reasonable and natural sounding that the public quickly latched on to it. It makes sense, and you can draw nice pictures to illustrate it. Don't feel too attached to it, though, because it's wrong.

If electrons did zoom around like little satellites, they would be accelerating. In physics it tends to be velocity rather than speed that's important. Velocity is a combination of how fast something is going, *and* the direction it's going in. Acceleration is just the rate at which velocity (not speed) changes. The electron's speed would remain the same as it flew around the nucleus, but its direction would be constantly changing – that means its velocity is changing, so it is accelerating.

Problem! It was already known when Bohr came up with his theory that an accelerating electron gave off energy as light. So any electron flying around an orbit should hurtle into the nucleus and be destroyed, like a moth spiralling into a candle flame. This clearly wasn't happening, or we wouldn't be around to realize it, because all our atoms would have imploded. So Bohr immediately had to replace the idea with one where electrons could only run on a series of tracks (confusingly called orbits), each closer to the nucleus than the last. The electron couldn't spiral into the centre as it lost energy, because it couldn't exist in the space between the tracks. But it could give off or receive a chunk of energy – a photon of light – and make that quantum leap between two of the tracks.

As quantum theory was developed it became obvious that Bohr's tracks were too rigid for the real picture. An electron doesn't have a position around the nucleus, just a range of probabilities as to where it might be found. So the best picture of an electron is as a fuzzy cloud that covers the outside of the atom. It would be better to imagine it is as the atmosphere around a world rather than a satellite.

WE JUST CAN'T BE CERTAIN

This uncertainty of where an electron is provides an illustration of another of the best known bits of quantum theory – the uncertainty principle. This simply states that the better you know one of a pair of linked pieces of information about a particle, the less well you know the other. For example, the more accurately you know where a particle is, the less accurately you can know its momentum (that's just its mass times its velocity). Know it's momentum exactly and the particle could be anywhere in the universe.

A good way of picturing the uncertainty principle is to imagine you take a photograph of an object that is flying past at speed. If you take the picture with a very quick shutter speed it freezes the object in space. You get a good, clear image of what the object looks like. But you can't tell anything from the picture about the way it is moving. It could be stationary; it could be hurtling past. If on the other hand you take a photograph with a slow shutter speed, the object will show up on the camera as an elongated blur. This won't tell you a lot about what the object looks like – it's too smudged – but will give a clear indication of its movement. The trade-off between momentum and position is a little like this.

Something else that can help in picturing this fuzzy distribution of an electron around its orbit is another fundamental of quantum theory rather grandly called wave/particle duality. It all started with trying to understand light. Newton had reckoned that light was made up of particles, but many others thought it behaved more like waves on the sea. A British doctor, Thomas Young, showed how light that was passed through a pair of narrow slits produced patterns like waves crashing into each other. These regular patterns where the waves interfered with each other didn't seem possible if a light ray was made up of particles. Yet Einstein showed different. In his Nobel Prize-winning paper, explaining how the photoelectric effect works (where light hits a metal and generates electricity), he had to assume that light came in particles – photons as they would soon be known.

It turns out that light can behave either like a wave or like a particle, but can't do both at the same time. In reality, it's best to bear in mind that light isn't either. Light is light, but it's useful to think of it as being like a particle or a wave, both phenomena we can experience with our senses, rather than its true nature in the quantum world. And the same goes for the other quantum particles. Not only can light act like a particle, an electron can act like a wave. You can get interference patterns from electrons, for instance. And another way of looking at that fuzzy cloud of an electron around the nucleus is to think of it as being a wave that circles the nucleus and joins up with itself, like the Norse serpent eating its tail.

BIGGER FLEAS HAVE SMALLER FLEAS

Down at the quantum level are the particles that make up everything. These particles combine together to make atoms of a single element, such as hydrogen, or carbon or oxygen. The atoms can also be joined, building-block fashion, to create molecules, which are just bigger particles containing more than one atom.

As we've already seen, it has been known that atoms are made up of smaller ('sub-atomic') particles for around 100 years. But of the four particles we've already met, only two are now thought to be fundamental – electrons and photons of light. The protons and the neutrons turn out to be made up of smaller particles called quarks. The current best description of what's going on down at the most basic level, called the standard model, describes a collection of twenty-four different particles (sadly, though this is the standard model, it isn't a *simple* model), plus an extra twenty-fifth that doesn't fit with the rest.

The twenty-four divide neatly into twelve bosons and twelve fermions. Loosely, fermions are the particles that make up matter, and bosons are the particles that enable fermions to interact with each other – particles that transmit forces. We've already met one boson, the photon, and it's joined by W and Z bosons, various gluons and the mysterious Higgs boson, which is thought to be responsible for giving other particles mass. (The extra twenty-fifth particle is also a boson – the graviton – a never observed, but theoretically existent particle responsible for gravity.)

Things are even messier in the fermion camp. Here we find neutrinos, positrons, muons and tau particles – particles produced when atoms are smashed together, or that come streaming through space from cosmic explosions such as supernovae. But more familiarly there is the electron and a whole mess of quarks. The quarks are distinguished by some distinctly odd characteristics, known to physicists as flavours (no, really). The different flavours are called charm, strangeness, top/bottom and up/down. (Even the more prosaic sounding names can be a bit odd, as every fermion has an anti-matter equivalent with the same mass but opposite charge. A positron, for instance, is an anti-matter electron with a positive charge. The existence of these anti-particles means that one of the quarks is the 'anti-bottom quark.') Protons and neutrons are made of combinations of three quarks each. The proton is two ups and one down; the neutron two downs and one up.

I won't go into the standard model in any detail, but will say a little more about quarks, as they do seem to be what make up protons and neutrons, which many people still think of as indivisible particles.

The word 'quark' is one of the stranger bits of naming in science. It was dreamed up by the physicist Murray Gell-Mann, and is properly pronounced 'kwork', though you will often hear 'kwark'. According to Gell-Mann, he had been using the spoken 'kwork' sound for a few weeks as a label for these then hypothetical particles, before coming across a line in James Joyce's *Ulysses*, which reads 'three quarks for Muster Mark!' (Gell-Mann admits he may have subconsciously lifted the word from there, as he had read the book several times before.) The way quarks come in threes made this line and the spelling very apt, but Gell-Mann wanted to keep his original pronunciation (Joyce clearly intended it to rhyme with mark).

No one has ever seen a naturally occurring quark, nor has anyone managed to break a proton or neutron into its component pieces. It is particularly difficult to do so, because of the peculiar nature of the force that holds the quarks together, which gets stronger as they get further apart, unlike pretty well anything else we know. As this is the case, it's difficult to understand how quarks were ever dreamed up. It's not exactly obvious that a proton or neutron should be made up of three pieces. The reason we believe that quarks exist owes its origins to a different type of physics that emerged in the early days of quantum theory.

As quantum theory was developed, two different ways of describing what went on emerged. One had clear parallels in the real world. This approach, developed by Erwin Schrödinger, talked about waves and other concepts that were relatively easy to grasp. Admittedly the wave didn't describe a movement, as it does with physical objects we experience. It was a probability wave, describing the likelihood of finding a particle in a particular place. But it was at least something that could be imagined.

The second approach, produced by Werner Heisenberg (he of the uncertainty principle), was known as matrix mechanics, and was purely mathematical. It was a big, mathematical black box into which you fed a set of numbers and got out a set of predictions that matched what was observed in the real world. But there was nothing to visualize – it was pure numbers, an elegant mathematical construct that did the job without any picture of what was going on. The British physicist Paul Dirac proved that the two ways of looking at quantum theory were identical, and they were eventually combined as quantum mechanics.

That first step into purely abstract maths was only a starting point. A range of mathematical techniques that even experienced physicists found confusing was increasingly used to make mathematical models of the quantum world that had no equivalents in the real world. Many of these models were rapidly shown to be useless – the predictions they made bore no resemblance to what happened in experiments – but some seemed to have hit on some sort of underlying truths. It was by building on and tweaking these purely mathematical concepts, until they very closely predicted what was seen in the real world, that the idea of the quark emerged. The existence of quarks themselves is not experimentally verified, but it is predicted by a theory which has had many other experimental checks.

Quarks, then, are like a visitor who has phoned ahead to say they are coming. And sent you a letter. And a text message. And you have online confirmation from the airline to say they are on their way. You haven't seen them, but you know they are on their way because of all the accompanying evidence. It's possible they won't turn up because of some unforeseen circumstance, and similarly it's possible things will go horribly wrong, and quarks will turn out not to have existed – but it's pretty unlikely.

THE BIG FOUR FORCES

There's one remaining aspect of quantum theory that's worth mentioning, as it's so amazing, but we'll leave that until we've dealt with relativity. First, though, we ought to consider the other fundamental requirement to build yourself a universe, which can either be thought of as forces or fields. That's not the sort of field with cows in – a field in the physics sense is a bit like the area of influence of a force like gravity. If we only had a collection of particles with no forces, then they would simply occupy space as a mist – to have anything happen, to make atoms and molecules and people and planets, there needs to be some way for them to interact with each other and of gluing things together. These are the forces, just four types of them in all.

The job of most of the bosons we've already met is to make these forces work. Perhaps the most familiar of the forces is the weakest and the hardest to understand: gravity. This is the wildcard. The reason the graviton, the particle that may be responsible for gravity, is excluded from the standard model is because our best theory of gravity – Einstein's general relativity (yes, we've almost reached relativity) – isn't a quantum theory.

No one has ever seen a graviton, but they are assumed to exist because, if we want to act on something that isn't directly connected to us, *something* usually has to cross the gap between us and the target. Often this 'something' is direct contact – I reach over and pick up my coffee cup, for instance, to get it moving towards my mouth. But if we want to act on something remotely without ourselves crossing the gap that separates us, there has to be an intermediary that travels from one place to another.

Imagine that you are at a coconut shy at the fair. If you want to hit a coconut and knock it off its stand, you can't just look at it and make it jump into the air by some sort of mystical influence; you have to throw a ball at it. Your hand pushes the ball, the ball travels through the air and hits the coconut; as long as your aim is good (and the coconut isn't glued in place), your target falls off, you smile smugly and you win.

Similarly, if I want to speak to someone across the other side of a room, my vocal cords vibrate, pushing against the nearest air molecules. These send a train of sound waves through the air, rippling molecules across the gap, until finally those vibrations get to the other person's ear. Now her eardrum starts to vibrate, stimulated by the air molecules, and the result is my voice being heard. In the first case, the ball was the intermediary, in the second the sound wave, but in both examples something travelled from A to B. That's the role of a boson, to be that 'something' in the four forces that hold the universe together.

Photons, the particles of light, are the bosons responsible for the next best known of the forces after gravity – electromagnetic force. This is what generates the pull of a magnet, or the force on a wire carrying a changing electrical current near a magnet that gives us an electric motor. It's electromagnetism that gives electrons a negative charge and protons a positive charge. Wherever there is an electromagnetic field, invisible photons are linking the parts affected by it.

The final two forces are the weak and strong forces, which both only apply to the atomic nucleus, provided by W and Z bosons, and gluons respectively. The weak force is a rather obscure one involved in certain types of nuclear decay. The strong force holds the nucleus together, despite the fact that all the positively charged protons in a large atom will be fighting to get away from each other as their charges repel.

Let's go back to electromagnetism, because it will provide the link between the two great foundations of modern physics, building a bridge from quantum physics to relativity.

Originally, electricity and magnetism were thought to be entirely different things, but Michael Faraday realized that the two were inextricably linked, and the Scottish scientist James Clerk Maxwell provided the maths to prove that they were two facets of the same thing, promptly if clumsily named electromagnetism. The clearest link between the two came with Maxwell's realization that a moving wave of electricity could generate an associated wave of magnetism, which itself would generate electricity and so on.

This remarkable example of hauling up by your own bootstraps would only work at one speed. The speed of light. By understanding how electricity and magnetism interact, Maxwell had revealed just what light was (at least, as we now know, from the wave point of view). A balancing act. A constant, self-creating marvel that has to keep moving to exist. Magnetism generating electricity generating magnetism and so on at 300,000 kilometres per second.

EINSTEIN'S MAGICAL MYSTERY DAYDREAM

So now imagine you're Albert Einstein. We're used to seeing pictures of Einstein as an old man, but you are Albert as a young man in his twenties. You are lying on a grassy bank in a park in Bern, letting the sunlight filter though your eyelashes. You know all about Maxwell's work, about light's nature. Seeing the apparently individual beams of light, flickering before your eyes, you imagine riding alongside the light beam, watching it side on, somehow seeing the light itself as if it were a physical object. And you realize there's a problem thanks to one word – relativity.

We are so used to associating the word 'relativity' with Einstein, that it's easy to forget that as a concept it goes at least as far back as Galileo. This relativity of the clockwork period is as natural and intuitive as Einstein's versions of relativity are not. All Galileo's relativity says is that you can look at the world from different viewpoints. (So things happen *relative* to the viewpoint you take.) If you throw a ball, you can see that ball in motion in different ways. You can think of the ball moving past the ground, or you can imagine yourself standing on the ball, in which case the ball is fixed in place, and the ground is moving past.

It works equally well with two things that are both moving. If you drive at 50 miles per hour towards a car that's already doing 50 miles per hour towards you, then the two cars head for collision at 100 miles per hour. And if both cars move in the same direction, you can make the other car stop (relative to you). If you drive alongside another car, both of you doing 50 miles per hour, as far as you are concerned, the other car isn't moving. This isn't some sort of optical illusion. You can reach out and touch it without being hurt. It isn't moving relative to your car, only compared to the ground.

Einstein was applying this sort of relativistic thinking to the beam of light. If he was flying along beside it, then from his point of view the light was stopped. But here comes the problem. Light can only exist if it is moving at light speed – 300,000 kilometres per second in a vacuum. If it were any slower, the whole interplay of magnetism and electricity would break down. There's no way to stop light by moving alongside it, because if it stopped, it wouldn't be there. It's crazy to imagine light would disappear every time anyone moved relative to it. We know that doesn't happen. So what Einstein was forced to accept was that, however fast or slow you go, in whatever direction, light would always be moving at the same speed.

It's the way light's speed stays the same whether you move towards it or away from it that triggers the counter-intuitive science. It has to be the case, or light could not exist – but the outcome is very strange.

LIGHT SPEED

Light is stunningly fast. A hummingbird's wings flap 4,200 times a minute, near invisible to the human eye. Yet in the duration of a single flap of those wings, a beam of light could cross the Atlantic Ocean.

Rather remarkably, light's speed was first worked out over 300 years ago by a Danish astronomer, Ole Roemer. He realized that changes in the timings of the orbits of Jupiter's recently discovered moons were caused by the difference in the time the light took to reach the Earth, and came up with a value of around 220,999 kilometres per second – about a third too low. Measures got closer and closer until 1983, when the speed of light was fixed – it is now exactly 299,792,458 metres per second, and always will be, however much better our measuring instruments get.

The reason is that, in 1983, the definition of the metre was changed to be 1/299,792,458th of the distance light travels in a second. Light now defines our unit of distance.

RELATIVITY CAN BE VERY SPECIAL

From the basic realization that light's speed would not vary came all of Einstein's special relativity. If something is moving close to the speed of light, everything takes on an Alice-in-Wonderland peculiarity. If you were sitting on the Earth, monitoring a spaceship flying away at near light speed, you would see everything inside the ship moving very slowly. For you, time slows down on the ship. It would get smaller and heavier too. But to the pilot on the ship, none of this would be true. After all, from her point of view, she is not moving. It's the Earth that is moving away from her at near light speed. To her, time on a contracting, heavier Earth would have slowed down. In case this sounds too bizarre to be true, it has all been demonstrated. In fact, the GPS satellites used for satellite navigation have to have a correction built in to cope with the shift in time caused by relativity.

Nothing solid can reach light speed itself. At that limit, mass heads for infinity; time stops. (Of course light can and must travel at this speed.) If it were possible to travel faster than light, time would reverse. A faster-than-light message would move backwards in time. This is because one of the other side effects of light's behaviour is that two things that appear simultaneous in the fixed world don't happen at the same time when you are moving with respect to them. If you could go faster than light, that simultaneity shift puts the 'later' event ahead of the 'earlier' one.

GETTING IN A TANGLE

I was always frustrated by this statement that a faster-than-light message would travel backwards in time. I couldn't quite understand why it was so. This is where quantum entanglement, a part of quantum physics I've already mentioned a couple of times, comes in. Entanglement is a strange connection between two quantum particles that works instantly across any distance. Because the link is instant, if you could use it to send a message, the signal would go backwards in time. I was able to make the explanation understandable for my book on quantum entanglement, *The God Effect*, but it does take a chapter to make straightforward – if, like me, you find it frustratingly puzzling, I'll have to ask you to take a look at that book (see www.brianclegg.net/god effect). There just isn't room here.

As it happens, entanglement can't carry a message – the information in the link is totally random and can't be controlled. But this doesn't mean entanglement isn't useful. It can produce unbreakable encryption to keep secrets safe, and makes possible incredibly powerful quantum computers where each bit in the computer is a quantum particle like an atom – computers so powerful that they can perform feats that would take an ordinary computer longer than the lifetime of the universe. And entanglement makes it possible to teleport a quantum particle – to transform another particle at any distance into an identical particle to an original (which is destroyed in the process). This is, in effect, a Star Trek style transporter, though it is unlikely to work for anything bigger than a bacterium.

Entanglement was a concept devised by Einstein in an attempt to disprove the quantum theory he so disliked. Einstein thought quantum theory must be wrong, because of the way entanglement would act instantly at a distance. Usually, as we've seen, a boson has to go from one place to another for something to happen, and they move at the speed of light. That's even true of gravity. If the Sun were to suddenly disappear, we would feel its gravitational pull for the same eight minutes that we would continue to see it, as its light covered the distance in between. But entanglement has no such delay. The connection between two entangled particles acts instantly at any distance, without anything having time to pass between them. That's why Einstein found it so disturbing (he called it 'spooky'), and why entanglement is so fascinating now it has been proved to exist. Gravity, though, Einstein found less of a challenge, and he managed to extend his ideas on relativity to deal with it.

THE GRAVITY GAME – RELATIVITY GOES GENERAL

The relativity we've seen so far is special relativity. Not 'special' because it's so amazing (though it is), but 'special' because it is dealing with a special case. Special relativity is mind-boggling, but it's not too complicated when it comes to formulae and stuff (don't worry, we don't need them), because it only deals with situations where nothing is accelerating. Everything is worked out for things that are moving at a constant speed.

In the real world, many things get slower or faster – they undergo acceleration. (In the science sense, acceleration is just change of velocity, which, remember, can be change in direction as well as speed. Getting slower is negative acceleration.) Einstein's second great revelation to shake the scientific world was general relativity. This does deal with acceleration. The maths is much more messy, but the results are very striking.

One thing Einstein realized is that the force we feel because of the pull of gravity and the force that is caused by being accelerated (when a car goes round a corner, or a rollercoaster drops down the track, for instance) are exactly equivalent. Indistinguishable. This was the breakthrough that would have the same impact on general relativity as the idea that light couldn't be slowed down did on special relativity. From it he would realize that gravity could bend light – or rather it bends the space through which the light travels. Gravity, Einstein would suggest, is like putting a heavy object onto a rubber sheet. The object distorts the sheet, causing a dip that other objects on the sheet slide into. Similarly, a heavy object like a planet distorts space enough for other things (like us and air) to be held in the distortion in space. Gravity keeps us in place.

The main limitation of the rubber sheet example is that the 'sheet' of the real world is not two-dimensional like a flat sheet of rubber, but four-dimensional. Three dimensions of space and one of time. Gravity doesn't just distort space, it distorts time as well, just as special relativity has an impact on both. Einstein's work resulted in the move in the scientific world from seeing space and time as totally separate to a unified concept of spacetime. In the everyday world space and time seem so different that we can't think of them together – it's another example of the counter-intuitive period at its best. Yet Einstein's theories suggest that spacetime is a more accurate reflection of reality. And like quantum theory, so far, relativity (both flavours) seems to have got it right.

By extending relativity to take in gravity and spacetime, Einstein had moved thinking out to encompass the whole universe. In a moment we'll see how the counter-intuitive age came up with a new idea on how the universe was formed, but before that we really ought to bridge the gap between quantum physics and relativity, the two great theories of how everything works. It would be wonderful if we could. But we can't. Both quantum theory and relativity are great at predicting what actually happens, but unfortunately they are incompatible with each other.

THEORIES OF EVERYTHING

For most everyday science this inability to merge quantum theory and relativity is not a problem. Gravity is such a weak force (compared with the other three fundamental forces) that it has very little influence at the quantum level, while quantum theory isn't directly applicable when you get to something much bigger than a molecule. But scientists have been frustrated that there is no way of pulling the two together to make what is sometimes called a Grand Universal Theory or a Theory of Everything. The best we have at the moment is string theory (more accurately superstring theory) and its derivatives, such as M theory. These do succeed in bringing the two together (sort of), but require there to be at least eleven dimensions of spacetime rather than the traditional four (most of them assumed to be curled up so tight and small we never notice them). While many scientists would agree that these theories are the best we have, an increasing number also predict that they are wrong.

The problem isn't that the theories are counter-intuitive (though they are), but that they are horribly complex, and though they are legitimate from the mathematical viewpoint, they have yet to make *any* connection with experimental reality. Although there have been many books written about superstrings and M theory, and hundreds of scientists have worked on nothing else for at least twenty years, some argue that this isn't even science at all, because the 'theory' has yet to produce a single testable prediction. Contrast this with the theory of quarks, which has lots of testable predictions that have proved true and made it more likely that quarks exist.

M theory and superstrings may shake down into something as solid as quantum theory and relativity, but for the moment they are a pretty weak guess, based on very abstract mathematics, and it's quite likely that a successful theory will only arrive when string theory has been consigned to the rubbish bin of history.

Meanwhile, back at the beginning. The trouble with finding out how the universe was formed is that when it comes to cosmology, the science that takes in the universe as a whole, we're almost back at the Ancient Greek stage of sitting around debating theories with no recourse to experiment. It's very difficult to do experiments to prove what happened when the universe began. We do get some clues. Because light takes time to get to us from distant stars and galaxies, as we look out in space, we look back in time. As telescopes get better, some in space, using visible light and other parts of the electromagnetic spectrum such as radio and infrared, we can see further and further back in time. But, like string theory, our best guess at how the universe was formed is still surprisingly fuzzy.

IN THE BEGINNING WAS THE BANG

It goes something like this. Somewhere between 12 and 20 billion years ago (best guess 13 to 14 billion years) it all started with a singularity, a sizeless point of, erm, something, that exploded into existence in the big bang. (This was originally a term of derision from astronomer Fred Hoyle who never agreed with the theory.) In that initial instant of formation, matter came into being that would eventually become atoms of the lightest elements such as hydrogen and helium. But very soon after the big bang, something inexplicable occurred. The universe inflated like a balloon (but here space expanded in three dimensions, rather than the two dimensions of a balloon's rubber skin). This happened immensely quickly. If matter had been moving through space at this speed it would have smashed the light speed barrier many times over. But because space itself was expanding, rather than anything moving within space, there was no speed in the normal sense.

Eventually, over billions of years, matter scattered through the universe was drawn together by gravity to form stars and planets. By this stage we are out of the fuzzy part and into the better supported theory. One thing that seems a bit puzzling is where the stuff to make planets came from. To begin with, most of the matter in the universe was composed of the lightest elements such as hydrogen and helium. When stars formed, more of the hydrogen was able to react to form the next heaviest element, helium, and so on – but that process can't go very far. The heavier the element, the more protons it has in its nucleus. Soon it becomes so hard to get the protons together to make the nucleus of a heavier substance that even the heat and pressure of a star can't produce the heavier atoms needed to make a planet – or a person. Instead it takes a supernova, an exploding star, to produce that matter.

Over time we ended up with the Sun and the Earth forming. How much time have they been around? Our solar system appears to be 4.5 billion years old. A fair amount of time. And that's just as well, because without a lot of time to play with, it would have been impossible for life to have formed. Evolution is a leisurely process.

NEXT ADD LIFE

Although it has flowered in the counter-intuitive period, evolution is really a Victorian concept – it predates the counter-intuitive and is, in fact, a thoroughly clockwork idea. The only reason it didn't crop up back in Newton's time (and, for that matter, is still challenged today) is that, though evolution was always entirely common sense, it didn't fit with beliefs that were accepted as unquestionable truths.

This doesn't mean that evolution is in any sense anti-religious. There is no clash between evolution and the core beliefs of the major world religions. But it does disagree with the creation traditions of most religions, and though these were never intended as scientific theories, there have been problems when evolution has been put up against a belief (for instance) that the world was created in six days around 4004 BC.

Evolution and natural selection together form something close to a self-evident truth. The only ingredient necessary to complete the picture is the understanding of how life works. If you are thinking 'only' is an underestimate of the complexity of the problem, I really mean the key elements of the chemistry of life, which became known well after evolution was put forward as a theory. If it had happened the other way round it's hard to believe there would have been such a challenge to evolution.

All life on Earth, and quite possibly any life in the universe, is dependent on the chemistry of a single element – carbon. Carbon is unique in the way that it can form links with other atoms. Carbon's flexibility is pretty obvious when you take a look at the pure forms of the element. There's graphite, where the four links of each carbon atom form a lattice a bit like a sheet of chicken wire. Because the links are all in a flat plane, these sheets of atoms slide over each other very easily, which is why graphite (pencil lead, for example) is so soft. Diamond, on the other hand, has a three-dimensional lattice, where any force on the carbon is spread through the lattice, resulting in an extremely hard material.

Much more recently discovered is a third form of carbon called the buckyball, more properly buckminsterfullerene. Named after the architect Buckminster Fuller, each molecule is a football-shaped array of sixty carbon atoms. But the structure can be extended to make tubes which – along the length of the tube – are even stronger than diamond.

Carbon's impressive ability to link up with itself in different ways is dwarfed by its ability to connect to other atoms. Nothing else has the flexibility to build the huge molecules that are essential for life. It has been occasionally suggested that it might be possible to have life based on silicon – the principal element in sand – as it comes closest to carbon in its ability to bond – but it really isn't in the same league.

It is thanks to carbon's flexible bonding that DNA – the chemical chains behind our genetic information – and proteins – the complex chemicals that regulate and run the body – are made possible. Thanks to carbon, we can reproduce. And here's where that ingredient for understanding evolution comes in. In the reproductive process, variation is introduced. In sexual reproduction there is variation as genes from the two parents are combined. And in all reproduction there will be small random changes to the genetic structure, for example due to impact from stray radiation.

The outcome is to produce variants and mutations. Despite what we're told by science fiction films, a mutant isn't necessarily a monster. Mutants are creatures whose set of genes contains random variations. In truth, we are all mutants. We all bear such subtle variants. Most have no effect at all. Many of those that do have an effect are negative, some deadly. A few will have a positive effect. So now, with this mechanism in place, we can see evolution at work.

A LITTLE CHANGE HERE, A LITTLE CHANGE THERE

Imagine we have a collection of creatures – it doesn't matter what they are, anything from bacteria to elephants. Let's say they are used to a warm climate. Suddenly, for whatever reason – perhaps there's an ice age – it becomes very cold. Many of the creatures will die. A few, with subtly different genetic makeup, will be rather better at surviving the cold. Perhaps they have thicker fur, a more insulating fat layer or a different body chemistry. Because they are more likely to survive, they will have more offspring, who will inherit the resistance to cold. After a few generations, most of our creatures will be better adapted to the cold.

That's evolution and survival of the fittest in a nutshell, and it makes such sense, that it's very difficult to see how anything else could be true. The only hiccup tends to be when applying this mechanism to the evolution of a complex creature, or even a complex structure like an eye. Partly this is because we can't really think on an evolutionary timescale, so it seems impractical that something like an eye could evolve through a series of tiny changes over millions of years. The other problem often raised is: what about the intermediate steps? What's the point of having half an eye? Evolution takes small steps at random, some good, some bad. There is no sense of purpose or direction, it's just that the living things with beneficial changes tend to survive better, and reproduce more. But how could you get from having no sight to something as sophisticated as an eye?

In fact it's not as much of a problem as it appears. It might be that there is an intermediate stage that has a different benefit – for all we know, creatures with half-formed eyes might have looked more attractive to potential mates. But, in fact, with the eye we know that there are intermediate benefits, because there are creatures out there still with pretty well every intermediate stage between nothing at all and a complex eye. Some have light-sensitive patches on the skin. Others have pinhole camera eyes – no lens, just a cavity with a retina. Some have very crude optics. And so on.

Evolution is sometimes knocked as being 'just a theory' by those who feel that it compromises their religious beliefs, but it really is up with the likes of quantum theory and relativity, with the added advantage for those trying to understand science that it doesn't conflict with common sense. *All* science is 'just a theory', but some theories are better than others, and this is one of the best.

Here ends the whirlwind tour of some of the bits of science that might not come up in the curriculum, but are essential background to understanding (and, I hope, delighting in) the position of modern science, rather than the Victorian version that is all too often equated with simple science. In the next three chapters we will take in the curriculum subjects, but don't worry – this isn't going to be yet another curriculum guide. I want to establish just what the key points are and how their innate wonder can be preserved against the duller aspects of curriculum-based teaching. The chapters are based on the main curriculum areas, but you will find a very different kind of content lurking within.

THE BASICS – ESSENTIALS

We've seen how science has gone through three broad phases – classical, clockwork and counter-intuitive. Almost all basic science as we now understand it comes from the counter-intuitive period, but most school teaching remains in the Victorian era.

The three most important components of basic science which won't come up in the curriculum, but are essential for putting the rest into context, are:

- quantum physics – the science of the very small, describing the behaviour of the fundamental particles that make up everything from atoms to photons of light, bizarrely delightful because of its probabilistic basis;
- relativity – in two parts: special relativity, from the realization that nothing goes faster than light; and general relativity, explaining gravity;
- evolution – a clockwork piece of science, but one that has come of age in the counter-intuitive world.

CHAPTER 4

AROUND THE CURRICULUM – LIFE

> Scientists have one thing in common with children: curiosity. To be a good scientist you must have kept this trait since childhood, and perhaps it is not easy to retain just one trait. A scientist has to be curious like a child; perhaps one can understand that there are other childish features he hasn't grown out of.
>
> Otto Frisch, physicist involved in the discovery of
> nuclear fission, in *What Little I Remember* (1979)

We could argue whether or not the right topics are in the Key Stage 1 and 2 curriculum – but realistically we have to make the best of what's there. Broadly, the topics that have been considered essential at this stage break down into life processes and living things (life), materials and their properties (stuff), and physical processes (workings). Those keywords are mine – the 'workings' word, for instance, emphasizes how the physical processes underpin everything else, including the biology. Because there was nowhere else to put it, the curriculum confusingly crams astronomy into physical processes. Although astronomy is normally a branch of physics, it doesn't really make sense here, but we're stuck with it.

What I'm *not* going to do is tell you what to teach or how to teach it. Instead I want to explore the topics you will be using with the children to help *you* understand that topic better. Much of the material here won't be directly usable in the classroom, but it's important that you understand just what scientists really think is happening. Apart from anything else, this is where a lot of that sense of wonder still exists. And I also believe that it will make it significantly easier to get the essentials across, if you have a better grasp of the underlying science. You can still simplify for the children, but you won't be faced with nasty gaps between your understanding and reality that might be challenged by difficult questions from the brightest students.

I've divided the information into three sections, corresponding to the three key topic areas. I haven't divided between Key Stage 1 and Key Stage 2, because the background you need – which is what I'm concerned about – is the same for both.

LIFE: IT'S ALIVE!

What makes something alive? It's not such an easy question as it appears to be. There is real debate, for instance, about artificial intelligence. If we managed to construct a computer that appeared to have all the characteristics of a living thing, would it be alive? No one is sure. Experts point out that they can now simulate something like a bacterium in incredible detail. At what point does the simulation stop being an imitation and start being a living thing?

Children, particularly in Key Stage 1, have the opportunity to explore this question of whether or not something is alive, which introduces them to two very common scientific tools – classification and properties. Classification is built on the very natural human tendency to build mental models of types of object. Our brains don't want to deal with every single tree we meet as a totally separate thing that we have to learn about from scratch, so we build a mental picture or model of what a general tree is like, which enables us to quickly recognize an object as 'tree' and know how to react to it without conscious thought. This is important if, instead of 'tree', the object to be recognized is 'tiger' or 'speeding car'.

This tendency we have to construct simplified mental models has its negative side. It's where stereotypes come from. However much we want to, we can't avoid classing things, or types of people, together.

In early science, classification was very important. It was often all that was possible. We couldn't explain why, for instance, a gorilla and a chimpanzee were similar but different, but we could see that this seemed to be the case, so produced a classification. As understanding grows, sometimes the old classifications make less sense, but they are a good starting point.

When dealing with life, children are starting to get the feel for what seems at first glance a very simple classification. Alive or not alive. (Or sometimes the classification that is one of the few things I remember from my infant school: alive, dead and never alive.) We want them to understand the difference between these classes. But how are they to decide which class to put an object in? This is where properties are involved (they are sometimes called characteristics, but property is probably the better scientific term). What makes something alive, or not alive?

Properties are generally things we can use our senses on and measure. Some fit neatly into tick boxes. 'Does it breathe?' for instance. Others are positioned somewhere on a continuous scale. 'What colour is it?' or 'How long is it?'

So let's get back to the alive/dead question. It's easy, particularly at the Key Stage 1 level, to get a response too quickly. The children haven't learned yet to check a range of properties – they might jump to conclusions because of a few immediate and obvious ones. Is a plane alive? Well, it moves, it can fly, so yes. Is moss alive? It doesn't move – it doesn't do anything really. No, it's not. You can also get caught out if the examples you use as teaching aids are themselves models. I have seen a

MODELS

It's crucial to understand the concept of models as used in science. We're not talking here about plastic kits or toy trains (or catwalk models). A model is a self-contained construct that behaves as much as possible like the thing that is being modelled. Different models might look like the target object, or behave like it, or both. Our mental models combine a visual representation of a generic object with expectations of how it will behave and what its significance is for us. Scientists' models are often mathematical, without a visual representation. They try to predict how the thing being studied will behave.

This isn't just a game, this is how scientific theories are constructed. The model reflects our guess of how this particular aspect of the world works. We can then throw at it different inputs – different situations – and see how it reacts. The better it corresponds to reality, the more useful the theory becomes.

teacher driven to frustration by a class who insisted on arguing that a plastic pig, brought in to illustrate the animal (because real pigs aren't very practical in the classroom), wasn't alive because it was made out of plastic. Logical, but not what the teacher had in mind.

The properties that make something alive or dead can make a good talking point. What can you think of that makes something alive? The essentials are often given as:

- breathing
- eating
- growing
- moving
- reproducing
- responding to stimuli
- producing waste.

In fact it's not always that simple. There are plenty of bacteria that don't need air (in fact many find oxygen deadly). And it's hard, when leaning against the trunk of an oak tree, to think that we're dealing with a creature that has much voluntary movement. Perhaps a property of life that has been missed here is attempting to survive. Similarly, some non-alive things have several of these 'life' characteristics. Think of lava, pouring out of a volcano. It breathes, or at least it consumes oxygen. It eats material it meets along the way. It moves and it grows. It hisses in response to the stimulus of pouring water on it. It leaves behind a waste trail of ash. Not a bad collection of living properties.

Something that really gets the thoughts going on this topic is a virus. Get hold of some electron microscope pictures of viruses from the internet (see Chapter 9 on getting information this way) – they look amazing, like anything from a naval mine to a moon lander. Viruses are not considered truly alive (which is why you can't kill them with an antibiotic). That gives us another property of being alive, incidentally – something alive can be killed. Viruses have many of the 'being alive' properties, but, crucially, they don't have the full set of capabilities built in. To reproduce, they have to use the genetic material of the cell they attack. So one essential of being alive is not just being able to do the things implied by the properties, but having that ability built in.

LIFE: SOMETHING THAT GOES

Although it's not really a property, life *goes*. It uses up energy to enable it to grow, it moves, reproduces and does all those other good, lifey things. This implies having some sort of power source. And the other properties are often about how the lifeform deals with energy production and the waste products of that energy cycle – hence eating and producing waste.

Plants have the most direct approach when it comes to getting hold of energy. Light energy, usually from the Sun, is used by the photosynthesis process to produce the chemicals (principally carbohydrates) that will fuel life. Photosynthesis is much more complicated than the apparently similar photoelectric effect used in solar panels, where light blasts electrons out of a special material to produce electricity. The chemical processes in photosynthesis are complex and often amazingly fast – some of the reactions are the fastest ever measured, taking place in under 1/1,000,000,000,000th of a second.

The light is absorbed by pushing up the energy of electrons in special colouring materials such as chlorophyll. This bit *is* like the photoelectric effect, but there's more. The energy from the light is then transferred in chemical form to an in-plant reactor, the photosynthetic reaction centre, where the fundamental reaction that produces the oxygen we breathe is performed. Different plants have different levels of oxygen production – despite all we hear about rainforests being the planet's lungs, it's actually plankton in the seas that make the greatest contribution. And a high-output photosynthetic species such as corn can produce enough oxygen to support over 300 people from each hectare of planting.

Animals don't share the plants' direct ability to convert light energy into food. They have to use an intermediary – either eating a plant, or eating another animal

MITOCHONDRIA

The cells in our bodies (and the cells of most complex living things) contain tiny structures called mitochondria. They are often called the power source of the cell, as they are responsible for production of a chemical called ATP, which the body uses to store away energy, like tiny chemical batteries. The mitochondria in your cells have their own DNA, separate from your normal genes – this mitochondrial DNA is only passed on from your mother. It's thought that mitochondria were originally separate bacteria which invaded primitive cells and over time have become part of the furniture.

(which itself will have eaten a plant, or another animal, etc.). Indirectly, though, the power source of all life is the Sun.

The oxygen business with photosynthesis shows the overlap of eating and breathing. The chemical reactions going on (whether it is a plant or a person) will usually involve the use of gases from the air, and the production of other gases. Luckily for us, plants are pretty handy at churning out the oxygen we need to deal with our food, and to function generally.

If you think about it, the purpose of most of these properties of life is to stay alive, so my suggested property of attempting to survive is an overarching one encompassing the others. The way most living things respond to stimuli – the senses in our case (and a surprising number of plants, for instance, will respond to touch and light direction) – is another mechanism to help stay alive. Think how difficult it would be to stay alive if you had no senses, no way to respond to stimuli. It would be a very short existence.

LIFE: THRIVING

It's one thing to live, another to thrive. Life is always a battle, but any living thing will have a set of conditions that help it survive most effectively. These can be the obvious requirements such as acceptable temperature, availability of water, sufficient nutrients and so on, or slightly less obvious requirements, whether it's getting enough sleep for a human or the pH of the soil for a plant.

An interesting exercise (which cunningly brings in a touch of astronomy too) is to look at different planets in the solar system and see what they would be like as a place to live. Take Venus, the most similar planet to the Earth. Until relatively recently everyone thought this was a good bet as a place for life to thrive, though no one could be sure, as the planet is permanently covered in cloud. Unfortunately, once probes had penetrated that cloud and brought back the reality of the Venusian environment, things weren't so rosy. There was good news, but not much of it.

The good news about Venus:

- average diameter: 12,103 kilometres (the Earth is 12,756 kilometres, so very similar in size);
- distance from the Sun: 108,200,000 kilometres (a bit close, but not impossibly so);
- surface area: 460,200,000 square kilometres;
- surface gravity: 0.9 Earth value (close to ours, but everything would feel a touch lighter);
- length of year: 225 days (reasonable for a life cycle).

The bad news about Venus:

- average temperature: 480°C – that's so hot that the metal lead is a liquid on Venus;
- maximum temperature: 600°C – that makes it the hottest planet in the solar system;
- atmospheric pressure: ninety times that of the Earth;
- length of day: 243 days;
- atmosphere: mostly carbon dioxide (97 per cent) with clouds of sulphuric acid;
- virtually no water;
- extremely volcanic surface.

Venus is no paradise. By looking at other planets we can see why life works so well on the Earth. In science, the need for certain conditions to enable life to thrive is sometimes referred to as the Goldilocks principle. That's because the particular requirement has to be not too extreme in one direction (not too hot, for instance), not too extreme in the other (not too cold), but just right.

Something that's relatively easy to overlook when considering the factors for survival of human beings is the capability of our brains. Although we haven't evolved in the last 100,000 years, we have pragmatically, if not biologically, become a totally different species. If an animal needs to be able to carry water to survive crossing a desert, it takes millions of years to evolve the capability. We buy a water bottle. If an animal will benefit from being able to fly from continent to continent there is a huge evolutionary timescale involved in developing wings – and because of the random nature of evolution, the chances are it will never happen. We can hop on a plane.

This special facility of the human impacts all measures of thriving. It also emphasizes the importance of some of the factors that may otherwise be ignored. For example, the ability to resist disease. Because we have an understanding of basic hygiene we can take action to prevent infection. It's one of the key factors enabling us to do more than scrape an existence – yet it tends to be overlooked as one of the requirements for thriving, because it isn't 'natural'. This is a misunderstanding. Our brains and their capabilities are natural, and so ought to be considered as part of our strategy for thriving.

LIFE: VARIETY IS SPICE

There's a whole lot of life going on out there. In the grand scheme of things, you can't beat bacteria. They've been around longest, and there are many more of them in the world than anything else. They are also incredibly successful. Consider, for instance, how much trouble a common little bacterium, staphylococcus aureus, causes when antibiotic-resistant variants cause the infection MRSA.

When working out how to categorize the complex mass of living things we revert to classification. Originally this was done on visible signs – classifying things together that look similar – though more recently we have started to rely on more fundamental genetic indicators, which have thrown up some surprising relationships. The elephant's closest living relative, for example, is the rock hyrax, which looks more like an inflated stoat than anything else.

The modern classification system leaves mammals almost sidelined, with practically everything we would normally think of as an animal (including birds, fish and reptiles) in just one of over thirty different animal groups (you might see eight listed, but things have got more complex since then). These large-scale groups in the classification of living things are called phyla (plural of phylum). Human beings are crammed into a single phylum with all the other animals with backbones, while nematodes – little unsegmented worms – get a whole phylum to themselves. In fact there is one phylum, placozoa (tubular animals), which only has a single member.

Combining the classification system with our understanding of evolution leads to one commonly held misunderstanding. Take this quote (with a little spelling correction) from a zoo poster about gorillas produced by Year 7s: 'Show some care for our ancestors and go and visit Bristol Zoo.' We seem to be haunted by the remnants of the Victorian concept that we are descended from the apes. Instead both we and the other apes are descended from a common ancestor. That common ancestor is closer to us and chimpanzees than it is to orang-utans. But it wasn't a human or a chimp. And it wasn't our immediate ancestor either. Between the common ancestor and homo sapiens there was a whole chain of different species, becoming gradually closer to a human. These chains can throw off dead ends – side developments that come to nothing, such as Neanderthal man. We may be from the same stock as other apes, and our ancestors probably were hairier and looked more like them than humans – but we aren't in a direct line of descent from gorillas or any other living apes.

LIFE: NOTHING IS CONSTANT

Life adapts. That's the idea behind evolution and natural selection. Animals or plants of the same species differ because of the way their parental genes have been combined and because of mutation. Some will fit a particular environment better than others. The variants that fit best tend to thrive better – so that variation is more likely to be passed on. (This is where human beings triumph, of course. We don't wait for biological change to provide the adaptation, we upgrade ourselves to deal with the problems we face, thanks to the capabilities of our big brains.)

It's easy to get confused about adaptation, a problem that resulted in an incorrect alternative to Darwinian evolution. The idea, called Lamarckism after the French biologist Lamarck, started from an obvious truth. We adapt to our environment. So, for instance, runners get bigger leg muscles. People who spend a lot of time in the sun get darker skin. But the mistake Lamarck made was to think that those changes are then passed on, to some degree, to the offspring. So we would expect a runner's children to have stronger legs than an average child. Someone who spends a lot of time in the sun would have darker-skinned children than the average.

You can see how easy it is to make this mistake when trying to work out, for instance, how giraffes got such long necks. Lamarck would say that, with years of stretching to try to reach high branches, the giraffe's ancestors slightly elongated their necks. The next generation had longer necks on average. They too slightly elongated their necks. Over time, the giraffe became what it is today. Note how subtly different this is from real Darwinian evolution. Darwin tells us that some of the offspring of the giraffe ancestors had slightly longer necks, some about the same, some slightly shorter. This had nothing to do with their parents' habits – it was random variation. The ones with longer necks were better able to reach the juicy, high-up leaves and survive. So there were more children born from them, and they too had slightly longer necks than average. Of those, some would be even more gifted in the neck area than their parents, some less . . . and so it goes.

The big difference between Lamarck and Darwin is that Lamarck thought the adaptation undergone by a creature would be passed on. Darwin thought that selection of the fittest from random variation would lead to an adaptation. Darwin didn't know how this worked. Now we know about genes it's much clearer that Darwin was right and Lamarck wrong. Physical adaptation of an individual has no effect on the genes.

LIFE: **NOT VERY WELL DESIGNED**

There's an awful lot of confusion about evolution, caused not only by those who object to the idea because it clashes with the timescale that they've deduced from (for example) the Bible, but also by those who have popularized the evolutionary message. Richard Dawkins' picture of 'the selfish gene' captured a generation with the idea that all of life is just the genes' way of replicating themselves. But we were never intended to take the idea of genes being selfish literally. Genes don't run the world.

Similarly, some evolutionary biologists (and some who try to mix biology and theology) speak of life as being designed. The proponents of intelligent design and other variants on creationism believe that the design was done by God. The evolutionary biologists are using the word in a much more abstract fashion. When they speak of evolution 'designing' a feature, they really mean that random chance has thrown this feature together and it has then proved useful.

It's impossible for science to answer theological questions – or for theological thinking to be used to give answers to scientific questions. The best thing is not, as Richard Dawkins or the intelligent design people do, to attack the other viewpoint, but to respect the separation of the two. So when I call this section 'not very well designed', it's not suggesting that animals and plants *are* designed, but looking at the quality of 'design' if animals and plants really were designed for a particular purpose.

In many ways biological design is superb. Many biological solutions to problems are very sophisticated, and do things we are only just starting to understand. An obvious biological success is reproduction – manufacturing is a much cruder way of getting to an end product. And there are also more bits of brilliance in biological 'design'. For example, there's a lotus flower that repels mud, so it comes up clean from a muddy pool. A similar technology is now being used to make 'self-cleaning' glass.

Equally, there are some clearly poor bits of 'design' in the human body which suggest that these features have been evolved rather than designed with a purpose in mind. For example, the optical nerves that sense light in the retina are back to front. Light has to travel through the 'wiring' of the nerve to the far end in order to start a signal that then heads back towards the retina down the nerve. And our throats aren't too good either. It really isn't a great idea to have solid objects going down the same passage as air, as anyone who has ever choked on their food will testify.

Yet some of the apparently poor design features that many children will spot if they think about the idea of being badly designed are a lot more complex – and wonderfully fascinating – than they might first seem. The other day I was out taking my dog for a walk. It was a cold day, and we were walking through a field of nettles and thistles. She didn't seem to notice any of this. I was chilled to the bone, and repeatedly scratched and stung. What possible good reason is there for us having such a delicate, unprotected skin? Why don't we have nice thick protective coats, as it's usually assumed our predecessors did? It seems totally anti-evolutionary to lose such a useful trait.

LIFE: WHY PEOPLE DON'T HAVE FUR

Sometimes, in order to gain something, we have to lose something else. Evolution through natural selection isn't directed. There is no mind, looking for the 'best' combination. Often a trade-off will occur that gives an overall benefit, even though it results in local problems – a sort of two steps forward, one step back, change. Our loss of that handy protective fur seems to have been a small negative side effect of a much bigger benefit – becoming human, a process that finished around 100,000 years ago.

Back then, our predecessors had already undergone huge changes from the ancestor they shared with chimpanzees and the other great apes. The pre-humans had lost most of their hair, leaving a delicate, thin skin exposed. They had shifted from a four-legged motion to walking upright. Their brains had grown out of all proportion with their bodies. Their mouths had become smaller, less effective as a biting weapon. The big toe had ceased to be an opposing digit that could be used to grip a tree branch.

Taken together, these alterations seem to be the entire opposite of everything we expect from natural selection. They made the pre-humans vastly more vulnerable to attack by predators. Their naked skin was pathetically easy for claws and teeth to rip through. Compared to the four-footed gait of the other apes, their tottering movements on two legs were slow and clumsy – even a rabbit could outrun this strange creature. The adaptations that survived in pre-humans don't seem to make any sense. Or at least, they don't make any sense until they're seen as side effects. Alone, they reduced the chances of survival, but taken alongside the change of behaviour that triggered them, they were an acceptable price to pay.

The physical modifications that made the development of a human being possible were the result of an environmental upheaval. As the global climate underwent violent change, our ancestors were pushed out of the protection of the forests into the exposed world of the savannah. Facing up to coldly efficient predators, they had to change behaviour or become extinct. Back then, most pre-humans could not function in large groups. This is still the case with our close relatives. The chimpanzee, for example, is incapable of forming large, cooperative bands. Get more than a handful together and the outcome is bloody carnage as battles for supremacy break out.

The pre-humans who first straggled onto the savannah around five million years ago were much the same. But the fast, killing-machine predators of the day – from the sabre-toothed dinofelis and the lion-sized machairodus to the more familiar hyenas – made sure that things would change. The most likely pre-humans to survive were those with a tendency to cooperate. Our ancestors began to operate in larger and larger groupings, giving them the ability to take on a predator and win, where a small roaming band would be torn to pieces. And this change of behaviour brought with it as a side effect all the physical oddities that we observe in modern man.

The characteristics that repressed aggression and enhanced the ability to cooperate are typical of young apes. Chimpanzees' inability to operate in large groups only appears with maturity. The individual pre-humans who were more likely to survive on the savannah, those with the immature ability to get on with their fellows rather than tear them to pieces, were also the least physically developed. The eventual outcome was lack of hair on most of the body, large head, small mouth – even the upright stance – all features of the early part of the ape life-cycle.

This mechanism of selecting for cooperative behaviour and getting an infant-like version of the animal as a side effect is something humanity has since managed repeatedly with its domestic animals. The dog, for instance, has much more in common with a wolf cub than with the mature wolf it was bred from. How this happened was demonstrated in a fascinating long-term experiment between the 1950s and the 1990s.

Russian geneticist Dimitri Belyaev selectively bred Russian silver foxes for docile behaviour and showed how early man managed to turn the wolf into a dog. Over forty years – an immensely long experiment, but no time at all in evolutionary terms – the fox descendants began to resemble domesticated dogs. Their faces changed shape; their ears no longer stood upright, but drooped down. Their tails became more floppy. Their coats ceased to be uniform in appearance, developing colour variations and patterns. They spent more time in play, and constantly looked for leadership from an adult. As they became more cooperative, they took on the physical appearance of overgrown cubs.

In the process of becoming more cooperative, more infantile (neotenous in the scientific jargon), the pre-humans had a physical resemblance to a modern human being for many hundreds of thousands of years, but still something was missing. They remained purely animal in their reaction to their surroundings. But with the final breakthrough around 100 millennia ago, something new, something unique in terrestrial biology, came about. The physical changes that had produced an infantile grown-up ape made possible one further change, the most dramatic of all.

Zoologist Clive Bromhall, who came up with the reasoning behind our child-like appearance, has described this last change as a partitioning of the brain, enabling the early humans to simultaneously experience an internal and an external world. Our ancestors began to scrawl pictures on rock walls, to represent in images animals that weren't present, or events that would happen at a different time. Something had changed in their brains, something that opened up the ability to see beyond the present. At the same time as reacting to the world about them, these transformed creatures were able to play around with 'what if?'s, to dream, to plan, to anticipate. To be conscious. And that would prove a dramatic gift – making possible all of civilization and science – for which our fragile, child-like bodies were a small price to pay.

LIFE: CRACKING THE DNA CODE

You will cover very basic aspects of reproduction with the children, but what you hear in the news won't help a lot with some of the key areas of biology that are coming up all the time – specifically cloning and stem cells. It's worth spending a minute or two on these subjects as they are widely misunderstood and might be brought up by some media-savvy Year 6.

Before we plunge into cloning, it's worth saying a little bit about how DNA works, because it's the engine for cell splitting and providing the 'recipe' for creating a living creature. There have been three big steps in the understanding of the workings of life. The first was the theory of evolution. The second was the concept of genes – little packets of information that we get from our parents and that tell the living creature how to grow. But as late as the 1950s, no one had any idea how genes worked.

The eventual discovery of the structure of DNA by the Cambridge team of Crick and Watson, largely thanks to data from the London pair Wilkins and Franklin (they couldn't really be called a team as they never got on), was the big breakthrough that was to provide that third step. DNA is a long, complex molecule that makes up our genes, which has two, helical (spring-shaped) outer chains, linked by a set of molecular 'rods' like the steps of a spiral staircase. The treads of the staircase consist of pairs of chemicals, and when a cell splits, the DNA divides in two, unzipping down the middle of each rung of the spiral staircase.

In all there are four different possible chemical components of the half of a tread that is left sticking out of one side of the unzipped 'staircase' – these chemicals, called bases, are adenine, cytosine, guanine and thymine, usually shortened to the first letter of their name. But the other half of the tread is always the same for a particular base. Adenine is always paired with thymine; cytosine is always coupled to guanine. This means that from the unzipped half you can always work out what the other half should be, and the genetic mechanism can reconstruct a full DNA double helix from the divided half.

Knowing the structure of DNA was half the battle. The other was working out what the different bases signified.

If you run along a piece of DNA and read off the bases, you are reading a code, not unlike the binary code a computer uses, except instead of having 0s and 1s, here there is A, C, G and T. After a lot of false starts it was discovered that the different letter combinations work together in groups of three to assemble amino acids – the chemicals that make up organic matter – into proteins, the much more complex chemicals that do most of the work in our bodies. Each group of three letters (called a codon) specifies a particular amino acid, so reading down the string of DNA, the mechanisms of the cell can effectively follow a recipe to produce the right proteins.

Two problems remain at this stage. One is the amount of information present. Some simple organisms have many more base pairs in their DNA than complex animals like a human being. The other problem is how the reading mechanism knows where the three letters of the codon start. It was discovered that three of the codons (for example, the combination UAA) act as stop signals, and one (ATG) doubles as both the signal for a particular amino acid and a start signal. This makes it clear where the triplets start, but also shows that huge amounts of the genetic information just aren't used. The bits that are used are called exons and the 'rubbish' codons are introns. No one is quite sure why we have this 'junk DNA' that doesn't do anything. Some of it seems to be older versions of the genetic code that have been replaced, but the jury is out on whether or not it still has a function.

LIFE: ANOTHER TAKE ON REPRODUCTION

Cloning is reproduction not by the combination of genetic material from two individuals, as in normal sexual reproduction, but by duplicating a single set of genes. When cloning an animal like the famous sheep Dolly, a piece of genetic material is taken from the original host (in the case of Dolly's parent, from the mammary, which is why she was named after singer Dolly Parton). The contents of one of the donor cells are used to replace the insides of an unfertilized egg cell.

With a touch of the Frankenstein, a tiny burst of electricity was used both to help the nucleus fuse into the egg that would become Dolly, and to give the process a kick-start. The egg, implanted in a host mother, began to grow in the normal fashion, and after the appropriate period of time, Dolly was born. Bear in mind that 'appropriate period of time'. Cloning in the movies often seems to produce fully grown adults in the space of hours or days. A clone is no different from any other animal of the species – it will take the same time to go from egg to newborn infant, the same time to grow up.

The previous paragraph is the 'no snags' version. If it were that easy, we would have clones popping up all over the place, and the few individuals who claim to have made human clones would be proudly displaying them, rather than making the claims but never producing any evidence. In practice it has proved hugely difficult.

Even getting to Dolly took many years. Although it had been possible to use this technique with frogs for some time, it just wouldn't work with mammals. The breakthrough was to use a cell in a different state from those that had originally been tried. Most of the time our cells aren't rapidly duplicating themselves as they do when a foetus is growing. All the original experiments had used cells that were in the right state to split. What the team at the Roslin Institute in Scotland (who came up with Dolly) tried instead was using quiescent cells, cells that had initially been splitting, but then had had their nutrients removed, so the growth process stopped. These proved effective.

The snags weren't out of the way yet, though. Although the quiescent nuclei did seem to work when transplanted into an egg, most were false starts. Out of 276 initial tries, only 29 showed any sign of activation, and of those 29 implanted in surrogates, only one – Dolly – lived. But surely, now we've had Dolly, it's easy to get better and better at the cloning business? Isn't it only a matter of time before we see those human clones?

No. First of all, although Dolly seemed perfectly normal, she died unusually young for a sheep, apparently from old age despite being only half-way through a typical sheep's life. One possible reason for this is that her cellular clocks thought she was the same age as her mother. Chromosomes, the packages of genes that make up our genetic instructions, have little tags at the end called telomeres. Each time a cell divides, its chromosomes lose a bit of their telomeres. It's thought this is a sort of age-tagging mechanism. Dolly's telomeres started identical with those of her 6-year-old parent. It seems possible that the older the parent animal, the less time the clone will have before the problems of old age set in.

Alternatively it could just be that Dolly's genes were damaged in the rough and ready process. Cloning is a bit like trying to repair a delicate watch with a hammer and chisel – you can get lucky, but it's much easier to do damage. Later studies of animal cloning have shown that the process tends to modify the DNA, damaging important genes and resulting in the inability of many embryos to survive. Those that do live tend to have serious problems. All the evidence is that these potential problems get worse with monkeys, worse still with apes, and it is quite possible that it may never be practical to produce a cloned human being (for which many people will breathe a sigh of relief). This doesn't mean that you can't clone human cells – we'll come back to that in a moment.

Even though we are unlikely to see the cloned Hitlers of the movie *The Boys from Brazil*, it is worth pointing out that the chances are very high that you have met a human clone. There may even be a couple in the class you teach. When thinking of Dolly, we are considering artificial procedures to manufacture clones, but a good number of natural clones are born every year. We call them identical twins.

There are two types of twins. Fraternal twins are the more common. Different-sex twins are always fraternal, as are many same-sex twins. Fraternal twins are born when more than one egg is fertilized at the same time. They are perfectly normal siblings, who just happen to be born together. Identical twins, however, are a very different proposition. They come from a single egg, which rather than initially dividing in the normal way to produce more and more cells in a single entity, has first split into two entirely separate cells. These cells contain identical genetic material – they are clones.

It ought to be stressed that identical twins aren't clones of either of their parents. They contain the normal half-and-half genetic material from the two. They are clones of each other. When you get to know identical twins, you can get a feeling for the way a manufactured clone would be. It's often assumed a human clone would be identical to the original parent. Yet identical twins can be quite dissimilar. This is in part because they aren't truly identical. We are all mutants. Our genetic material undergoes small random changes from the impact of natural radiation, for instance. This will differ between twins. But also the twins will differ because of environmental reasons.

They won't eat and drink the same things. They won't be exposed to exactly the same conditions. Over time they will grow more and more different. There is good evidence that much of our personality that isn't genetic comes from our interaction with peer groups. These interactions will be different for the two twins. Adult identical twins not only often look fairly different because of environmental pressures, they will also differ significantly in personality. Anyone egotistical enough to want a clone so they can have a 'mini me' will be sadly disappointed.

LIFE: FIRST CATCH YOUR STEM CELL

The reason human cloning isn't a total dead end brings us to the second headline-grabbing aspect of this kind of biological manipulation – stem cell research. What lies behind this is part of a total transformation that has quietly happened to medicine. For thousands of years, medicine was a matter of guesswork and experience. Most theory was once based on the Ancient Greek idea of the four humours. The Greeks thought that the body contained four essential fluids – blood, black bile, yellow bile and phlegm. In good health these four humours were in balance. When someone was ill, the humours had got out of balance. Most of us, it was thought, had a dominant humour that came through in our personality. So someone with blood dominant was 'sanguine', with phlegm dominant 'phlegmatic', with yellow bile 'choleric' and with black bile 'melancholic'.

This idea was responsible for many of the most disastrous failures at curing the sick. All the way through to the nineteenth century, medicine resorted to blood letting and the use of emetics to try to relieve an excess of one humour or another. The result was generally the weakening of the patient, and a worse chance of survival than if nothing had been done at all. Other cures were largely down to rumour and experience, often driven by coincidence. If someone happened to get better after a certain kind of branch had been waved over them, then that was clearly good for the cure. Diseases were often thought to be caused by breathing foul air – 'miasmas' that carried with them the taint of illness.

It was only with a better understanding of the body and the recognition of the existence of bacteria and viruses that medical attitudes began to change. But even thirty years ago, there was very little idea of how illnesses and medicines worked. The revolution has been a better (though still very incomplete) understanding of how we work at the cellular level, and how diseases and drugs impact us right down to their effects on individual molecules.

When really effective medicines were introduced, it used to be because of an accidental discovery. These true medicines still started with traditional experience-based cures, but they were then tested, and the effective component isolated (or the old wives' tale was dismissed). Over time, for instance, it was discovered that chewing a particular kind of bitter bark helped reduce pain – the active ingredient was extracted and refined to aspirin. In the 1930s it was noticed that a particular mould killed dangerous bacteria – the active ingredient would eventually be refined as penicillin. But this was finding something that worked without understanding why. Recent medical breakthroughs have involved knowing how a particular chemical will be handled by the body, and designing a drug that will have the required effect – much more science and less guesswork, but a very lengthy and expensive process.

Stem cell research, with all its accompanying debate and scandals, is one of these new lines of medical thinking, based on a better understanding of how the body builds itself and mends itself. All cells are not created equal – some are much more flexible than others. If you look at the cells in the body, they are not all the same. This is pretty obvious. The cells in your skin are visibly and tactilely different from the cells in your hair, your blood or your flesh. Yet all your cells came from a single, original cell that divided over and over again as you were developed in the womb.

The very first embryonic cells to form are totally flexible. They can become anything. But as cells divide they begin to differentiate. As they become more and more different they become more specialized. By this time a particular type of cell is only likely to split to make more of the same kind of cells. Cells that can become different types of cell are called stem cells.

So far, so good. But there are two broad types of stem cells – embryonic stem cells and adult stem cells. (The 'adult' word is a bit misleading, since children have these stem cells too.) Adult stem cells are more specialized. In principle, an adult stem cell from a kidney could produce all the cells required for a new kidney – but it couldn't produce a new liver. Embryonic stem cells can do anything, become anything.

In principle – and it's a long way off – stem cells could be a real miracle tool for medicine. In the long term they could enable us to grow replacement organs and to treat cancer or repair damage to internal organs and systems. More short-term, but still important possibilities are treatments for conditions such as Parkinson's disease and diabetes. However, the only way to get hold of those particularly effective embryonic stem cells is to destroy a human embryo. This is at the stage when it is still a collection of a few cells – nonetheless such an action presents a real moral problem to many people.

Even so, scientists are often bewildered by the resistance to stem cell research. For example, in 2006, US president George Bush vetoed a bill to enable limited embryonic stem cell research. This would have made use of cells from excess embryos created during *in vitro* fertilization (IVF) treatment for infertility. These embryos are normally destroyed – it's hard to see how destruction is better than making use of the cells to develop therapies that have the potential of being life-saving.

Cloning comes into this issue because the body is very good at destroying invaders. Our immune system is designed to spot foreign material, like bacteria, and to destroy it before it can do too much harm. But when using cells for therapeutic reasons, all the way up to organ transplants, we need the body to accept foreign cells. The immune system has to be fought into submission, which puts the patient at risk of infection, and there is always the possibility that it will fight back and reject the implant.

However, if it were possible to start with cells that were clones of the patient's own cells, there would be no rejection – the new cells would be recognized as 'one of ours'. So there is a huge amount of interest in therapeutic cloning – the production of cloned stem cells that can be used to help repair the original donor. This therapeutic cloning is banned in many countries and remains controversial, not because of its application, but because the source of the cloned cells is, in effect, a very early embryo.

Acceptance of the procedure was not helped by one of the biggest scientific scandals ever. A South Korean scientist, Woo Suk Hwang, who claimed to have made big steps forward in the cloning of human stem cells, was shown in early 2006 to have faked all his research. Hwang was disgraced, and the whole process thrown into temporary disrepute. Stem cell research and therapeutic cloning are not going to go away, but the process has suffered a significant setback.

We like to think of science as being cool and objective, but we can't do science without being aware of its moral consequences. The scientists who worked on the Manhattan Project creating the atomic bomb were well aware of the ethical issues they faced. So are scientists working in fields like stem cell research today. There are some areas that society will decide are not appropriate. But such a decision should be based on a good understanding of the science, not a knee-jerk reaction to emotive terms.

LIFE: PASS THE ENERGY

To all intents and purposes, the whole Earth is powered by sunlight. (Okay, there is some heat energy from the Earth's core, which is seriously hot – about the same as the surface of the sun, at around 5,500° Celsius. That heat is partly because it was hot to start with, from the impact when the Earth was first formed, and partly maintained by energy produced by radioactive decay. Some of the heat seeps through to the surface, but not much.) One way of looking at life is as a mechanism for passing around that energy.

Energy can neither appear from nowhere nor can it disappear into nothing. (Strictly speaking, this isn't true, thanks to that masterful manipulator of the counter-intuitive, quantum theory. This predicts (and it has been shown to be true), that empty space isn't truly empty. Particles keep springing into existence and disappearing. Normally the net result, added over time, is that energy isn't appearing from the void, but in a confined locality, over a short space of time, it can happen.)

It can seem that energy does sometimes appear from nowhere, but what is usually happening that is one type of energy is being transformed into another. At the extreme, for example, the Sun appears to generate energy from nowhere, but in fact a very small amount of matter is being transformed into energy – and matter is the equivalent of such a vast amount of energy (this is the subject of Einstein's famous equation $E = mc^2$, where E is energy, m is the mass of the matter, and c is the speed of light, a very big number, which is then multiplied by itself).

While it would be foolish to say that the 'purpose' of life is to transfer energy from one form to another, it certainly is one of the major functions of life. Everything living is part of an energy chain, starting with energy from sunlight and passing it

SELFISH GENES AS A MODEL

Zoologist and science writer Richard Dawkins famously gave us the image of the selfish gene. The idea here is that one way of looking at life is that it is a mechanism for genes to reproduce. What Dawkins also said, but is often missed, is that this is just a way of looking at life – it's not a definitive truth. It can be useful as one vehicle for understanding life and how it works, but there's a lot more to life than just this. Similarly, life can be looked at as a mechanism for converting energy into different forms. Like Dawkins' selfish gene, it's a very blinkered view if you take it as the only factor – but it is useful to understand one aspect of life.

through myriad variations and forms. Although such a view of life is simplistic, it can also be surprisingly beautiful.

As we've already seen, from Einstein's viewpoint, matter and energy are really just variations on a theme – and in the next chapter we move on to matter, covering the stuff that makes up living creatures and all the rest of the material world.

LIFE – ESSENTIALS

In the life section of the curriculum areas, we've seen how to identify what is alive, using our natural tendency to classify and list properties. We've seen how life is something that 'goes', using energy: it's an energy converter. The different planets have provided a useful mental laboratory for testing the requirements for life to thrive, and we've seen the variety and tendency to adapt that have resulted in the rich diversity of life on Earth. Not directly curriculum-linked, but an important addition, is an understanding of cloning and stem cells.

CHAPTER 5

AROUND THE CURRICULUM – STUFF

One thing I have learned in a long life: that all our science, measured against
reality, is primitive and childlike – and yet is the most precious thing we have.

Albert Einstein, quoted in Banesh Hoffmann,
Albert Einstein: Creator and Rebel

There's something very satisfying and touchy-feely about stuff. It's basic. It's . . .
what everything is made of. So materials, what they are, how they work, provide a
very sensible core aspect of the curriculum. Life is an important topic because being
alive is important to us on Earth. Stuff is more versatile than that – it's universal.

STUFF: WHAT SORT?

When we move onto materials, we're back to classification. What is an object made
of? What are its properties? The great thing here is that there's less hidden than in
biology. What you see is often what you get. Having said that, it's not all obvious
on the surface with materials. If you look at some sulphur, some salt, and some
custard powder, it's not obvious that the sulphur is a pure element, one of the chemical
building blocks of matter, while the salt is a compound – a substance that combines
two or more elements in a particular structure. The elements in the salt (the metal
sodium and the gas chlorine) are linked, so instead of being made up of individual
atoms or molecules of an element, it has molecules that contain one part each of
sodium and chlorine, linked together. Custard powder is a mixture – a mixture contains
two or more different types of atom or molecule, but there is no bond between them,
they are just mixed up together.

It's also not so easy to take a look at gases, most of which are invisible, and
can be present in a confusing mixture like air. That's why it took so long to sort out

what air was, and to dismiss the idea of phlogiston. It was thought for many years that when something was burned it gave off a substance called phlogiston. This seemed natural, as burning tends to give things off – smoke for instance. (Good old common sense.) The phlogiston idea eventually fell apart when it was discovered that the total remains of a burned substance were usually heavier than the original weight. Though some tried to cling on to phlogiston by deciding it had negative weight, it was more likely that burning involved something out of the air being combined with the original material – a 'something' that we now know to be oxygen. But the whole phlogiston business shows that classification of substances isn't always easy.

A common way of classifying materials – one that's easy to use from an early age – is to use the division between natural and manufactured. Be careful, though, not to follow that classification with a starry-eyed, unscientific green outlook. There is no value judgement in the terms 'natural' and 'manufactured'. Our ability to survive beyond our biological capabilities is largely driven by manufactured materials.

What's more, many simple manufactured products are identical to their 'natural' counterparts. The only difference between natural salt, taken from a salt mine or the sea, and manufactured salt, made by chemical combination, is that the natural salt is more likely to be contaminated with poisons. Chemicals themselves are neither inherently natural or manufactured, inherently bad or good. The most deadly poisons in existence can be obtained from nature.

Bear in mind also that manufacturing can include manipulating a natural material into an unnatural structure – so paper, for example, contains natural material, but not in a form you would find in nature. Manufacturing can also involve purely synthetic materials like plastics.

The immediately obvious way to classify materials is by their physical properties. How hard a substance is, for example. But children will also find it natural to classify on use – the things a material is used for. This is rarely a very scientific method of classification – it really just tells us indirect information about the other properties, and these can be very fragile. For instance, when classifying by usage, a computer and a piece of paper are both in the class of 'things I write on'. But this is very little help in understanding the materials involved.

What isn't in the curriculum – a bizarre omission – is the heart of the nature of materials, atomic theory. This is neither new (it goes back to the Ancient Greeks), nor does it have to be complicated. There are plenty of analogies available, for example, Lego® bricks. While there's no need to go into the structure of the atom, a basic understanding of atoms and molecules is very helpful to understand the nature of materials, the differences between solids, liquids and gases, and why different materials *have* different properties. Don't leave it out.

ATOMS AND MOLECULES

You probably know already, but just to distinguish what's going on, an atom is the single smallest particle of an element. It has a substructure – the protons and neutrons in the nucleus and the electrons somewhere fuzzily outside – but it is as small as you can get and still have a bit of an element. A molecule contains more than one atom, joined together. This joining takes place by sharing electrons. Some atoms have a few electrons to spare – others are rather short of them. In bonding, one or more electrons from one atom are attracted by the nucleus of the other atom – this tug of war over the electron forms the bonds.

A molecule can be a pure element. For example, a molecule of oxygen contains two oxygen atoms, joined together. But it can also have more than one element, whether it's a simple molecule like sodium chloride or one of the immensely long DNA chains that make up the complex molecules that support life.

STUFF: TRANSFORMERS

Stuff wouldn't be nearly so interesting if it couldn't be changed. We are surrounded by materials that have been manufactured – transformed from their natural state. In Key Stage 1 a lot of emphasis is put on the different ways materials react to manipulation – squeezing, twisting, stretching, as well as heating and cooling.

The differences between materials happen at the quantum level. It's a matter of how the atoms link together – as we saw with carbon, the difference between the soft, easy sliding planes of graphite and the rigidity of diamond is purely down to the shapes which the atoms form in joining together. The material's properties also depend on how the molecules – the groups of atoms – interact. This can be down to attraction or repulsion of bits of the molecule. Water molecules, for instance, are attracted to each other like little magnets, with the positively charged hydrogen being attracted to the negative oxygen in a different molecule. (This kind of attraction is called a hydrogen bond.)

The effect of this bond is that water molecules stick together more than you might expect. This makes water boil at a higher temperature than it should. Much higher. Water boils at 100°C at sea level. (The boiling point falls as air pressure drops and rises with higher pressure, which is how pressure cookers work. The increased pressure in a pressure cooker means the cooking takes place above 100°C.) If it weren't for hydrogen bonding, the boiling point of water would be well below $-70°C$. Water just wouldn't exist as a liquid on the Earth – and no water means no life.

Water has lots of unusual properties – one that may come up is that solid water (ice) is less dense than the liquid. This is why ice floats on top of a drink – it also explains why it is dangerous to put a glass bottle full of water in the freezer. As the water turns solid it expands (to have the same weight but be less dense, it has to have a bigger volume). The inflexible bottle has nowhere to go and the glass shatters.

I have seen it said in children's science books that this decrease in density on freezing is a unique property of water – unfortunately it isn't, though it is very unusual. Most things shrink as they solidify, but there are other substances that behave like water – for instance acetic acid (the acid in vinegar) and silicon are both less dense as a solid than as a liquid. This behaviour of ice is well known to adults, but not why it happens.

It's down to those hydrogen bonds again. The shape of the normal crystal form of water, a six-sided lattice, won't fit with the way the hydrogen bonds pull the hydrogen of one water molecule towards the oxygen of another. To fit into the structure, these bonds have to stretch and twist, pulling water molecules further apart than they are in water's most dense form (at around 4°C). It's a bit like the way you can keep construction kits in a smaller bag than you need for the a model you make out of the bits.

ICE NINE

While we're on the subject of water, fans of the US science fiction writer Kurt Vonnegut may have already come across the concept of Ice Nine, which appears in his novel *Cat's Cradle*. Vonnegut describes a newly discovered form of ice, so stable that it only melts at 114° Fahrenheit (45° Celsius). If water ever got into an Ice Nine form, the chances are that under normal weather conditions it would never get out of that form. Should a seed crystal of Ice Nine be dropped into a lake or an ocean it would spread uncontrollably from shore to shore, locking up the water supply and devastating the Earth.

Luckily, Ice Nine doesn't exist (though it was a wonderful concept), although there is a type of ice that forms at very low temperatures with the intentionally similar name of Ice IX. This, however, isn't stable at room temperatures, and presents no danger to our water supply.

STUFF: BACK TO THE BEGINNING

An important concept to get across when dealing with changes in stuff is reversibility. Some changes are reversible (for example, the change from water to ice and back to water). Other changes are not reversible – for example, unburning a piece of wood, or getting the milk back out of your coffee. Strictly speaking, even these processes are reversible at the quantum level – you could imagine using a pair of quantum tweezers to pick out the molecules that came from the milk bottle one at a time – but they are much harder to put into reverse than they are to run forwards.

This difficulty of reversal illustrates one of the least well understood areas of science, thermodynamics, and specifically the idea of entropy. Thermodynamics is the apparently simple study of the way heat or energy is moved from one thing to another. Entropy is a fuzzy-sounding concept (though it is described mathematically in physics), which is usually described as a measure of disorder. The more messy something is, the more entropy it has.

Thermodynamics has two famous 'laws' (remember these are really theories that solidly match reality). The first is that energy can't be destroyed or come from nowhere.

QUANTUM TWEEZERS

The idea of picking individual molecules out, one at a time, seems far-fetched, but the technology does exist to manipulate individual quantum particles. In 1980, Hans Dehmelt of the University of Washington managed to isolate a single barium ion (an ion is an atom with electrons missing, or extra electrons added, giving it an electrical charge). The ion was suspended in electromagnetic fields that held it in position. Incredibly, when illuminated by the right colour of laser light, the single barium ion was visible to the naked eye as a pin prick of brilliance floating in space.

In 1989, scientist Don Eigler at the Almaden Research Center used a scanning tunnelling microscope, which it was discovered could manipulate tiny things as well as see them, to spell out the letters IBM with individual xenon atoms. At the same time other fields of science have made major steps forward in nanomanipulation, the handling of particles around a nanometre (1/1,000,000,000th of a metre) in size or less.

So called optical tweezers use tightly focused laser beams to trap particles, while biologists have constructed 'molecular tweezers' where large molecules – typically DNA strands – are combined to make arms that can catch other nano-level objects and manipulate them.

The second says that energy tends go from being concentrated in one place to being spread out. Or to put it another way, entropy increases.

When your milk is separate from your coffee, there is more order in thermodynamic terms. Milk here, coffee there, clear separation between the two. After mixing they're all somewhere in the middle – there's less order.

It's easy to find an apparent hole in the second law of thermodynamics. How come our planet exists, with its excessive order instead of a totally random collection of elements? The thing is, you are allowed to reduce entropy locally, as long as you make things worse universally. It's a bit like global warming. We bring order to the Earth at the price of creating more disorder in the rest of the universe. We have to put more energy into the process than is being used to bring a little local order. Nothing is totally efficient – that extra energy contributes to disorder elsewhere. This is one system that you can't beat.

STUFF: RIDING THE ECO-SURF

It's impossible to turn on the TV these days without finding a politician trying to be more green and eco-friendly than his or her rivals. The impact of global warming is being taken seriously by world governments at last, and from an early age, encouraged by TV programmes like *Blue Peter* and *Newsround*, children become enthusiastic to save the planet.

It can be worth harnessing this enthusiasm for taking a good, ecologically sound approach, though the decision to put it here in the stuff section emphasizes that it doesn't fit awfully well with the main curriculum areas. In part this is about stuff – limited natural resources like gas, oil and wood. In part it's a workings issue, because green issues mostly have energy at their heart. And it's a life issue too – because it's about our survival and our impact on the life on our planet.

Most of the science involved in taking on ecological issues is quite basic – there are really no new points to make that aren't covered elsewhere. The essential in dealing with green science is to make sure that the science is realistic. Too often, the green agenda results in token actions that are all show, rather than providing real benefits. Although children will inevitably take a simplified view, the information they are presented with doesn't have to be oversimplified to the point of incorrectness – and it's important that you understand the real picture.

Take two powerful examples of how green science can be misrepresented. In 2006, David Cameron, at the time the leader of the opposition, made a big thing about riding to work on his bike, rather than using the official car he was provided with. Unfortunately, it came out that his official car was following him, carrying all his papers – so there was no positive impact on the environment. Then there's the example of the Reading wind turbine. Also in 2006, a single electricity-generating wind turbine was erected alongside the M4 motorway near Reading. Unfortunately, because of its sheltered position, it doesn't get much wind, so it doesn't do much . . . but it looks impressive.

Wind power and recycling are two examples where even at primary level it should be possible to take a scientific attitude to green ideas, rather than a purely knee-jerk, propaganda-driven view. A wind turbine is good because it generates electricity without using up scarce resources like gas and coal, and because it doesn't generate greenhouse gases, as do fuel-burning power stations. But make sure you take in the full picture. As it happens, the picture isn't uniformly rosy for wind power.

First there is the environmental impact. Wind turbines are not visually to everyone's taste (though I have to say I prefer them to cooling towers), and for them to be effective they are best placed on high ground (hence the weakness of the Reading site), which often results in spoiling some of the country's best views. They can also cause significant noise pollution, and can have a negative impact on wildlife, killing migratory birds.

Then there's the whole concept of renewable energy. Wind, solar and wave power is usually called 'renewable' in the sense of not using up a resource. But the danger with this label is the assumption that nothing is being used up in the process. When using solar cells, this isn't too bad an assumption. The solar energy they absorb would have been lost whether or not the cells were there. But things are subtly different with wind and wave power. Heavy use of wind power will change weather patterns; and use of wave generators can change the conditions for wildlife in the sea. Technically none of this energy is renewable – there is enough of it to outlast the human race but it will eventually run out. It does nothing for children's understanding of energy conservation if we call it renewable. And it isn't impact-free, which renewable suggests.

The final, and probably most important, problem with the assumption that wind turbines don't have a bad impact on the environment is that this view doesn't take into consideration the energy and materials used in constructing the wind turbine and in modifying the grid to take its input. Making such a large and complex device generates a lot of greenhouse gases and uses a lot of energy. This has to be earned back from the negative side of the balance before a wind turbine makes any positive contribution to the environment.

Recycling also has problems from the impact on the environment of the processing involved. Recycling *is* a great idea, but as yet quite a lot of recycling can have a negative impact on the environment. This is because the processes required to take an old item, turn it back into raw materials, then manufacture something else, use so much energy, and generate so much greenhouse gas, that it may be worse than starting from scratch. To make matters worse, many countries don't have good enough facilities to recycle some materials, and have to ship the waste abroad, resulting in even higher environmental impact.

GREENHOUSE GAS ISN'T JUST CARBON DIOXIDE

It would be easy to think from the simplistic media coverage that carbon dioxide was the only greenhouse gas. It isn't. Methane (famously produced in large quantities by farting cows) is twenty-three times more powerful as a greenhouse gas than carbon dioxide.

Reuse is much better than recycling – this cuts out the remanufacturing cost in terms of energy use and waste generated. It's also worth bearing in mind the impact of movement around the country and around the world. Vast amounts of energy and greenhouse gas production are involved in stocking our supermarkets from all over the globe. Just eating locally produced food can have more effect than much more painful, but more visible (and hence more popular for politicians), green efforts.

The message for good green science is clear. What's important is taking into account all factors, not just what's visible on the surface.

STUFF: GETTING IN A STATE

Matter, as we've seen and as we experience in everyday life, can come in several flavours, technically referred to as states. Children will be very familiar with two of these states – solids and liquids – but have a fuzzier feeling for a third state – gases. Most gases are invisible, which makes it a lot harder to get a grasp on their existence. We are reliant on second-hand sensations – the feeling of wind on the hand, the sight of branches blown by the wind, gas bubbles in a liquid – rather than the direct experience we have of solids and liquids.

The curriculum stops with the clockwork science three states of matter, but there are five states altogether. The fourth is one that all the children will have experienced – it is much more obvious than a gas – but because our primary science is so strongly locked into the clockwork world, even many adults don't know it exists, except in one particular application (large screen TVs). It's plasma.

One potential for confusion needs clearing up here. This has nothing to do with blood plasma. (Actually neither of the uses of the word fits particularly well with its origin, as it originally meant something formed or moulded, and plasmas are very obviously formless.) Blood plasma is the colourless liquid in which blood corpuscles float – it's the liquid part of blood. Plasma in the physics sense is a fourth state of matter, beyond a gas.

WHAT IS GLASS?

When we're teaching children to classify, it's not uncommon for one of the choices to be between solid, liquid and gas. Watch out, though. Apart from the obvious trap that pretty well anything can be in any state, depending on the temperature, one or two materials are downright deceptive. Take glass. What is glass at room temperature? A solid, of course. But don't be surprised if you see it said that it's a liquid.

It's often thought that glass is a very viscous liquid because medieval window glass is thicker at the bottom than at the top – but this merely reflects the way glass was made at the time. Much older Roman glass, for instance, doesn't show any signs of flowing. This appears to be the scientific equivalent of an urban myth. However pitch, such as the tar used in roads, *is* a liquid at room temperature, despite appearing solid.

To show how plasma isn't understood, my dictionary defines plasma as being a gas in which there are ions rather than atoms or molecules. Let's not worry for a moment about those ions, but note how the dictionary was thinking clockwork style. To call plasma a gas is like calling a liquid 'a very dense gas with fluid properties'. A plasma is more like a gas than a liquid, just like a gas is more like a liquid than a solid – but it is still something else, a different state of matter.

I mentioned that children are more likely to have direct sensorial experience of plasmas than gases. The sun is a huge ball of plasma. Every flame contains some plasma, although flames are pretty cool in plasma terms, so are usually a mix of plasma and gas. Just as a gas is what happens to a liquid if you continue to heat it past a certain point, so a plasma is what happens to a gas if you continue to heat it far enough.

As the gas gets hotter and hotter, the electrons around the atoms in the gas are bumped up to higher and higher energy states. Eventually some have enough energy to fly off. In general, depending on how many electrons they have furthest away from the nucleus, atoms have a tendency to find it easier to either lose one or more electrons or gain one or more electrons. Atoms that easily lose electrons do so, and end up as a positively charged ion. Atoms that easily gain electrons hoover up the spare electrons from the positive ions and end up negatively charged. This is a plasma.

Plasmas are very common once you consider the universe as a whole. After all, stars are pretty big. In fact it has been suggested that up to 99 per cent of the universe's detectable matter is plasma. Although plasmas are gas-like in not being hugely dense, they are very different from gases. For instance, gases are pretty good insulators – plasmas are superb conductors.

CHANGING THE STATE OF CUSTARD

We usually think of material changing state as a result of variations in temperature. Cool down water and it becomes ice. Heat up a piece of metal and it becomes molten metal. But pressure can also have a dramatic effect on some materials. Thixotropic non-drip paints change from gel form to liquid when stirred. But the most dramatic and fun demonstration of the effect of pressure on state is provided by custard.

Mix custard powder with water so you get a thick yellow liquid. Pour some into a bowl. Now put your finger and thumb into the liquid a few centimetres apart and squeeze them together. The liquid becomes a dry powder under the pressure of your fingers. As long as you keep the pressure up, it will stay solid – you can easily lift it out of the bowl – but as soon as you relax the pressure it will return to liquid and drip from your fingers.

STUFF: CATCHING THE COLD

The fifth state of matter (it's not custard) is wholly part of the counter-intuitive world. On a good day, scientists can come up with impressively snappy terms. Plasma is pretty good. So are photon and quark. But all too often they come up with a term that no one in their right mind wants to say (try this one after a few drinks). The fifth state of matter is a Bose Einstein condensate.

This is a material down the other end of the temperature scale from a plasma. In fact, before we visit the condensate, it's worth just briefly thinking about temperature. What is temperature? Well, it's how hot things are. To heat them up we have to put energy into the stuff. But what is happening as we do so? The atoms or molecules in the material speed up. Even in a solid, atoms jiggle with energy. In a liquid they shoot about, while in a gas they positively rocket around the place. Temperature is a measure of how much energy there is in those speeding particles. (If you aren't sure about there being a difference in energy just because something's moving faster, imagine being hit by a tennis ball at 5 kilometres per hour, then at 500 kilometres per hour. The second one would hurt a lot more, thanks to all that extra energy.)

Unless you knew that temperature was about the movement of the atoms in a material, you might imagine that you could just cool things down indefinitely, getting colder and colder. In practice, though, you can only slow down the atoms or molecules so much. Eventually they would stop. That temperature, unreachable because quantum particles can't conceive of being entirely stopped, is absolute zero. This ultimate minimum temperature is around $-273.16°C$. Scientists quite often use a temperature scale that has the same size units as Celsius, but starts sensibly with zero at absolute zero. This is the Kelvin scale, so 0°C is about 273K. (For those who like pedantic detail, the units of the Kelvin scale are kelvins, with a small K. Unlike Fahrenheit and Celsius there are no 'degrees' – it's 273K, not 273°K.)

When materials get close to absolute zero, they begin to behave very strangely. By now you won't be surprised to discover it's a quantum effect. When the materials become a condensate (technically there are two variants, Bose Einstein and fermionic, but let's not worry about too much detail here), it's almost as if the particles within the substance lose their individuality. This can result in strange behaviours like superfluidity – where the substance has absolutely no resistance to movement. Superfluids climb out of containers of their own accord, because there is no resistance to the random movement of the molecules. If you start a superfluid rotating in a ring it will go on for ever. Then there are superconductors with no electrical resistance.

The *pièce de résistance* of the condensate world is the way a Bose Einstein condensate deals with light. Because the condensate is half-way between normal matter and light itself, it can interact with light in a strange way, slowing it to a crawl or even bringing it to a complete standstill. This weird mix of light and matter is called a 'dark state', a romantic name that well fits such an odd phenomenon.

So that's five states of matter. Up the top, plasma, a collection of high energy ions. Next a gas, then a liquid, then a solid. Finally, at the extreme limits of cold, the Bose Einstein condensate. Who said stuff was ordinary? Although we think of the different states of matter varying in their physical properties, the key difference is the energy of the atoms or molecules that make up the substance – and it is energy and other essential workings that keep the universe ticking along that provides the subject for our final curriculum chapter.

STUFF – ESSENTIALS

Materials take us back to classification and properties. A particularly important aspect of stuff is its transformation, whether in complex manufacture or simply changing between different states, such as solid, liquid and gas. (But remember there are also plasmas and Bose Einstein condensates. And custard.) Some changes are reversible, others not – generally speaking, entropy increases. Increasing entropy is something we're doing with global warming, and green issues can make great teaching aids – but make sure it is done honestly, taking in the whole cost of adopting a green approach, as well as the benefits.

CHAPTER 6

AROUND THE CURRICULUM – WORKINGS

[A] schoolboy now can predict what a Faraday then could only guess at roughly.
Oliver Heaviside, physicist who predicted the existence
of a charged layer in the atmosphere that reflected radio
waves, in *Electromagnetic Theory* (1893)

I'm biased – I need to admit it straight away, my first degree is in physics and I can't help but love the subject. It's because this is about how everything works. If stuff seemed fundamental, now we can go in one stage deeper and say: what is that stuff made of? Why does it behave the way it does? This is as central to understanding science as it gets.

WORKINGS: ELECTRICKERY

One of the more common aspects of the workings of the universe in everyday modern life is electricity. Some basic electrical work is included in the curriculum, but you can play with batteries and lights to your heart's content and never really grasp what electricity *is*. In a sense this isn't too surprising – electricity, like pretty well all the 'workings' of physical science, operates at the counter-intuitive quantum level.

Electricity is often described using a model that pretends it's like a flow of water – but this isn't really an effective model. If it were, we would have to plug up empty electrical sockets to stop the electricity flowing out. Even so, thanks to the early adoption of this model, we've plenty of fluid-based terms, such as current and the early electronic switching device, the valve, now replaced by the transistor.

Electrical current works because conductors, such as metals, have loose electrons floating about, shared between the atoms in the substance. Put a positive charge on one end of a piece of metal, and these loose electrons will be attracted towards it.

But there's a problem. As all the electrons bunch up at one end, the other end of the piece of metal is short of electrons. Shortage of electrons means that the far end of the metal has a positive charge – so there's a counter-attraction – net result, not much happens. But provide a negative charge at the far end – effectively some spare electrons – and the build-up of positive charge is neutralized. So electricity will only flow when there's a complete circuit – unlike water.

It's rather unfortunate that the people who devised the model of electrical current didn't actually know about electrons. The direction current flowed was decided upon arbitrarily – and it happens to be the opposite way to that of the true flow, the movement of the electrons.

The other problem with the water model is that it suggests that all that happens is that electrons pour down a 'tube'. But if that were all that were happening, we would have a lot of time to wait before electrical devices kicked into action. An electric light, or more dramatically a phone on the end of a long cable, seems to react pretty well instantaneously when the switch is thrown. Yet if you measure the speed of electrons down a wire, they saunter along at less than walking speed. (This is a bit misleading – they actually shoot around at high speed, but all over the place. Most of these movements cancel each other out, but add them all together and you get a gradual drift towards the positive pole.)

What is coming from a battery is not just a bunch of electrons, but an electromagnetic field – the field of influence of electromagnetic energy, and it travels at the speed of light. This invisible, light-like wave (or stream of photons) is what gets the electrons moving at the far end of the wire – they don't (thankfully) have to travel the entire length of the cable from the battery.

WORKINGS: ILLUMINATION

This leads us neatly onto another of the fundamentals, light. Light, as we've seen, is beautifully subtle. Like all quantum particles, photons of light can act like waves, and because waves are often the easiest way to explain light's behaviour, the tendency, at primary school level, is to ignore anything else and say that light *is* a wave. But a moment's reflection should cause concern – at least if you understand waves.

Think of some waves. A wave on the ocean. A Mexican wave, passing from spectator to spectator through a crowded stadium. A sound wave rippling through the air. A wave is a regular movement in something – a medium. It's the wave that travels, not the stuff itself. Otherwise your spectators in the stadium, who are the medium for a Mexican wave, wouldn't stay in the same seats, they would shuttle around the stadium. But there has to be a medium for the wave to exist – otherwise, what moves to produce the wave?

Light doesn't know about this restriction: it travels across empty space. Other waves can't. Take the air out of a jar with a ringing mobile phone inside and the sound of the ring tone will gradually die away. As the *Alien* posters said, in space no one can hear you scream. But light (or the radio waves carrying the phone call) merrily blasts through space without problem. For a long time, the only explanation was to assume that there *was* something in space, the ether (or aether), a strange material that was dreamed up solely for the purpose of giving the light waves something to ripple in.

The ether had to be very strange indeed. It was totally undetectable – it put up no resistance to normal physical objects moving through it – yet it also had to be perfectly rigid. Any tendency to floppiness and light would gradually lose energy as it caused the ether to flop around; before long, the light would run out of energy and stop. In practice, light doesn't lose any energy travelling through space, so the ether had to be perfectly rigid.

In the late nineteenth century, it was proved that the ether didn't exist, with an experiment that looked for the effect of the Earth travelling through the ether on light – it found nothing. Light can't be a wave in the normal sense. But it still remains convenient to refer to it as acting like a wave for most of the circumstances that we will come across in primary school.

The main problems with the wave approach to light come when the light is generated or absorbed. So, for example, in an electric light bulb, or in a plant where photosynthesis is happening, the process is only really describable in terms of little packets of energy – photons, particles of light.

The great physicist Richard Feynman, who specialized in the reactions between light and matter (known as quantum electrodynamics, or QED for short), made it clear that light is *light* – neither a particle nor a wave – but if you want to go with one, he felt that the particle description was the only choice. So there's a real quandary. Waves make it easier to explain some aspects of light, such as colour, but they aren't the ideal way of describing it. Even so, we're stuck with waves as far as the curriculum is concerned.

WORKINGS: GETTING TO THE SOURCE

The other big issue, as far as light is concerned, is the difference between a light source and a reflector. Here's a strange distinction, where a child's view is in some ways closer to our best, counter-intuitive theories than is the usual explanation.

Looking up into the sky, there are plenty of sources of light. The Sun is intensely bright, the Moon duller, stars duller still. But we make a significant distinction between the different lights in the sky. The stars (including the Sun, nothing special in stellar

WHY DO MIRRORS REVERSE LEFT AND RIGHT?

A common question from children about mirrors is why they swap left and right, but not top and bottom. There are two answers, both of which amount to 'they don't really swap left and right at all'.

The first answer, which unfortunately is incorrect, is to say that the left/right switch is because our eyes are on a horizontal plane, so mirrors swap in the plane of your eyes, rather than left/right. But this doesn't stand up very well. If that were the case, what would happen if you closed one eye?

The real answer is that mirrors swap front and back, not left and right. Your reflection in a mirror seems to be as far into the mirror as you are away from it. The reflection of the closest part of an object to the mirror – which to you is the back of the object, becomes the closest part of the reflection – to you, the front of the object.

Let's make that a bit clearer with a real example. Take a magazine and hold it with the front cover facing you, while standing in front of a mirror. The front of the real magazine is the front cover. But the front of the mirror magazine, the bit facing *you* (not your reflection), is the back cover of the magazine. What the mirror effectively does is turn the object back to front – not by rotating it as you would to see the back cover, but by pushing the back through to the front, so that we see mirror writing, rather than writing the right way round. The reason we get confused and think there is a left/right swap is that we put ourselves in the place of the unreal person in the mirror by doing a rotation, and say 'his or her right hand is the reflection of my left hand'. But the version of you in the mirror *isn't* rotated, its back has been pulled through to the front (like pushing out a rubber mould).

terms apart from being close by) generate their own light. The Moon doesn't – like the planets, it reflects light.

Similarly, young children can confuse a local source of light – a torch or a candle flame – with a local reflector like a mirror. Look in a mirror where a candle is reflected and you see light shining out of the glass. You can even use a mirror to send a light around the room. Quite a lot of young children believe that taking a mirror into a dark place will brighten it up.

The distinction between reflection and emission of light seems quite clear, but the children's version is closer to the fact than we like to admit. Once again, it's a faulty model that helps us draw the line neatly. The argument is that a light source emits light – like a gun shooting out bullets. A reflector like the moon or a mirror doesn't emit anything: it just allows the 'bullets' of light to bounce off. In fact reflection isn't like that.

To begin with, a photon isn't like a bullet. It is insubstantial. It's also tiny compared with the huge empty spaces in an atom. On the whole, if light bounced like a bullet (or, perhaps better, like a tennis ball off a wall, since bullets don't generally bounce far), it would pass straight through most atoms and out the other side. Instead, something more interesting happens. The photon – electromagnetic in nature – interacts with the electromagnetic field caused by that fuzzy probability mesh of electrons around the outside of the atom. The photon is absorbed. An electron gains energy. But shortly after, it drops back to its original energy level and emits a second photon, back out of the reflective material.

So a reflector *does* emit light, like any other light source. The big difference is that a traditional light source is powered by the energy contained within the source – whether it's the nuclear energy of the sun, the electrical energy of a light bulb or the chemical energy of a candle flame. A reflector is powered by the energy of incoming photons of light. Without the incoming photons, the reflector doesn't emit. But taking the light away is like disconnecting a battery, not like having no source in the first place. For convenience, though, I will continue to describe the process as reflection.

There is one 'traditional' light source that works surprisingly like a reflector – the fluorescent tube (watch your spelling here – it's very tempting to write *flour*escent and I have seen this in science books for teachers, despite spellcheckers). Fluorescence is a physical process very similar to reflection. The difference is that in fluorescence, the photon that comes out is a different energy (different colour, for example) from the photon that hits it. The most common form of fluorescence is when ultraviolet light – invisible to our eyes – hits a material that re-emits the light in the visible spectrum. This is why fluorescent card looks so bright – it is adding the photons from converted ultraviolet to the ordinary reflected light. This effect is also seen in some plants that almost seem to glow in the dusk.

In a low energy light bulb, the ultraviolet is generated inside the bulb, hits a fluorescent coating on the outside, and this coating transforms the ultraviolet to visible light.

WORKINGS: REFLECTING ON THE PHOTON

Reflection of light really isn't at all like a ball bouncing off a wall, once we understand it at the quantum level. In fact, when a photon hits a mirror at a particular angle it could reflect off at any old angle. Imagine a beam of light hitting a mirror and bouncing up to your eye. Quantum theory says it doesn't have to travel to the middle of the mirror and reflect to your eye at the same angle, like those optics diagrams most of us did at school. It could hit anywhere along, then bounce up at a totally different angle to reach the eye. But when you add up the probability of all the different routes occurring (remember, at the quantum level, probability is the driving force of reality), most of them cancel each other out. The final outcome is that the light travels along the path that takes the least time – which usually happens to involve reflection at equal angles.

But just because all those other probabilities are cancelling each other out doesn't mean they don't exist. And you can prove this. If you chop off most of the mirror, leaving only a piece to one side, you obviously won't get a reflection from the missing middle. But put a series of thin dark strips on the remaining segment, to only leave available those paths whose probabilities add together, and it begins to reflect, even though the light is now heading off in a totally inappropriate direction for reflection as we understand it (see Figure 6.1).

You can actually see this happening without fiddling around with mirrors and dark strips. Visible white light is a mix of different colours of light, each of which will be reflected at a different angle by such an off-position mirror with dark strips on it. Shine a white light onto such a special mirror and you will see rainbows. Practically everyone has a mirror like this – a CD or DVD. Turn it over to see the shiny playing side and tilt it against the light. The rainbow patterns you see are due to the rows of pits in the surface cutting out all the paths with certain probabilities, leaving light reflecting at a crazy angle into your eye.

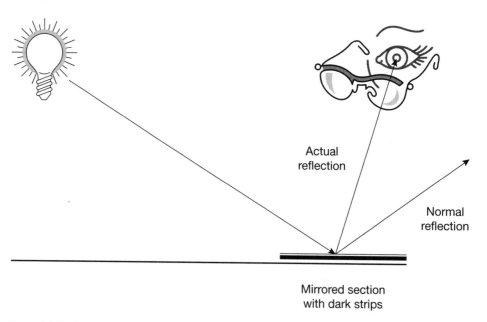

Actual
reflection

Normal
reflection

Mirrored section
with dark strips

Figure 6.1 Reflection at a strange angle due to quantum effects

WORKINGS: REFRACTION MEETS *BAYWATCH*

Another aspect of light's odd behaviour is best examined using a discovery made by Pierre de Fermat, the seventeenth-century originator of the mathematical challenge that became known as Fermat's last theorem, a mathematical proof so difficult that it wasn't solved until the end of the twentieth century. But his idea about light involved no complex maths. Instead it relied on the idea that nature is lazy.

Fermat was trying to explain refraction – the way light bends when it passes from one substance into another. The best known example is the effect at the boundary between air and water. Put a pencil into a cup of water and it seems to bend. There's the old trick where you put a penny at the bottom of a cup, position yourself so you just can't see it, then pour in water, and the bending of the light brings it into view. But what's happening?

Before looking at Fermat's result it's worth thinking for a moment about the way he went about it. So often great breakthroughs have come by looking at a problem in a totally different way. Such an approach may require no new information, but suddenly the problem is transformed. The technique that Fermat used is a singularly powerful one for exploring the workings of the world. It's exactly the same technique that Richard Feynman would use to explain the fundamental nature of light many years later. It is called the principle of least action or the principle of least time, but what it amounts to is that nature is lazy.

In the world of solid objects, the principle describes why a basketball follows a particular route through space on its way to the basket. It rises and falls along the path that keeps the difference between the ball's kinetic energy (the energy that makes it move) and potential energy (the energy that gravity gives it by pulling it downwards) to a minimum. Kinetic energy increases as the ball goes faster and decreases as it slows. Potential energy goes up as the ball gets higher in the air and reduces as it falls. The principle of least action establishes a logical balance between the two.

This principle can also be applied to the way light behaves. The whole business of refraction seems odd to begin with. Light is travelling happily along in a straight line through the air. It hits a piece of glass. Suddenly, for no obvious reason, it changes direction down into the glass, carrying on in a whole new straight line. This doesn't make a lot of sense until you apply the time version of the principle. The principle of least time says that light wants to get to where it's going as quickly as possible.

We are used to straight lines being the quickest route between any two points – but that assumes that everything remains the same on the journey. In this case, light was travelling faster in air than it does in glass. Because of this, a straight line was no longer the quickest route. To see why this is the case, compare the light's journey to that of a lifeguard, rescuing someone drowning in the sea.

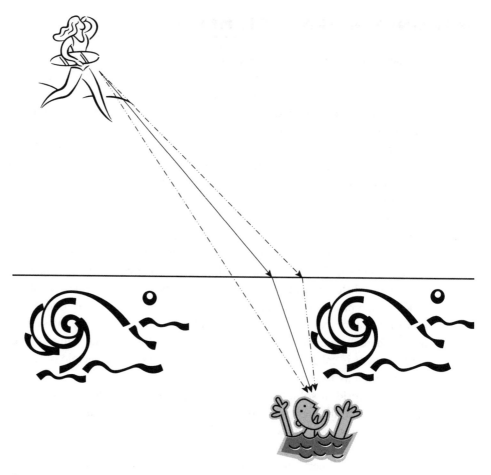

Figure 6.2 The Baywatch Principle – a straight line isn't the fastest route

The obvious route is to head straight for the drowning person. But the lifeguard can run significantly faster on the beach than she can run or swim in the water. By heading slightly away from the victim, taking a longer path on the sand, then bending inwards and taking a shorter path in the water, the lifeguard can get there more quickly (see Figure 6.2). (This analogy has led to Fermat's principle sometimes being called the Baywatch principle.)

In just the same way, a light ray could get from its start point in the air to its end point in the glass by making a straight-line journey. Or it could travel a bit further through the air, but then bend when it hits the glass so it still reaches the same end point. Because of the change in angle it will have a shorter distance to travel through the glass. And because light moves faster in air, it will take less time to follow the bent route than the straight line. But bend the light too much and it has to travel too far in the air to overcome the advantage of less time in the glass. The angle that minimizes the journey time is exactly the one that actually occurs.

WORKINGS: SEEING THE LIGHT

One of the most significant features of light at the primary level is the connection between light and sight.

It is only natural that sight comes early in our consideration of light – it's how we experience the phenomenon. The earliest theories of what light was were tied in with sight – and these ideas which were then 'common sense' now seem so bizarre it is worth getting an idea of what they were, as they may crop up as children's early ideas today.

As far as (many of) the Ancient Greeks were concerned, light was a fire that poured from the eye, connected with the subject and enabled us to see it through that connection. This seems ridiculous, because if this was all there was to it, then you should be able to see in the dark. The Greeks spotted that problem and threw in an effect from a light source like the Sun. This acted as a sort of conduit for the fire from the eyes – without it, the eye-light was dispersed and you couldn't see.

The fire part, which itself seems pretty unlikely – eyes aren't exactly fireproof – was an example of the very human tendency that once we've accepted a theory we stick to it, despite significant evidence to the contrary. A Greek philosopher,

YOU CAN'T SEE LIGHT

There's a subtle but important distinction to be made here. Light, hitting your optical nerves, causes the sensation of sight. We see things when light reflects off them and hits our eyes. But you can't see light as it passes by, because light doesn't reflect off other photons of light. It's just as well. The space around you is filled with an inter-penetrating web of light and other electromagnetic radiation. Sunlight, artificial light, radio, TV, mobile phone signals, wireless networks – they are all the same stuff, and if they did bounce off each other then we wouldn't be able to use them, or to see. If you shine a bright light down a black tube with the side cut away, you won't see anything – the light going past the hole is invisible. It's only if there's something in the tube that scatters the light away from its path – such as the smoke used in laser displays – that you can see a beam.

Empedocles, had decided that everything was made up of four elements – earth, air, fire and water. (Actually five elements – he allowed an extra one for the universe beyond the moon, which was considered special. This was the ultimate element, and because it was the fifth was called the quintessence.) In one sense, Empedocles wasn't far from the real truth – the four things he described weren't true elements, but were pretty close to four of the states of matter (earth – solid, water – liquid, air – gas, fire – plasma), and even closer if we allow the quintessence to be a Bose Einstein condensate (see page 75) – but that last parallel is being rather generous.

To make the fire idea work, it was assumed there were special water-lined passages in the eye to protect the flesh from burning. The real reason this theory ever came into being was that it was difficult to accept that the eye was a passive receptor. In reality, seeing is something we have done to us rather than something we do – but it feels like a conscious act because we can direct it and switch it off by closing our eyes. Even when it was realized that eyes were reacting to a totally external phenomenon – light – it was easy to misunderstand just how our eyes work. We are very good at getting it wrong with sight – that's why optical illusions can be so striking.

Take a look at the optical illusion at this web page: http://www.popularscience.co.uk/features/feat16.htm.

The illusion shows a chessboard with a cylinder sitting on it that casts a shadow. The text tells you that one of the dark squares on the chessboard (at the top, out of the shadow) is exactly the same colour as one of the light squares (in the shadow). But it seems impossible that this could be true. The squares appear to be very different shades indeed. It is so convincing that I have had many e-mails from people who are convinced that I have got it wrong. But if you do the test suggested on the page you will find that it's absolutely true – the two squares are the same shade.

The reason optical illusions work is that we think what we *see* is the same as the image cast on the retina by the lens at the front of the eye. We think of the eye as a sort of biological camera – and that is very misleading. It's the same problem as the explanation of persistence of vision (see pages 16–17) – the image we 'see' is a construct, a model, not the real thing.

A good example of the way sight doesn't correspond directly to the light coming into the eyeball is the way our eyes can correct for different levels of lighting. Our eyes try as much as possible to make any light level look the same. First thing in the morning, you might be surprised when, in apparently bright light, a security light is tripped by a motion sensor. Its light level detector, used to avoid switching on in the daytime, can tell that it's still really quite dark, but your eyes tell you that it's normal daylight. And then there's moonlight. Okay, it's obviously a lot dimmer than sunlight, but you can see pretty well by moonlight. In fact it's around 300,000 times dimmer (and that's with a full Moon).

HOW BIG IS THE MOON?

While we're on the subject of optical illusions and the Moon, the size of the full moon provides a classic optical illusion. Sometimes the Moon looks much bigger than at other times, but what is its actual visual size? Imagine you held a coin at arm's length – which coin do you think would look around the same diameter as the full Moon? Take a guess.

In fact all the coins are too big. The Moon's visual diameter from the Earth is only the size of the hole in a piece of standard punched paper held at arm's length – remarkably small. Try it out, if you don't believe it. Look at the full Moon through a punched hole at arm's length – you will see the whole thing.

WORKINGS: COLOUR ME EXCITED

From our selfish viewpoint as human beings, colour is an important feature of light (unless you are colour-blind), and one that causes plenty of confusion. It would be useful to start off with knowing how many colours we're dealing with. Assuming that a rainbow is a typical example of the colour range of visible light, how many colours are there in a rainbow?

If you answered seven (red, orange, yellow, green, blue, indigo, violet), you are following a tradition started by Isaac Newton, and one that is still popular today – but there is no good reason why you should go for that number. Take a look at a picture of a rainbow. It's very difficult to pick out seven distinct colours. Most of us would say that there are five or six clear colour bands. Newton made a totally arbitrary decision in saying seven. Some people think this is because he thought seven was a lucky number, but it's more likely he equated the rainbow colours with the seven notes in the musical spectrum, and in his clockwork universe expected an equal number of each.

Equally you can go the other way and say there are millions of colours in the rainbow, each very subtly distinguished. If you play around with a computer paint package that lets you alter individual components of the colour used, you could easily find yourself dealing with 16 million different colours – and that's only limited by the number of electronic bits you use. You can go as far as you like.

Incidentally, one of Newton's seven colours was at the time a recent innovation – orange. Until Elizabethan times, orange was just the name of a fruit, not a colour. It was only shortly before Newton's day that the name of the fruit was also used to describe its hue.

ACROSS THE SPECTRUM

What we usually mean by 'light' is actually 'visible light' – the light that our eyes are capable of detecting. This is just part of a much bigger spectrum (or range of colours). The only difference between light and other parts of the spectrum is the frequency (how fast the wave ripples) if you think of light as waves, or the energy of the photons if you think of it as particles. The spectrum goes from high energy gamma rays, down through X-rays, ultraviolet, visible light, infrared, microwaves and on to radio waves. At risk of overemphasizing the point, these are all the same stuff.

Colour particularly causes confusion because we use the word to mean two different things. The colour of light is a measure of the energy (or wavelength) of the different particles (waves) making it up. The colour of an object is actually the colour of the light reflected back from it when white light is shone on it. White light contains (pretty much) all the colours of the visible spectrum. Most objects absorb a fair amount of this light. What isn't absorbed and gets reflected back provides the colour. So when we say something is red, what we really mean is that it absorbs all the colours except red and only reflects red back to the eye.

The primary colours, from which all other colours of light can be produced by mixing different amounts, are red, green and blue. A traditional TV or computer monitor (before LCD (liquid crystal display)) works by combining little dots of red, green and blue to make up all the colours. Confusingly, the primary colours for pigments, like paint, are different – they are cyan, magenta and yellow. These are the colours you will find in an inkjet printer. The pigment primaries are called subtractive primaries to avoid confusion with light's additive primaries.

Unfortunately the pigment primaries, the ones for mixing paints, are the ones young children will come across first, and to keep things simple, cyan, which is a turquoisy blue, is often referred to as blue, and magenta, a reddish purple, is called red. This leads to the often stated but entirely incorrect statement that the primary colours are red, yellow and blue. That's just wrong, but it's based on the assumption that young children can't cope with 'cyan' and 'magenta', and over the years everyone has come to forget that 'red, yellow and blue' was just an approximation.

One difference between the two types of primary colours is that mixing all the light primaries results in white, while mixing all the pigment primaries results in black. With light, black is just the absence of light; with pigment, white is the absence of pigment. This means that a light-based system can only produce a black as dark as the screen when it's switched off. If you look at many TVs, the screen is actually grey when switched off. There are no blacks on that TV darker than the grey – it's just your brain, overriding the facts as usual, that makes you think you are seeing the strong black of space in a science fiction show, or the black of the night sky.

The fact that we can see colour at all is down to some complex arrangements in the eye. We have four different types of sensor in our eyes. One just handles black and white. There are about 120 million of these rods, which are significantly more sensitive than the 7 million or so cones that handle colour. When light is low, the cones give up entirely. In low light conditions, we see the world in black and white – something many people, children and adults, just won't believe until you demonstrate it. The colour-detecting cones are concentrated around the middle of the eye – if the light is very weak, you can see things better if you don't look directly at them, using the abundance of rods at the edges of your vision.

The cones could be said to handle red, blue and green, though actually they overlap strongly. Not all animals have the same set of sensors. Many are colour-blind. Others, like dogs, have limited colour vision with two sets of cones. On the other hand, many birds have a fourth set of cones that work in the ultraviolet. This means they can see things we can't. Some flowers, for example, have ultraviolet patterns, invisible to us, but not to creatures that sip their nectar.

Perhaps the most dramatic use of ultraviolet sight is in the hawks that are often seen hunting small mammals by the roadside. The mice, shrews and voles they are

WHY IS THE SKY BLUE?

One of the most obvious occurrences of colour in nature is the blue sky, and you might be faced with the tricky question of why the sky – even a clear, clean sky with just transparent air in it – is blue. There have been lots of attempts to answer this over the years, such as saying that it was the reflection of the sea. In fact it's another of the quantum effects of light interacting with small particles – in this case the molecules of the air.

As light passes through the atmosphere, some of the photons interact with air molecules and go shooting off in a new direction – this is called scattering. Sunlight contains all the colours, but the higher energy photons at the blue end of the spectrum get scattered more than the low energy reds and yellows. This means that the sky takes on a blue tinge from the more heavily scattered blue content of the sunlight. It is also why the sun looks yellow when high up and red as it sets. When the sun is setting, the light has more of the atmosphere to get through. More of the higher end light gets scattered, leaving a stronger red component.

out to catch are very difficult to see. The light brown fur of these small mammals hides them well against the grass roots. From the height the bird hovers, they haven't a hope of seeing their prey. But these little animals urinate a lot. And their urine is highly visible in ultraviolet. What the hawk does is not spot its prey, but instead follow the clearly visible trail of urine and pounce at the end of it.

WORKINGS: HEAR, HEAR

Sound tends to get lumped in with light, which is a bit of a pity as it's nowhere near as fundamental a part of science as light is. But it is still an essential for us as people, and provides some interesting opportunities to think about waves and other physical phenomena. The clearest natural demonstration that helps to contrast light and sound is a thunderstorm – if there has been one recently, it's a useful way of seeing that these two things, thunder and lightning, are both coming from the same place at the same time. But because light and sound are very different, we experience them differently – light, being much faster, gets to you first (unless the thunderstorm is right on top of you). The sound from a strong thunderstorm is very obviously a pressure wave. You don't just hear it, you feel it.

A slinky spring is often used to demonstrate the differences between a lateral or transverse (side-to-side) wave like a water wave and a compression or longitudinal wave like sound. You can send both types of wave down the slinky and see them in action. But I think it's also very helpful (and fun) to get the children themselves to be the medium for different kinds of wave. Get them standing in parallel rows, quite close to each other. Using the front row, demonstrate a sound-type wave. Get them all facing left to right along the row. Then, get the person at the left-hand end to take a step forward, gently push the person in front of him or her, then take a step back. As soon as the second person feels the push, they do the same. This is a compression wave.

You can then demonstrate a transverse wave by getting the front row to face forwards. The left-hand person in the front row is asked to take a step forward, away from the other rows, then a step back. Each person in the front row does this as soon as he or she sees the previous person step back. Then get all the rows sitting down. You can also demonstrate a transverse wave in a middle row by getting them to do a Mexican wave – the first person stands up, raises and lowers their arms, then sits. As the arms come down, the second person does the same, and so on.

With older children, you might want to point out that there is one combination that is impossible to do – send a transverse wave through the middle of the medium. Now they might argue that they've already done that with their Mexican wave. But in fact this was on the edge of the medium, as far as the direction the wave went in (up and down), like a wave on the sea. If the middle row tried to go back and forward as the front row did, they would collide with the other rows, and the whole thing would collapse in chaos and noise. The same is true with real waves – which is another way of demonstrating that the ether doesn't exist – as light appears to be a transverse wave which merrily ploughs its way through the middle of the medium.

WORKINGS: FEEL THE FORCE

The way forces work provides some of the deepest confusion in basic physics. Although this is clockwork stuff, what actually happens falls more into the counter-intuitive bracket. Forces don't seem to obey common sense.

Take a common idea – centrifugal force. If you are in a car that corners sharply, or on a theme park ride that is taking a corner, you are pushed out, away from the direction of the turn, and this is caused by centrifugal force, right? Well, no. Because unfortunately there is no such thing as centrifugal force. Common sense says, 'yes there is, that's how I ended up sitting in my neighbour's lap after that tight turn', but physics knows better.

This is another example where the Ancient Greeks' totally incorrect ideas seem to make sense from experience. The Greeks thought that things had a natural tendency to stop. Unless you kept pushing things, they would stop moving. After all, that's what happens if you push a car or a brick – stop pushing, and the thing stops moving. But that tendency to stop is the effect of gravity and friction. As astronauts know, in space, give something a push and it just keeps going.

It was Newton who spotted what was really happening (without going into space). The Greeks had got it totally back to front. What really happens is that once something is moving it keeps moving in a straight line, unless you push it to change direction, or push it to slow it down. It just so happens that everyday objects on the Earth are always being given a push to change direction by gravity (for instance, when you throw a ball, it goes from travelling horizontally to curve down towards the ground), and given a push to stop, thanks to friction. (They can also be given a push to change direction by spinning them, as when a football is 'bent' around a wall of players.)

So now let's get back to that imaginary centrifugal force. Let's say you're on one of those teacup rides at the fairground. As you are spun round, it feels like there's something pushing you outwards. But all you are trying to do is carry on in a straight line. The outside of the teacup won't let you head outwards and it pushes in on you to keep you in the cup. The force is not actually outwards (centrifugal) but inwards (centripetal), resisting your natural tendency to travel out in a straight line.

Take another example where forces often confuse. Imagine you have got a ball and you hurl it up into the sky as hard as you can. In which direction is the force on the ball just after you have let go? What direction is the force in at the point at the top of the ball's trajectory when it isn't moving at all? And what direction is the

MASS AND WEIGHT

In science you have to watch your terms. As we've already seen, velocity, which is the term used for rate of movement, contains more information than speed, as velocity also includes the direction of motion (essential if, for example, you are going to add two velocities together). Similarly mass is used in science rather than weight, although popular science books, including this one, will sometimes use 'weight' where they mean mass, to be more approachable. Mass is a fundamental property of an object – broken down to detail, it is a measure of the number of particles that make up the object. On the Earth, under our particular gravitational pull, we define weight so it happens to be the same as the mass. But take the same object up into space and it weighs nothing, yet the mass remains the same. Mass lets you know how hard the object is to accelerate – force is mass times acceleration, so the mass reflects how much force is needed to achieve a particular acceleration.

force in as it falls back to the ground? Think about it for a moment and make sure what your answers are. To avoid cheating, jot your answers down before reading on.

I've seen a whole roomful of intelligent adults (and I've heard of a good number of secondary school science teachers) getting this wrong. The answer is down in every case. Once it has left your hand, the only force acting on the ball is the force due to gravity, which is always the same way (at least on the surface of our planet) – towards the centre of the Earth.

I think the reason that force is tricky is that we're quite good at coping with how things move – it's moving this fast, it's moving in that direction – but we find acceleration, the rate at which the velocity changes (remember this can be a change of direction, or speed or both), confusing. Force is intimately related to acceleration. The bigger the force on a particular object, the greater the acceleration.

You can see this confusion again when it comes to the old chestnut about Galileo dropping balls off the leaning tower of Pisa. As far as we're aware, incidentally, Galileo never did this. The only reference to it is in a document written by one of Galileo's assistants in the great man's old age. Galileo was a superb self-publicist, and it is very unlikely he would have done the experiment and not told people about it. Instead he did his experiments by rolling balls down slopes, which has the same effect, but is easier to control and measure.

However, the point, really, is that, just like the Ancient Greeks (yes, them again), most children and many adults think that a heavy ball will fall faster than a light ball. But gravitational attraction has no interest in mass, it's a pure acceleration –

the same rate, however heavy the item. What can cause confusion is that large but light objects suffer more from being slowed down by the air as the object bumps into air molecules on the way down. So a feather or a polystyrene ball will tend to fall more slowly than a piece of metal – but it has nothing to do with its mass, and everything to do with the amount of air resistance that slows it down.

WORKINGS: OUTER SPACE

There are two aspects of science that more than any others seem to inspire that hoped for sense of wonder in children. One is dinosaurs – which makes it quite surprising that they aren't more explicitly in the curriculum. And the other is space. Perhaps it's because space is something exotic and distant, yet we can all see it on a clear night. For many years now, astronomy has been the only science where amateurs regularly make useful contributions – and it doesn't seem any surprise that the longest-running TV show with a single presenter is Patrick Moore's *The Sky at Night*.

The sheer scale of the universe is well beyond our direct grasp. Light travels at 300,000,000 metres per second, yet takes years to reach us from the nearest star – and because of this, as telescopes penetrate further and further, we see back into the past. Light that reaches us from a source a billion light years away has taken a billion years to get here. Anything could have happened to that source since. The star or galaxy could be long gone. But we see it as it was then.

What is usually classed as astronomy broadly divides into three areas. There's astronomy itself, which is largely a matter of visual exploration, cataloguing and classifying. Then there's astrophysics, which describes how features of the universe such as stars or galaxies work. Then there is cosmology, which takes the big view and tries to explain how the universe as a whole was formed and evolved.

It shouldn't be necessary, but it's probably worth throwing in the usual warning that astronomy is not the same as astrology. The whole concept of astrology started off as one of those ancient, nearly-made-sense ideas, but instead of dying away as would seem natural for such an off-the-wall idea, it has got even more bizarre in the form we now see it appearing.

The original idea was not that the stars influenced our future, but that they influenced our present. It was thought that the celestial configuration when you were born would tend to shape your personality and the way you felt about things. Although it had no scientific basis, this didn't seem too unreasonable given that, for instance, most of us feel more positive on a nice, sunny day than we do on a dull, wet, winter day, so the Sun seems capable of influencing our moods. But to then bolt onto it some sort of mystical ability to predict the future is outstandingly bizarre. The survival of astrology tells us a lot more about human gullibility than it does about the stars and their influence.

Some of the early astronomers – in fact, all the way up to Galileo – were expected to cast horoscopes by their patrons, but they saw this chore as a necessary evil to keep in favour with the rich and powerful, rather than something they believed in.

However, in our enthusiasm to put astrology in its correct place (in the bin), we do have to be careful not to overrate the accuracy of some aspects of astronomy, especially cosmology. When you think about it, we ask a lot of our astronomers. Physicists, chemists and biologists can usually study whatever it is they're interested in in their laboratories. It's not always easy. A biologist might have to go out in the jungle to track down a particular species. A physicist might have to put detectors in the deepest mine workings to detect particles so insubstantial that they generally shoot straight through the Earth unnoticed. Even so, their experiments are largely under their control. A cosmologist has to make sense of the universe.

As we've seen, the best guess for the age of the universe put it at around 13 billion years old. That is a big picture to cover. Astronomers will never be able to pick up a piece of the Sun, or travel to a distant galaxy. Instead they have to rely on what reaches us across the vast distances, whether it's visible light, or more recently other electromagnetic radiation such as radio, infrared and microwave. That means that most theories here are much less well tested than those in normal science.

WORKINGS: DINOSAURS AND STANDARD CANDLES

The astronomer is in an even worse position than those who try to work out what dinosaurs were like (to link those two classic bits of child-inspiring science). Each is trying to look back across time, though the dinosaur theorists have a far shorter timespan to cover. Each has to assemble intelligent guesses based on limited evidence and common sense. But remember that common sense is an awesomely bad guide when it comes to science – the chances are they are still getting a lot wrong.

Before we lose those dinosaurs, let's take two classic visual representations of dinosaurs that have become possible thanks to modern computer graphics – the film *Jurassic Park* and the 'factual' TV programme *Walking with Dinosaurs*. In *Jurassic Park* we saw the mighty Tyrannosaurus Rex chasing and eating pretty well anything that moved, and the awesomely deadly Velociraptor tracking down its prey in a pack. Yet since the film was produced, some doubt has emerged that Tyrannosaurus was a hunter – it might have been a scavenger – and the latest idea of the appearance of a Velociraptor makes it look as frightening as an oversized chicken, even though it was still a vicious pack hunter.

Similarly, *Walking with Dinosaurs* showed us the colours of dinosaur skins, the sounds they made, what their family life was like – and perhaps because it was a 'factual' show, many viewers assumed that this was how dinosaurs truly were. Yet these were all guesses based on what we know of living creatures that share some characteristics with a dinosaur. We just don't know what dinosaur skin was like, or what sounds they made. There's only so much you can learn from a fossilized skeleton.

If all that seems difficult, pity the poor astronomer. We are confidently told, for example, how far away various astronomical features are. With the relatively close stuff, these distances are pretty accurate. Astronomers can use parallax to get a good idea of (astronomically) near distances. This sounds very technical, but parallax is something all of us who have two eyes use to judge distances every day. The view from our two eyes is subtly different. Hold up your finger in front of your face and look past it at something in the distance. Close one eye. Then open it, while closing the other. Alternate the two eyes and you will see the two objects, your close finger and the distant one, moving with respect to each other. The closer an object is to your eyes, the more it seems to move.

Astronomers can use a large-scale version of looking with one eye and then the other by looking at something in the sky from opposite sides of the Earth's orbit around the Sun. It's not exactly instant – you have to wait six months for the Earth to move into position – but the two observations will be taken around 300 million kilometres apart, not a bad size for a scientific instrument.

Unfortunately, as things get further away, so the shift due to parallax gets smaller and smaller. Before long – well before we reach the distance of a galaxy – it isn't working any more. Now we get to one of the big guesses used by astronomers – standard candles. If this sounds a bit woolly and medieval, it's not quite as bad as it appears – but it is still pretty awful.

The theory goes something like this. If I take a bright object – say, a candle – the further away it is, the dimmer it gets. So if I have a way to measure the brightness of what I see, knowing how bright a candle is close up, I can work out how far away a distant candle is. We have very accurate instruments for measuring brightness – some can detect individual photons of light. (This isn't as impressive as it sounds. It only takes about a dozen photons to trigger the optical nerve in the human eye. On a clear, dark, unpolluted night a candle flame is visible to the naked eye 14 kilometres away. But the detectors don't just see the light, they measure how often those photons arrive to give a clearer picture of brightness.)

So, if we knew how bright a particular star was, and how bright it looked, we would know how far away it was. The catch is, we don't know how bright any particular star is. What the standard candle theory does is to say that there are some types of star that are particularly consistent in their brightness. If we assume that all these stars are of the same brightness, then by identifying this particular type of star, and finding how bright it looks, we can work out its distance. But that's a big assumption. We don't know these types of star are all of the same brightness. We just have to hope.

It might seem that finding out the type of star at a great distance is equally difficult, but there's plenty we can discover about stars despite their remoteness. We know what's in them, for example. The spectrum of light colours given off by stars has black gaps in it, corresponding to the energies of photons that are absorbed by the different elements that make up the star. Using spectroscopy, the technique of analysing the colours emitted (and hence energies), it's possible to work out how the different stars are made up. Some stars also have very particular habits. One of the most commonly used standard candles is the Cepheid variable.

Variable stars, as the name suggests, seem to vary in brightness, pulsing in a regular fashion. Cepheid variables are named after the constellation Cepheus. Astronomer John Goodricke discovered the first variable, Delta Cephei (hence the name), in 1784. From observation of a good number of Cepheid variables that we can get a parallax distance on, it seems very likely that the speed of flashing of these variable stars is directly linked to their brightness. Cepheid variables pulse over a period of days to months and it seems that they are actually shrinking and growing to make those changes in brightness. So finding a Cepheid in a distant location makes it fairly likely that we know how far away it is.

WORKINGS: MEASURING THE UNIVERSE

Standard candles are totally solid ground, though, when compared with one of the best known cosmological theories – the big bang. As we've seen (see pages 42–3), the big bang theory suggests that the universe came from an infinitely small point, then expanded to the universe we have. For a long time in the mid-twentieth century it was rivalled by another theory – that the universe was in a 'steady state' where the expanding universe was continuously replenished by new material, rather like a three-dimensional river flowing out from its centre.

Technical evidence proved the steady state theory unlikely – but new evidence is just as likely to shake the big bang theory in the future. These are essentially top of the head theories that match as much of the data as is known at the time the theory is put together, but there really is limited evidence to be sure. The big bang is growing in solidity as a theory, thanks to observations from space satellites that seem to show the background residue of the beginning – but this is a very indirect observation based on distribution of temperature. It reinforces the big bang, but the evidence is still relatively limited compared with that supporting an earthbound theory like quantum theory.

In fact the original big bang theory was seriously flawed. The universe we can see is too consistent at its furthest reaches. The trouble is, the entire lifetime of the universe wasn't long enough for information to travel from one side of the universe to the other and make things so even. Because of that, it's thought that shortly after the universe started to expand it went through a sudden, short, mega-expansion – what's known to cosmologists as inflation. This was vastly quicker than the speed of light, but, as we've seen, doesn't break the constraints of relativity because it was space itself that was expanding, not the atoms in space moving away from each other.

Again, there is no real evidence for this inflation beyond the uniformity of temperature, nor any idea of a mechanism by which the inflation process could have happened – it's just a patch on the big bang theory to keep it consistent with what's observed. The point here is not to knock the big bang – it's the best theory we've got for how the universe started – but to emphasize how much guesswork there is in cosmology.

If the big bang did happen, and there was inflation, it gives us an intriguing puzzle about the size of the universe. We can see about 13 billion light years in each direction – seeing back to the earliest existence of the universe – so a natural assumption might be that the universe is around 26 billion light years across. (Big enough. Just one light year is around 9,500,000,000,000 kilometres.) But because of the limitations of light speed, the limits on what we can see aren't the limits on the size of the universe, as long as that hyper-fast inflation really did occur. Best estimates as of 2006, based on the distribution of the cosmic background radiation that dates back to the earliest existence of the cosmos, suggest that the present universe is at least 156 billion light years across.

WORKINGS: INTO THE BLACK

One of cosmology's best known and most dramatic ideas is the black hole, which Hollywood has got its hands on and distorted almost beyond recognition. Black holes are another good example of the 'best theory so far, we're pretty sure it's right, well, fairly sure' school of science. We can't say for certain that black holes exist, in the same way we can say with some confidence that ordinary stars exist. It seems likely that there are black holes, but they aren't the sort of thing you can observe very easily, and it's entirely possible that there is another explanation for phenomena that have been blamed on black holes, as we will see a little later.

First of all, though, what is a black hole? It's a seriously collapsed star. Normally stars like the Sun exist in a rough equilibrium. All that mass of material provides a big gravitational attractive force – but it is balanced by the repulsion of the charged ions, and by the outward pushing force from the nuclear reactions that power the star. But as a star grows older, the equilibrium can be pushed out of kilter. The material in the star can collapse in on itself.

Below a certain mass, the outcome of this process is a neutron star. This is a very dense body with a mass between 1.5 and 2 times that of the Sun condensed into a sphere with a radius as small as 10 kilometres. We are fairly certain we have detected neutron stars, some of which pulse very regularly and quickly due to spinning round at a speed that would be impossible for a normal body of that mass. But if the mass is big enough, nothing can stop the collapse. The gravitational field is so strong that it distorts space in on itself. The result is a singularity – a point object in space. So strong is the distortion around a black hole that nothing that comes within a certain limit can ever escape. Even light is trapped by the massive distortion of spacetime – hence the name 'black hole'.

Black holes, if they exist, have some remarkable properties. If you fell into a black hole, the gravitational pull is so strong that the difference between the force at one end of your body and at the other would rip you apart. According to general relativity, time slows as you encounter this powerful gravitational field, effectively coming to a stop as you pass the limit where nothing can escape.

Strangely, though, one thing black holes shouldn't be is entirely dark. As matter is sucked into the hole and accelerated it gives off light, so a black hole should be surrounded by a haze of glowing matter on its way to oblivion. It's partly through observing these sorts of phenomena that astronomers think that they have found black holes. But bear in mind that the evidence is always going to be indirect. We have a theory that fits that evidence – black holes – but we can't prove that's why the evidence is there.

The most remarkable black holes scientists have predicted are supermassive black holes. These are thought to sit at the centre of galaxies, like our own Milky Way. The way stars near the centre of the galaxy behave suggests that there is something very massive there. Also some of the distant galaxies (hence far back in time) are intensely bright – much brighter than anything should be at that distance. It is thought that these 'quasars' (short for 'quasi-stellar objects', because they look like stars) are lit by black holes eating up all the spare dust and gas lying around in the centre of the galaxy. Once the debris has been scavenged, the bright emissions stop – in an older galaxy like ours, the central black hole has largely gone dark.

WORKINGS: WORMHOLES IN SPACE

Some scientists believe that black holes may give us a means to cross vast distances quickly and to be able to travel backwards in time. When science writer Carl Sagan wanted a means to cross interstellar distances for his fictional book *Contact* (later a film with Jodie Foster), he asked physicist Kip Thorne to suggest a mechanism. Thorne came up with the idea of using wormholes in space. These are a side effect of Einstein's general relativity, which as we've seen (pages 40–1) considers gravity to be the effect of space being distorted into a curve, so things effectively roll down into the curved well around a heavy body.

If this is the case, then it's tempting to wonder what would happen if space got so curved in on itself that it broke through into another region of space. The result is a wormhole – a tunnel through spacetime itself, where in principle you can enter at one point in space and come out somewhere totally different. This is one of the few ways anyone can think of to cross interstellar distances. It also provides a time machine, because anything travelling faster than light travels backwards in time (see page 39), so jumping through space also pushes you back in time.

Unfortunately, about the only way anyone can think of to generate a wormhole is from the distortion of space generated by a black hole, and, as we've already seen, travelling into a black hole is not good news. Although there are various speculative attempts to find a way to survive the transit, in reality the chances are that even if wormholes do exist (we have no evidence they do), they would be impossible to enter.

The implications of black holes are great fun, and make good science fiction, but remember that the evidence even for the existence of black holes is all indirect. As recently as July 2006 it was suggested that the whole idea of black holes in the centre of galaxies may be wrong. The same evidence could point to a clump of a strange substance called dark matter, which some believe makes up around 90 per cent of the content of the universe, but which is largely undetectable. It's thought that such a cloud of dark matter would emit regular bubbles, bursting out from it, broadcasting regular bursts of light. It has now been found that the central mass of the galaxy does give out bursts of X-rays every twenty minutes or so, which seems more likely to be caused by one of these dark matter bubbles than a black hole. The jury is out – and may always remain so. That's the way it is with cosmology.

WORKINGS: SOLAR SYSTEM

The facts about the far reaches of the universe are inevitably hard to pin down. We are, thankfully, a lot clearer about what is going on in our own spatial backyard, the solar system.

The Sun formed around 6 billion years ago, with the planets following a little later, though the Earth is still a respectable 4.5 billion years old. Stars like the Sun formed largely from the elements produced in the big bang. Over billions of years, hydrogen and helium atoms clumped together, each atom attracted by the tiny gravitational pull of the other atoms. As the clump got bigger, the attraction got stronger, pulling in more and more gas until we ended up with the huge ball that is the Sun. (It's around 1.4 million kilometres in diameter, compared with the Earth's 12,700 kilometres.)

We'll come back to how a collection of gas turned into the power source of life on Earth, but in the meantime, other matter was being attracted by the increasingly massive Sun. Earlier stars had already formed, lived and died, ending with vast explosions we call supernovas. Nova is just 'new' in Latin – supernovas appear as

HOW MANY PLANETS?

As of 2006 there is one less planet out there. Pluto, for seventy-six years considered the ninth planet, is very small and has an irregular orbit. Since Pluto's discovery quite a few of these planetoids have been found, so in August 2006 Pluto was demoted. The planets are now Mercury, Venus, Earth, Mars, Jupiter, Saturn, Uranus and Neptune – just the eight of them – and any textbooks that say different are out of date, though at the time of writing there are still those who would like Pluto to be reinstated.

new stars, because they are much brighter than the pre-explosion star. The 'super' part is to distinguish the exploding supernova from a nova, which is a star that suddenly brightens by eating up surrounding matter, but doesn't explode. In the process, supernovas produced the heavier atoms like carbon, oxygen and the metals that would be essential for planet formation. It's this stardust that was caught up in orbit around the new Sun and gradually clumped into the planets as we now know them. (Further out, there was more gas that wasn't pulled into the Sun, so planets like Jupiter and Saturn have a more gaseous makeup.)

How the Sun works was a mystery for many years. It clearly appears to be on fire, so early attempts to explain it assumed that it was very similar to a fire on Earth. The trouble is, as we got to know more about the Sun – its size, external temperature and composition – it was possible to calculate how long it could sensibly burn as a conventional fire before running out of fuel. The answer was in the millions of years range. This was okay, because at the time there was little idea of just how old the Earth was, and the best guess based on biblical study was around 6,000 years.

Discoveries in geology started putting pressure on the physicists to re-think the workings of the Sun. An understanding of the Earth's structure and how mountains were formed soon put the age of the Earth as significantly greater than the estimated lifetime of the Sun. Something was horribly wrong. It took the discoveries of the counter-intuitive age to come up with an alternative mechanism for the Sun that would give it a vastly greater lifetime.

WORKINGS: ENERGY FROM ATOMS

There are two processes down at the quantum level that can relatively easily release large amounts of energy. The first is nuclear fission. This is the power source behind all present nuclear power stations and the atomic bomb. In fission, one unstable element splits apart. The energy in the bonds that are broken is given out – and because nuclear forces are very strong, there's a whole lot of energy generated. What was realized in the 1930s was that this simple process could be made part of a self-running chain reaction. This is because the simplest way to get an atom to split is to load an extra neutron into the nucleus of an already unstable atom.

When, for instance, the right kind of uranium undergoes this reaction, as well as producing energy it flings out two or three neutrons. If these neutrons then go on to hit other uranium nuclei and these nuclei split, the neutrons flying out grow in number very rapidly. Although it's called a chain reaction, that sounds too linear. Actually it's more a tree reaction, with one splitting nucleus branching out to trigger two or three more, each of which can trigger two or three more and so on. When moderated – usually by putting in material that will soak up extra neutrons – this results in a steady flow of power. When left to its own devices, with enough unstable material, it will result in meltdown and catastrophe. (Getting it to explode is a lot harder, because you've got to get it all happening in a short space of time in a confined space – but that's a different story.)

This isn't how the Sun works, though. Fission requires big, heavy atoms like uranium. The Sun is powered by hydrogen, which only has a single proton as its nucleus: there's nothing to split. Instead, the Sun uses fusion power. This is a mechanism that has been used in some experimental reactors, and it provides the extra kick of a hydrogen bomb. It would be hugely preferable to fission for nuclear power stations if it could be used effectively, because fusion doesn't produce nasty radioactive end products. Unfortunately we haven't seen fusion reactors springing up all over the place because running a fusion reactor is like trying to handle a piece of the Sun. Not easy. The fusion reaction is likely to destroy any material it comes into contact with, and has to be kept isolated in mid-air by strong magnetic fields – it's just very difficult to manage.

The fusion reaction produces even more energy than fission. It is produced typically when two 'overloaded' hydrogen atoms get together. A hydrogen nucleus is just a single proton. The next biggest element, helium, has two protons and two neutrons. But there is a fairly stable variant of hydrogen called deuterium which has a neutron as well as a proton in its nucleus. Get two such atoms together and the result is helium and an outpouring of energy. (These 'heavy hydrogen' atoms are themselves formed when two hydrogen nuclei get together. One proton ends up being converted to a neutron and throws out a positively charged variant of an electron. But that's not really important.)

One of the good things about fusion reactors is that they are never going to run out of control. It's very difficult to make fusion happen at all. This is because the process requires the positive protons of the hydrogen nuclei to be pressed closely together. Very close. But, just like trying to get two north poles of very strong magnets together, the positive charge on the hydrogen nuclei means that there's a huge opposing force. They really don't want to be together. It was thought when fusion was first put forward that the only way to make it happen was to put the hydrogen under huge pressure and temperature.

The Sun is massive – so there is a fair amount of pressure. But the temperature of the Sun on the surface is around 5,200°C. This is nowhere near high enough. As more was found out about the Sun, the internal temperature was put at around 14 million °C – but even this wasn't enough. The Sun shouldn't work. The supporters of the fusion theory were seriously worried, until quantum theory came to the rescue.

Remember how a quantum particle doesn't have a fixed position – but rather has a range of probabilities as to where it might be. This is true even when there's something in the way. Put quantum particles in a box, and some of them will appear on the outside of the box. They haven't passed through the box, they are just on the other side, because that's one of the places they might be, admittedly with a much lower probability than being inside the box. This process is confusingly known as quantum mechanical tunnelling – confusing because there is no tunnel; the particle jumps from being inside the container to being outside without passing through the wall.

Tunnelling was to come to the rescue of the star scientists. The repulsive force of the hydrogen nuclei is no different, as far as a quantum particle is concerned, from any other sort of barrier. The chances are a particle will be outside the barrier presented by the repulsion, but there is a small probability that one of the nuclei will jump to be within the barrier – to be so close to the other nucleus that fusion occurs. There are so many atoms in the Sun that this is happening all the time, and it is only thanks to this bizarre tunnelling process that we have the Sun's light and heat to keep us alive. (I've referred to hydrogen atoms, but in fact the material in the Sun is a plasma (see pages 73–4) – it's a sea of nuclei with the outer electrons stripped off by the heat.)

WORKINGS: IS ANYBODY OUT THERE?

One last consideration that often occurs to children is the possibility of alien life. Are we alone in the universe, or can we expect aliens (whether friends or invaders) to drop in any time soon? Popular fiction treats aliens as an everyday occurrence, but the reality is that we are pretty unlikely to see any visitors from another world. Simple reason – where are they going to come from?

In the early days of science fiction – H. G. Wells and the like – there were only really three sources of alien invasion – Mars, the Moon and Venus. None do very well on close examination. Venus (see page 52) is an overheated hell hole, while the Moon and Mars lack the water and air to sustain life in anything close to the forms we know. The outer planets are too cold and those like Jupiter that are gas giants totally lack a practical environment.

About the best bet for life outside the Earth in the solar system is Europa, the second moon of Jupiter. It's not exactly warm out there. The everyday surface temperature on Europa is around 160°C below zero. Compare that with the coldest temperature ever measured on the Earth's surface of −90°C. But Europa has a surprise in store. Probes have detected a frozen ocean, and underneath the icy crust it's entirely possible that there is liquid water, kept warm by a combination of the huge tidal strains put on the moon by Jupiter's powerful gravity and the kind of radioactive furnace that keeps the Earth's core molten.

If Europa really does have a liquid water ocean, with enough warmth to help life keep going, it's entirely possible that creatures have developed there. And with relatively mild conditions and all that useful water, Europa is one of the few places in the solar system where life could have evolved. Even so, the chances are we'd only be dealing with something like bacteria – far and above the most flexible and successful lifeforms in terms of long-existence life on Earth. Not much danger of flying saucers invading from there.

Intelligent life is much more likely to come from the planet of a distant star. Remarkably, given the distances out there, we know that there are planets around hundreds of stars. The first were spotted by the wobble the planets caused in the star itself – these extra-solar planets were all big Jupiter-like giants. But other techniques have since been used to block out the output of the star itself (the star usually renders planets invisible), and planets that are more Earth-like have been discovered. Even so, to date, despite throwing lots of effort into trying to find signals from other worlds, we have failed to do so. Earth now has a jacket of radio emissions around it around

FLYING SAUCERS

Flying saucers are a good example of how relying on reports of third party 'experience' can result in very poor science. In 1947, pilot Ken Arnold saw some strange objects in the sky. Not only did they look strange, these objects moved in an unusual way. They flew erratically; Arnold said they moved 'like a saucer if you skip it across water'. The newspapers, picking up his story, made up the dramatic headline 'Flying Saucers' – but Arnold never saw a saucer-shaped craft, his mysterious objects were roughly spherical. As soon as the term flying saucers came into popular use, people started seeing saucer-shaped craft – but never before that.

100 light years thick – we would expect something similar if other intelligent lifeforms have developed parallel technology.

Even if we did spot another intelligent lifeform at a 'neighbourhood' inter-system distance of, say, twenty light years, we couldn't expect to make much headway with meeting and greeting them. If we used radio for a conversation, we would have to wait forty years every time we asked a question to get a reply (that's after working out how to communicate). That would mean some seriously careful phrasing.

As for visiting, it's pretty well out of the question. We are seriously challenged by the technological difficulties of sending a human being to Mars – just four light *minutes* away on a good day. It's estimated it would take six months for a manned mission to reach Mars. Our 'neighbourhood' star is more than 2.5 million times further away. Without some technology that allows us to bend the restrictions of light speed like a Star Trek warp drive (and despite all the fun 'Physics of Star Trek' type books have with this, the chances are it will never happen), there just aren't going to be interstellar visits.

Don't let this put you off, though. The universe is a wonderfully vast, fascinating place. And we don't need flying saucers to take a trip around it. Science gives us a great vehicle to explore and understand it.

WORKINGS – ESSENTIALS

Electricity is usually described at this level as being like a fluid, but be aware of the limitations of this model. Light is wonderfully mysterious – like a wave and a particle – but really is just light. Bear in mind the differences between emission and reflection of light – but also how they are more similar than you might think. When it comes to colour, the primaries for light are red, blue and green. Just how many colours there are in the rainbow is a difficult one – but it's not likely to be seven.

Although force is a solid part of clockwork science it can be counter-intuitive. Remember that things keep going unless a force is applied, rather than the 'natural' assumption that forces are needed to keep things moving.

When we're looking out in space, bear in mind just how much has to be taken on trust, when we say how big the universe is or how far away a distant galaxy lies. Even black holes may not exist – but they are pretty amazing if they do. When we get closer, looking at the solar system, remember the amazing mechanism of the Sun which relies on quantum tunnelling, and the small chances of ever meeting up with an alien.

CHAPTER 7

GETTING HANDS-ON

Hands-on experience at the critical time, not systematic knowledge, is what counts in the making of a naturalist. Better to be an untutored savage for a while, not to know the names or the anatomical detail.

Edward Wilson, American entomologist and sociologist, who was an expert on ants and social behaviour, in *Naturalist* (1994)

Children like doing things. They like getting their hands dirty. Telling you this is, I'm sure, like teaching your grandmother to suck eggs, but bear with me.

Most of the school hands-on science I can remember as a pupil is from secondary school – but that doesn't negate the point that I found most of it dull. And this was as someone who was already very interested in science. It was all too often tedious and repeated measurement and observation of not very exciting phenomena (like the angle a beam of light was bent when passing through a lens).

It may well be a good thing that secondary school science contains a fair amount of tedious repeated measurement, because it's a realistic preparation for the real thing. The everyday practicalities of grown-up science can be intensely tedious along the way to an exciting result. But this is no way to get children excited by the wonders of science, so it seems reasonable to limit the amount of repeated measurement that primary children experience, provided they get enough to understand and have experience of the techniques of recording and checking data.

So what's the alternative? I would like to suggest ten key ways to keep hands-on science exciting:

1 make sure it's *their* hands;
2 things should happen;
3 stimulate the senses;
4 look for the unexpected;

5 explore error;

6 make results live;

7 everyone loves a gift;

8 dress to impress;

9 use your external resources;

10 if it's too dangerous, go virtual.

Let's look at each of these in a bit more detail.

MAKE SURE IT'S *THEIR* HANDS

Here's a simple scenario. You haven't got enough equipment for everyone to do the experiment, even in groups. Or you haven't had time to prepare multiple copies of the experiment before the lesson. Who does? Or you know that someone in your class is bound to make a mess. (You probably even know who it is.) Or you just know the children will take for ever over it and you have to get on to something else. Or . . . any number of other excuses. So instead of letting the children do the experiment, the teacher or the teaching assistant will do it for them as a demonstration. What difference does it make? They still see the experiment, still have a chance to get excited by the science.

But watching isn't doing. There is a huge difference between the engagement induced by getting your hands on things and the interest that arises from watching a demonstration. If you have any doubt, watch children go around a museum and see the difference in enthusiasm between the exhibits that are objects in glass cases and the interactive exhibits. I can still remember going around the Science Museum in London as a boy, at a time when interactivity and museums didn't really go together. It was absolutely thrilling when you got to the gallery where there were buttons to push and wheels to turn (and even a door that opened automatically with an 'electric eye' – it's still there and modern children find it difficult to believe just how exciting this was back then). If you are a parent, think how often you've said 'don't touch!'

The urge to interact directly is extremely strong in children. (In fact it's strong in all of us, but we tend to play it down as we get older, and we have been socialized into not touching strange things in case they break or prove dangerous.) So when those excuses to avoid a hands-on experiment turn up, be creative about overcoming them. Don't give in.

THINGS SHOULD HAPPEN

It might seem obvious, but something should happen in an experiment. Although measurement and observation are important, and need to be learned, make sure that this isn't a purely static experience. Often the 'something happened' can be part of what is being observed or measured. Even with a static object like a stone, this can be incorporated into the experiment – for example by requiring the children to find or dig up the stone, effectively introducing fieldwork into the experiment. But if it's not practical to have action as part of what is being observed, that 'something happened' will have to be introduced as part of the process. Can you make taking the measurement or the observation more interesting? Can it be recorded in a way that makes something happen – perhaps by recording the information in a computer programme that instantly does something dramatic with the results?

When looking for something to happen, it's often a case of thinking through the impact on the senses – which leads neatly into the next category.

STIMULATE THE SENSES

Our senses form our interface with the outside world. They provide an excellent guide to making the experience of 'doing' science more exciting. If the experiment engages one or more senses in a dramatic way, it is likely to capture the imagination.

When thinking about sight, use colour and movement. If you are setting up an experiment, for example, with liquids, using a drop of food colouring to give them dramatic colours gives the experience a little edge. (Yes, it could result in stained clothing, but science always has attendant risk.) Watching a live animal is very different from seeing a picture of one. It should be a more exciting experience than handling a stuffed one too, but the relative rarity of stuffed animals these days might induce a certain shock factor, especially if the children can handle them, so stuffed animals are well worth trying. Chemical experiments that result in physical motion, such as a traditional vinegar and baking powder volcano, grab the attention very effectively.

Sound can be equally powerful. If an experiment generates a noise, either directly or by triggering a measuring device to ring a bell or sound an alarm, it adds strongly to the excitement. Think of those games where you have to trace a complex-shaped wire with a metal ring on a stick, and a loud buzzer sounds if you let the ring touch the wire. There's something almost tangible about the impact of that loud noise. Of course loud noises in the classroom aren't always appropriate – but they are worth using occasionally.

At the other extreme, very quiet noises can be doubly effective. The fact that it's necessary to really try hard to hear them can make the experience more intense – and as a side effect you might get a very quiet classroom for a little while.

Taste is a sense that has to be handled with care in this context. While it's good to encourage children to taste appropriate things – different fruits, for example – there are many circumstances when tasting items in the laboratory can be dangerous, and it is important even at this early stage to get children into the habit of not putting fingers to the mouth when performing experiments. It would be best to very carefully separate taste experiences from your normal hands-on science.

Probably the Cinderella of the senses is touch. We can learn a lot from touching, and the result can be quite intense, especially if the sensation is unexpected. When giving a class on creativity to primary school children, I normally take in a cauliflower with some gel on it in a canvas bag and ask the children to feel the contents without looking inside the bag, to get an idea of what the surface of the brain is like. The fact that the contents of the bag are never identified as not being a brain adds to the effect. Similarly, being able to touch a stuffed animal will dramatically heighten the impact.

Both these examples emphasize a popular way of extending and amplifying sensory interaction – by making the experience in some sense 'disgusting' or 'gross'. As you can't have missed, children love things they consider disgusting, from bodily functions to slime, and careful use of these can really strengthen the impact the experiment has on the senses. Often the grossness can be deceptive – as in the use of a gelled cauliflower as a brain.

LOOK FOR THE UNEXPECTED

Unexpected outcomes also tie well into our sense of surprise, helping to make an experiment more memorable and more enjoyable. In the brain-in-a-bag example above, I have in the past also taken in a second, identical bag with a 'bumble ball' – a ball that bounces around randomly under its own power. After the children have identified the contents as a brain, the bags are switched and one of them is handed the bag to look after, at the same time as the ball is switched on. It begins to jump around, causing a great dramatic effect.

If all that happens in a hands-on experiment is what was expected, it's easy for the children to get a little blasé. It's much better if you can find experiments where the outcome is not what they expect, giving a stronger learning impact. For example, I can still remember an experiment we did when I was at primary school. It involved two table tennis balls, held up by threads. You had to write down what you thought would happen, then blow between the balls. Everyone duly wrote down that the balls would move apart – but when they tried it, the balls moved closer together. That was then a great opportunity to explore what was happening.

In that particular example, the teacher was quite clever at overcoming one of the excuses for not letting the children do experiments detailed on page 106. He only had one pair of table tennis balls. If we had done the experiment in open class, the element of surprise would have been lost very soon. Instead, he set up a series of experiments scattered around different locations in the school. The table tennis balls experiment was tucked away in a cubby hole, so no one else could see your results. The effect was doubly powerful – the experience of moving around from experiment to experiment was fun in its own right.

Of course that sort of set-up is a little complex for everyday classroom science, though it would work well as part of a science week, or other special science event. However, it is still possible to look out for opportunities to give the children a surprise and give hands-on science an edge.

EXPLORE ERROR

Experiments go wrong. It has long been the practice to allow for and explore a range of answers in the arts, but in science, where there are usually clear right and wrong answers, it's easy to take the sort of depressing action described by a friend of mine who tells of an experience in a music class in primary school. It might not be science, but the effect is all too familiar from science classes:

> We were played a piece of music, which I now know to be Tchaikovsky's 1812 Overture. Then our teacher said to us, 'What does that music make you think of?' I was brought up in the countryside, and I could hear all the elements of the hunt in the music. The huntsmen's cries, the hounds, the beat of the hooves. I put my hand up excitedly. 'I can hear a fox hunt, miss!' The teacher looked at me for a moment. She may even have raised an eyebrow. 'No, that's not right,' she said, 'what does anyone else think?'

That's a lesson he never forgot, but for all the wrong reasons. This doesn't mean we should say 'there is no right or wrong answer'. Even in quantum physics, where many answers are probabilities rather than one figure, there's no need to stray into the fuzzy postmodernist thinking that denies the existence of objectivity. Quantum theory is excellent at predicting the phenomena we experience, but there has always been argument over the interpretation of it, and this 'fluffiness' appeals to some who want to link quantum physics and traditional Eastern philosophy and religions.

Michael Shermer, *Scientific American*'s resident sceptic, points out the ease with which 'New Age scientists' can pick up a little quantum jargon to spice up their ideas with a little improperly used science. Shermer picks out a great example of this in a film called *What the **** Do We Know*. Shermer quotes a scientist in the film as saying, 'The material world around us is nothing but possible movements of consciousness. I am choosing moment by moment my experience. Heisenberg said atoms are not things, only tendencies.' Shermer encourages the quoted 'scientist' to jump off a twenty-storey building and challenge the tendency of the ground to flatten him.

The scientific approach is not to say there is no right or wrong answer, or nothing is objective. But science does recognize that scientists are human and will make mistakes. We can get things wrong in experiments, and have to acknowledge that. What's important is the response to an incorrect result: it should be significantly different from 'no, that's wrong'.

It's important to emphasize the opportunity for error in experiments. Scientists need to look out for everything that could go wrong and allow for it. They use a wide range of techniques to avoid error as much as possible – repeating the experiment, having different people undertake it in different locations, using controls, reducing the opportunity for human error, and so on. Even then, experimental results are often produced with 'error bars', showing the range of likely error, rather than a single-figure result.

Much of this is too complex for the primary school, though it doesn't do any harm to introduce the concepts. But it is possible, rather than simply to say a result is wrong, to compare results across all the children, and if a few differ significantly from the rest, use that as a first way of separating those results off, rather than simply identifying them as wrong. Although scientists should never ignore incorrect results, it's not uncommon to temporarily put conflicting results to one side as 'experimental error', until the experiment can be repeated or redesigned to remove the opportunity for error and test whether or not it was acceptable to reject those numbers.

It isn't always true that you can reject a few odd results, of course. They may be telling you something. It's even possible that these are the only correct results, if there was a systematic error. There's no doubt that simply ignoring results that disagree with your premise isn't good science, hence this joke:

A mathematician, a physicist and an engineer are trying to work out if all the odd numbers are prime (can't be divided by another number to produce a whole result). The mathematician quickly counts off: 1, 3, 5, 7, 9 – no, nine isn't prime, it can be divided by three, so the theory is not true. The physicist does much the same: 1, 3, 5, 7, 9 – hmm, 11, 13 – yes, he says, odd numbers are prime, nine was just an experimental error. Then it's the engineer's turn: 1, er, er, 3, erm . . .

Apart from being enjoyably insulting to engineers, this makes the point about a potential bad habit for scientists. Nonetheless, a good starting point when you get a few wrong answers is to compare the results across the class and ask why some were significantly different. Try to get the children to understand that mistakes happen and it is necessary both to look for ways to minimize the risk of error in the first place, and then to check the results and look for where things could have gone wrong. Always establish *why* the hands-on experience produced a doubtful result.

MAKE RESULTS LIVE

This is an extension of 'something should happen'. Don't just collect a series of results from an experiment – do something with them. At the very least, look at different ways of presenting the information. Give the children a chance to be creative in the way they display the information, using graphs and other visual means of display as well as tables.

This is a good opportunity to discuss with them what the point of presenting the results in different ways is. It's easy to forget that presentation of results is usually for a purpose. What are you trying to achieve? If it's just to show a single value – what was best, or biggest, how many there were of something – a number is better than a graphic. Visual presentation comes into its own for comparisons and to follow changes.

It's also possible sometimes to give results more impact by bringing in some external comparison. It's difficult using numbers or graphs to really grasp the difference in scale between an atomic nucleus and the overall size of an atom. The comparison of it being like a fly in a cathedral gives a great visual image and makes the scale come alive. Look for similar opportunities to accompany numbers by physical comparisons that can make the results more striking both to those doing the experiment and those seeing the results.

EVERYONE LOVES A GIFT

Everyone, adults and children, gets a disproportionate thrill as a result of being given something. A gift (with the possible exception of socks) pretty well always feels more impressive than the equivalent cash, even when – and this is where human psychology gets odd – you want the gift less than something else you could buy with the money.

If part of the aim of hands-on science is to be memorable, to give that little extra, then the opportunity to include a 'gift' as part of the experiment is an easily achieved bonus. We aren't talking end-of-term presents here, but simply having something out of the hands-on experience to take away. If the budget will stretch to it, it could be a little working torch or some other electrical gizmo, but it could equally be the traditional batch of cress or some other very cheap plant.

DRESS TO IMPRESS

An enthusiasm for the dressing-up box lasts through pretty well all of primary school. Hands-on science can be given an extra boost by having interesting gear to wear while doing an experiment. Although there's a slight danger of reinforcing the white-coated stereotype, there is something exciting about putting on a special coat, or protective goggles or gloves. Even if it isn't strictly necessary for the experiment, provided it won't stop the children doing what they are meant to be doing, donning protective gear gives that 'dressing-up' fun, emphasizes that you do need to take care when doing experiments, and makes the experiment seem more dangerous (and hence exciting) than it actually is.

There aren't many primary schools with a full set of protective clothing for the children – a bit of ingenuity can go a long way here. Consider getting enough to cover one class and move it around from class to class. Ask parents for help – you can improvise with gardening gloves or the sort of goggles used for handling a strimmer, as long as the experiment doesn't need the real things (and that's unlikely in a primary school). See if the local secondary school or a parent's workplace has any cast-offs. This one isn't essential, but it can add to the sense of drama that will make the hands-on science more memorable.

USE YOUR EXTERNAL RESOURCES

In the previous point there was a suggestion of taking a first step into using external resources – asking the local secondary school for help with cast-off lab clothes, or seeing if something can be begged from a parent's workplace. But these external resources can be taken much further. Many secondary schools, particularly those with science or technology specialist status, can help out with equipment, and with experiments you don't have the opportunity to undertake with a primary school's resources.

If you are lucky, the secondary school will have some sort of outreach programme with its feeder primaries. If not, don't be shy to contact the head of science and see if you can arrange something. The secondary school fed by my local primary offers a plethora of equipment, from robolab remote-controlled buggies and a felt bag of bones to cylindrical mirrors and a 'sink or float exploration kit'. They also go out and visit primary schools, and occasionally (though not frequently enough) have primary classes in to their labs to perform experiments that can't be done in the primary school. Push these opportunities for all you can get.

You aren't limited to schools here either. Subject to the usual safety considerations, look at the opportunities for experimental materials and experiences from local businesses. They are often enthusiastic to be seen as an active part of the community.

IF IT'S TOO DANGEROUS, GO VIRTUAL

One of the saddest things about the way science has gone in secondary schools is the need to avoid anything potentially hazardous. Experiments that would once have been done by all the class are now often confined to demonstrations by the teacher. Some just aren't done at all. One of the most memorable demonstrations when I was at secondary school was the old trick of filling a metal coffee tin with holes punched in the top and bottom with gas, then lighting the gas. When the air/gas mixture gets to the right proportions, the gas explodes, blowing the top off the tin. It's dramatic, loud and incredibly popular. I suspect it's not allowed any more even as a demonstration, in case anyone copies it at home, because it is dangerous in the wrong hands (don't try it at home, as they say).

This isn't the place to analyse the changing attitude to risk and children. We have to accept that there are many experiments that are no longer considered safe for children to undertake – and most of them were never done by primary school children anyway. However, modern technology does give the opportunity to try out virtual experiments with no personal risk. It has to be emphasized that this is always second best. A virtual experience, however loud and colourful, does not have the lasting personal impact of real, physical hands-on. But it is much better than nothing.

With a smartboard or individual PCs and appropriate software (see Chapter 9 for more information on finding virtual experiments), your class can experience a modelled experiment that is hugely risky – playing with X-rays, explosives and atomic piles, for instance – without any personal danger. Look for virtual experiments where there is an opportunity to modify the process. A pretty video is better than nothing, but it's much better if you can choose ingredients or materials, press buttons, move things around and generally interact with the experiment to find out the results.

GETTING HANDS-ON – ESSENTIALS

The essential here is simple but easily overlooked. Even if you are teaching the most basic recording, observation and measuring skills, by adding a little something extra it is possible to make a potentially dull chore into a memorable experience.

CHAPTER 8

OUT IN THE WORLD AND ELECTRIC EXPERIENCES

> We have to understand that the world can only be grasped by action, not by contemplation. The hand is more important than the eye . . . The hand is the cutting edge of the mind.
>
> Jacob Bronowski, Polish-born British science
> writer, in *The Ascent of Man* (1973)

There's something delightfully *ad hoc* about using the world as a natural demonstrator of scientific theories and principles. We are used to going about things in a highly structured way, building what we will do on what we need to teach. This approach refreshingly inverts things. Instead, when using the world as a laboratory, we have to look around, see what there is available and look for the opportunities to demonstrate and explore the science that it presents. This might sound lacking in structure and messy, but it can be one of the best ways to produce effective results.

LOOKING AROUND ME

To give a feel for what's possible, a good starting point is to take a look around you. I can see, amongst other things, the PC I'm writing this book on, a mobile phone, a wooden desk, CD-Rom blanks, a toy light sabre (don't ask), a gel pen – and through the window, a tree, some ivy climbing a wall, a bird scratching around in leaves and a goldfish circling a pond.

INSIDE THE MACHINE

Each of these could be used as a world-based opportunity for learning. The computer is one of the most complex examples of manufacture the class are all likely to be familiar with. If you are feeling brave, open up a computer so they can see inside it – how the different components fit together and work together. (If you aren't comfortable opening up a PC that's in regular use, ask the school or parents for an old one that's no longer regularly used – there are plenty of them out there.)

See how many different materials you can find inside the computer, how they are joined together, and try to get an idea of the different tasks they undertake. Although they are rapidly becoming obsolete, you may still have some diskettes – the little squareish disks that hold about 1.4 megabytes of data. Get hold of an old one no one wants any more (again schools and parents will have these lying about) and crack it open. This will immediately get the children's interest – you are breaking something! Inside you will find the disk itself, a flimsy sheet of magnetic material, with a piece of fabric-like material either side to protect it from wear.

Let the class feel the different materials. Get hold of a magnet and show how the inner disk, despite feeling like a sheet of plastic, is a magnetic material thanks to the tiny fragments of metal distributed through it. If you are careful in the disassembly, you can also show how the protective metal cover slides back and forward, pushed back into place by a spring (it's best if you can have two disks, one that remains in one piece, to help with this demonstration).

The computer screen is also an interesting demonstrator when thinking about light. How does it manage to display all the different colours? In a traditional cathode-ray screen, there are clusters of three dots that glow different colours when hit by electrons. Each cluster contains one of each of the primary colours of light – red, blue and green (if you don't think these are the primary colours, see page 88). Electromagnets inside the box control the beams of electrons that scan across the screen, building up the picture. This is a useful, different approach to the mixing of coloured lights to produce new colours.

A computer screen is also a useful demonstrator of how the picture you 'see', thanks to your brain's complex action, is different from reality. Get an image on the screen with some rich black – perhaps a space scene. Everyone can confirm that they see black. Now switch the screen off and ask the children what colour the screen is – the chances are it's grey. That is as dark as it can get. The only way it can change is by lighting up and getting brighter. Anything apparently darker than that is down to your brain's clever manipulation.

You can demonstrate the workings of a traditional screen by bringing a strong magnet (the ones that act as a base for those magnetic sculptures are good) near the screen – it's very impressive the way the colours shift and develop interesting patterns as you move the magnet around. Unless you are using an old screen that you don't normally use, don't do this too often – the colour distortion can eventually become permanent. (If it does seem to stick, turn the screen off and on again: this uses a static discharge to get rid of any remaining charge, which will remove temporary effects.)

GETTING MOBILE

If you have the modern LCD flat panel screens you can't do the magnetic demonstration – there is no beam of electrons nor are there any magnets involved – but the light aspects of the learning work just as well. Light also comes into a mobile phone – or at least the full electromagnetic spectrum of which light is just a part (see page 88). Mobile phones work by radio, an invisible form of light. They are a handy way of demonstrating that some forms of electromagnetic radiation consider walls as transparent as light does glass.

They are also useful for thinking about the way different light beams don't collide with each other. If they did, all those phone signals (and light, and wireless networks and so on) would end up in a tangled mess and nothing would work. Another useful way of using the mobile phone is to compare sound and electromagnetic radiation, as they make use of both. And they are one of the most common battery-powered devices, so give you a chance to talk about how we use electricity and batteries.

DESKS AND LIGHT SABRES

You can see how this is working, and I won't labour each of the examples I noticed around me in detail, but I would like to bring out a few more points. The wooden desk, for example, provides a good opportunity to look at materials and how they are used. Why is my desk made out of wood and not out of paper or rubber or water? What are the differences between a wooden desk and a plastic or metal one? Where does the wood come from? How does it get from being a tree to being part of a desk? What are the differences between the wood when it's in a tree and when it's in a desk? There are plenty of questions that start to emerge when you look at such a familiar manufactured item.

The light sabre is good to help think a little more about light, and it doesn't do any harm to bring in a bit of popular culture when illustrating a point. Assuming that what comes out of the end of a light sabre is a beam of light, there are a couple of very odd things about it – ask if anyone can spot them. First, the light beam goes a certain distance, then stops. Can they think of any example of this happening? A torch beam hitting a wall might come up. You can use this to look at how light moves in a straight line and doesn't stop until it hits something that absorbs it or reflects it. This isn't the case with a light sabre, which is very strange.

Second, see if anyone knows what a light sabre looks like as it is switched on or off. The light beam visibly grows to full length, or shrinks to nothing. You could use a guess at how long it takes (a second?) to see how fast it is going. This can then be used to work out just how fast the speed of light is – and to explain that in reality you will never see a light beam move, as it travels much too fast. (If you want to give them an explanation of the light sabre, you'll no doubt find one on a Star Wars website – I would guess it's not actually supposed to be light, but a tube of plasma (see pages 73–4) contained by magnetic fields, or some such thing, which would explain its behaviour.)

One last point, which again shows how it isn't always the obvious curriculum topic that something around you can illustrate. The ivy might naturally come into the living things part of science – and there's no harm in that – but you can also use it to illustrate workings, for example, in the way that it sticks to the wall.

BUILDING YOUR HIT LIST

Try the same exercise yourself. Wherever you are as you read this, take a look around you and jot down the different objects and phenomena you can see. One obvious object is the book itself – and don't forget your body and what you are wearing. Think about the items in your list in terms of the main curriculum topics. What could they be used to illustrate?

You can repeat this exercise at school (if you aren't there at the moment). Take a look around the classroom, the rest of the school buildings and the playground. You could pick on anything from recycling bins to autumn leaves. You should have an embarrassment of real world illustrations. Don't worry about that – it's better to have too many rather than too few. What you then need to do is highlight several things about each object or phenomenon. What point or points can you use it to illustrate? How dramatic and interesting is the example? How easy is it to get the class to see the example? These criteria will enable you to build a shortlist of ideal real world illustrations.

MOVING OUTSIDE THE SCHOOL

More than with any other subject, there are brilliant opportunities to make science come alive for children by giving them experiences above and beyond what's possible in the classroom and school environment. Look out for these opportunities:

- hands-on science museums
- science festivals
- major institutions
- touring facilities.

HANDS-ON SCIENCE MUSEUMS

Science museums have come on in a huge way since the first static exhibitions. Most cater for school parties, and the range of hands-on activities is often quite stunning. Take a look at the suggestions in the next chapter for finding information on the web. Some museums provide general science exhibits, like the Science Museum in London and @Bristol, while others specialize in a particular aspect of science. Consider making use of your most local museum, but also travelling further to make use of one of the big centres.

SCIENCE FESTIVALS

A growing resource for school science is the science festival. You can expect talks with plenty of dramatic demonstrations, and there is often also an area to experience hands-on exhibits. See the next chapter for details of finding out about science festivals. Perhaps the best known is the Cheltenham Festival of Science – worth a trip from anywhere in the Midlands, south and southwest – but there are many more to choose from.

MAJOR INSTITUTIONS

Many higher education institutions offer services to schools, whether it is speakers to come and visit, talks at the institution, or the opportunity to see science in action in a real laboratory. Even if there isn't a history of school visits, it is worth contacting nearby universities and asking if they would be interested in giving talks, or providing tours of their science departments, suitable for your age group.

There are also some specialist organizations, most notably the Royal Institution in London (www.rigb.org), which provide excellent science presentations. Although many of the RI's talks are aimed at adults or Key Stage 4, they also put on a range of events for children, including the famous Christmas lectures established by Michael Faraday in the nineteenth century and still going strong. You may have mixed feelings about these if you saw them on TV when you were young. Maybe you were forced to watch them because they were educational, and developed a bit of a dislike for them. If so, forget what you saw. They have become more child-friendly, and experiencing them live is totally different from watching on a TV screen.

TOURING FACILITIES

We have already looked at the resources that might be available from your local secondary school (see page 112), but there are plenty of other sources, from universities to local authorities and science organizations. Facilities that can be brought to your school range from portable planetariums to samples of moon rocks and meteorites that the children can touch and examine. See the next chapter for finding such resources.

Apart from exhibitions and resources you can bring in, there are also a number of speakers who specialize in coming into schools and giving entertaining talks and demonstrations. Take a look at www.popularscience.co.uk/talks.htm and other recommendations in the next chapter.

OUT IN THE WORLD AND ELECTRIC EXPERIENCES – ESSENTIALS

I am not suggesting that all your science is taught this way, but using real world examples has several real benefits. First, this is the science of the world the children know. Detached scientific examples – for example, lenses, or a battery circuit, or an illustration of the blood circulation system – aren't part of everyday life in the form you present them. These things are. That gives them an extra sense of presence and purpose.

Second, it can make the investigation a bit more of an adventure, especially if it involves getting out of the classroom. And finally, by using real world examples you can illustrate key scientific points in a way that combines the abstract science with application.

The approach is simple. Survey your environment. Look for things at home you can take in, or things around the classroom, school and playground you can make use of. List the science topics they can illustrate, score each item on the value of the point, how exciting the demonstration is and practicality, then select your shortlist to build into your teaching. It will take a little while, but it's a one-off exercise, and well worth that investment of time.

Once a year it's also worth updating your list of what's available beyond the school. Check out science museums and festivals on the web (see the next chapter). Look for opportunities to make use of universities and facilities like the Royal Institution. And see what is available in terms of touring exhibitions, shows and speakers – all ways to help bring science alive.

CHAPTER 9

SCIENCE WEB

> Nature, displayed to its fullest extent, presents us with an immense tableau, in which all the order of beings are each represented by a chain . . . The chain is not a simple thread which is only extended in length, it is a large web, or rather a network . . .
>
> George-Louis Leclerc, Comte de Buffon, French naturalist and philosopher, in *Des Mulets* from *Oeuvres Philosophiques* (1774–9)

We will look in the next chapter at how you can keep yourself up-to-date and expand your personal knowledge of science. For now I want to examine how to use one very significant resource – the web – not so much to enhance what you know, as to find new material – both information and demonstrations – that will help your class get more into science.

This material may be to use in front of them on a smartboard, for them to interact directly with on computers or just to provide old-fashioned 'recipes' for successful science. Equally, you may be looking to get hold of information on science festivals and museums, or looking for resources that can be brought into the school for special occasions – the web is a superb source for all this information.

GETTING IT RIGHT ON THE WEB

Everyone knows how to get onto the web and type a few keywords into a search engine, but there is a lot you can do both to make your searching more effective, and to ensure that the results you get are true. Sad to say, not everything you read on the web is true. I have gone into detail on how to do this in my book *Studying Using the Web*, but I want to pick out some of the highlights to make sure that you get the best out of the web as a source for science.

In print, most facts are checked. An academic paper is reviewed by experts. A book or a newspaper article is edited. A company's accounts are audited. None of this is foolproof, but there is some form of checking in place. The web is very different. Anyone can put material onto a website. It might be true. It might contain mistakes. It could be a hoax or a deliberate attempt to mislead. The web is the best source of information we've ever seen – but it has to be handled knowingly. Web users can't afford to be naive.

So how can we ensure that we're hitting the best information? The first step is to improve searching, and specifically to know how to ask the right question. Knowing what you want ('How does a petrol engine work?' or 'Where can I find a piece of moon rock my children can see?' – or whatever your brief happens to be) is not the same as knowing the right keywords for a search engine.

Let's say you wanted to research the history of computers to give a little background to this familiar piece of technology, and typed 'computer' into Google (www.google.co.uk). I tried that, and was told there were 1.6 billion places to look. (This illustrates

---

BETTER SEARCHING

Search engines provide simple shorthand to make searches more effective. Try these:

- **"Blips"** – surround a set of words with double inverted commas to search for an exact phrase.

- **Forget upper case** – search engines either ignore upper case or think you only want upper-case words. Searching for **trade** will find trade, Trade, TRADE (and even tradE).

- **Increase results displayed** – most search engines have a setting in the preferences section for number of results on a page. Google defaults to ten: try increasing it to fifty.

- **Use brackets and Booleans** – you can use brackets and special connecting words that were originally used in the branch of logic called Boolean algebra ('NOT' and 'OR', for instance) to make things clearer. What does the search phrase **dogs and rabbits or guinea pigs but not cats** mean? I'm not sure, and a search engine won't know either. But type **dogs (rabbits OR 'guinea pigs') NOT cats** and the search engine knows you want dogs combined with either one of rabbits or guinea pigs, but don't want cats. Note 'and' and 'but' are ignored, so can be left out.

TEN TIPS FOR A TRUSTWORTHY SOURCE

1 **Avoid anonymity**. Look out for clear ownership and means of contacting the author. Be suspicious of anonymous text.

2 **Don't trust a messy site**. Be wary of amateurish presentation. This doesn't mean a site has to be fancy – some of the best university sites are plain – but it should have reasonable spelling and layout, and should avoid using garish backgrounds, lots of fonts and too many text sizes.

3 **Suspect the over-flashy**. If a site is packed with animations and clever graphics, the content may be shallow or sales-oriented.

4 **Check for consistency**. Internal inconsistencies suggest a badly checked site.

5 **Are basic facts right**? You wouldn't use the web if you knew all the answers, but if basic information is wrong, the specialist content may also be suspect.

6 **Use the hierarchy**. There is a rough hierarchy of trust. Government sites (apart from propaganda), university sites and peer-reviewed journals come top. Next, TV, newspaper, magazine and well-known encyclopedia sites. Then non-governmental organizations and information sites. Then company sites. Finally, general user sites and blogs. Treat these last as opinion rather than fact.

7 **Use multiple sources**. Don't rely on a single site, only on information you've found on several, making sure they aren't word-for-word copies.

8 **Watch out for lies, hoaxes and misdirection**. Not everyone out there is telling the truth.

9 **There isn't always one right answer**. Many issues are debated. You may have to collect a range of opinion, rather than fact.

10 **Distinguish between factual debate and belief**. There is nothing wrong with belief, but don't put it up against fact.

how the web has grown – I did the same experiment five years ago and got a mere 66 million responses.)

It's essential to make good use of keywords to focus the search. The search engine is dumb; it doesn't know what you are looking for. Type **computer history**, or even better, **"computer history" or "history of computing"**, covering two different ways of referring to your requirement. Or you might look for a specific computer resource such as **"history of computing" timeline**.

Take a look at the hints in the 'Better searching' box to improve your search terms. Then, when you get a search result, scan through the first couple of dozen for obvious patterns that will help refine what you are searching for. It's also worth temporarily moving off your favourite search engine and seeing if a meta-search like Dogpile (www.dogpile.com) or Jux2 (www.jux2.com), which combine results from several different search sources, works better for you.

Once you get some results, overcome the temptation to accept them immediately as absolute truth. You can't be sure whether any single source is trustworthy. If you think a convincing-looking website implies truthful content, take a look at www.petroldirect.com, apparently selling petrol through the post, or www.bonsaikitten. com, a site that pretends to be a source of tips on growing kittens in glass bottles to make them interesting shapes, so convincing that it has been investigated by the FBI.

It's worth giving a specific piece of advice on Wikipedia (www.wikipedia.org). This is far and away the biggest encyclopedia on the net. In fact it's the biggest encyclopedia anywhere. But because it can be edited by anyone, some entries are inevitably incorrect (see page 132 for more details on using Wikipedia safely) and, more to the point, the science entries, though often very detailed and effective, are usually at much too high a level for direct use with primary school children. Wikipedia is great for your own exploration, but has limited value when searching for material for school.

The rest of this chapter is mostly for reference – take a glance through it now, but make use of the specifics when you want to get some practical information.

INFORMATION FOR SCHOOLS

There is now a good range of websites providing basic science information for your lessons, worksheets, lesson plans and more.

Use a search engine such as www.google.co.uk (click on the 'pages from the UK' button to get better focused results) to search for **"primary school science"**. The examples below were current at the time of publication:

- **ScienceWeb** – primary school worksheets and interactives. There is a charge, but it is relatively low. www.scienceweb.org.uk

- **Primary School Science** – schemes of work, lesson plans, worksheets and much more. It's a subscription site, but a limited amount is available free. www. primaryschoolscience.com

- **Planet Science** – a glossy science information site with a specific 'under elevens' section. www.planet-science.com

- **Primary Resources for Science** – a mixed collection of resources with both information and activities and presentations. www.primaryresources.co.uk/science

- **Kent NGfL** – a good collection of resources on Kent's National Grid site. www. kented.org.uk/ngfl/subjects/science/qca/index.htm

- **Physics for Primary Schools** – rather messy, but useful site from Bristol University. www.phy.bris.ac.uk/groups/particle/PUS/Primary.html

- **ABPI Science Resources for Schools** – medical-based resources from the British pharmacological industry. www.abpischools.org.uk/

ONLINE DEMONSTRATIONS AND ACTIVITIES

Extending beyond the simple information, many sites also provide demonstrations and interactive websites that can be used to give a visual illustration, or can be used directly by the children. A fair number of sites provide both these and information.

Use a search engine such as www.google.co.uk (click on the 'pages from the UK' button to get better focused results) to search for **primary science (demonstrations OR activities OR interactive)**. The examples below were current at the time of publication:

- **Planet Science** – a glossy science information site with a specific 'under elevens' section which includes demonstrations and activities. www.planet-science.com

- **Primary Resources for Science** – a mixed collection of resources with both information and activities and presentations. www.primaryresources.co.uk/science

- **Smart Education** – site with a wide range of smartboard resources, including a fair amount of science. www.smart-education.org/uk

- **First School Years Science** – the science section of this free resources site has a good collection of resources under the individual curriculum topics. www.firstschoolyears.com/science

- **Crick Primary School** – this school's site has some excellent Flash online demonstrations. www.crick.northants.sch.uk/Flash%20Studio/cfsscience/cfsscience.htm

■   **BBC Dynamo Lab** – as you might expect, the BBC's interactive material is fun
and visual. www.bbc.co.uk/education/dynamo/lab

SCIENCE TALKS

It can help to have a different face presenting on science, particularly if that face
belongs to a science expert or author. A number of sites help with finding the right
science talk for your school.

Use a search engine such as www.google.co.uk (click on the 'pages from the
UK' button to get better focused results) to search for **school science talks**. You will
find that a lot of the talks are aimed at secondary level, but there are some primary-
focused events too, so it's worth filtering through them. The examples below were
current at the time of publication:

■   **Popular Science** – details of talks provided by popular science authors. Some
are aimed at secondary level, but many are available for primary schools.
www.popularscience.co.uk/talks.htm

■   **The Creative Science Centre** – talks and demonstrations provided by the Centre
at the University of Sussex at Brighton. Check the list for primary level talks.
www.creative-science.org.uk

■   **Science Live** – an online guide to science presenters and outreach shows.
www.sciencelive.net

■   **Glasgow University** – schools liaison page for physics and astronomy.
www.physics.gla.ac.uk/teachers

■   **Strathclyde University** – a range of talks and resources. Note the offer of school
talks by departmental staff part way down the page. www.phys.strath.ac.uk/public

MUSEUMS

Science museums are much better than they used to be for primary children, with a
wide range of interactive exhibits. Pretty well every museum can be found on the
web.

Use a search engine such as www.google.co.uk (click on the 'pages from the
UK' button to get better focused results) to search for **science museums**. You may
also want to try **science museums schools** to find information specifically for schools.
The examples below were current at the time of publication:

- **24 Hour Museum** – an excellent listing site with loads of information on science museums. At the time of writing, the best way of getting to them was via this trail: www.24hourmuseum.org.uk/trlout/TRA11863.html. Alternatively, put **science** in the search box at www.24hourmuseum.org.uk

- **The Science Museum** – the national museum in London with a large exploratory science section and plenty of schools interaction. www.sciencemuseum.org.uk. For those in the West Country, see also www.sciencemuseum.org.uk/wroughton

- **The Natural History Museum** – the dinosaurs are always popular, but of course there's much more (and don't forget the building itself). www.nhm.ac.uk

- **The Museum of Science and Industry** – Manchester's often neglected but excellent museum. www.msim.org.uk

- **Glasgow Science Centre** – stunning high-tech buildings house this new and dramatic museum. www.gsc.org.uk

- **@Bristol** – Bristol's modern hands-on museum remains very popular. www.at-bristol.org.uk

- **Discovery Museum** – Tyne & Wear's relatively small but friendly science museum. www.twmuseums.org.uk/schools/discovery

FESTIVALS

Building on the success of literary festivals, science festivals are rapidly becoming hugely popular, combining talks, demonstrations and hands-on science aimed at all ages.

Use a search engine such as www.google.co.uk (click on the 'pages from the UK' button to get better focused results) to search for **science festival**. The examples below were current at the time of publication:

- **Cheltenham Festival of Science** – one of the most dynamic of the science festivals, usually featuring a good hands-on area. Takes place in June. www.cheltenhamfestivals.com/whats_on/science_festival.html

- **Edinburgh International Science Festival** – early April festival with plenty of content. www.sciencefestival.co.uk

- **The BA Festival of Science** – the British Association for the Advancement of Science holds an annual festival at a different location each year. Check the website for details. www.the-ba.net

- **Cambridge Science Festival** – one of the smaller festivals, but very lively. Held in March each year. www.cambridgescience.org

- **Newcastle Science Festival** – a growing festival in the northeast, also in March. www.newcastlesciencefestival.co.uk

- **Wrexham Science Festival** – takes place every two years, but quite sizeable and handy for Wales and the Midlands. www.wrexhamsf.com

- **Brighton Science Festival** – an early festival (February): useful to have something in those dark winter months. www.brightonscience.com

TOURING FACILITIES

We've already looked at science talks, but it is also possible to bring resources to your school, ranging from travelling planetariums to pieces of moon rock.

Use a search engine such as www.google.co.uk (click on the 'pages from the UK' button to get better focused results) to search for **science roadshows schools, touring science schools** and **in-school science events**. The examples below were current at the time of publication:

- **Association for Science Education** – the ASE's site has a list of contacts for in-school events. www.ase.org.uk/htm/teacher_zone/pta_science/pta_contacts.php

- **Generation Science** – the touring wing of the Edinburgh science festival, providing a range of events around Scotland. Okay, they may not come to your school, but they are more local. www.sciencefestival.co.uk/html/schools.html

- **Moon rocks and meteorites** – impressive free loan packages from the Particle Physics and Astronomy Research Council. www.pparc.ac.uk/Ed/LS/moon.asp

- **CHaOS Science Roadshow** – touring fun science events in the Cambridge area. www.chaosscience.org.uk

- **SciFun** – the Scottish science technology roadshow. www.scifun.ed.ac.uk

- **Astrodome, Hereford Starlab, Armagh Stardome, Glamorgan Starlab** (and more – search for **portable planetarium schools**) – portable planetariums with operator to visit your school.
    - www.astrodome.clara.co.uk
    - www.hereford-starlab.co.uk
    - www.armaghplanet.com/html/stardome_primary.htm
    - www.glam.ac.uk/roccoto/planetarium.php

INSTITUTIONS

Universities, colleges and specialist institutions often have programmes to help with school science.

Use a search engine such as www.google.co.uk (click on the 'pages from the UK' button to get better focused results) to search for **public science lectures children, public science talks children** and **university science "primary schools"**. The examples below were current at the time of publication:

■ **The Royal Institution** – the UK's premier organization for presenting science to the public has a range of children's events, including the famous RI Christmas Lectures. www.rigb.org

■ **Bristol University** – runs a range of events in collaboration with local primary schools. www.chemlabs.bris.ac.uk/outreach/primary

■ **Cambridge University** – has a wide range of activities both in-school and visiting the university. www.cam.ac.uk/schooloutreach/local.html

■ **Queen's University, Belfast** – provides events at university facilities and in schools. www.qub.ac.uk/home/QueensintheCommunity/OutreachDirectory/Project List/index.html?prog_cd=PRIMS

CHAPTER 10

KEEPING UP-TO-DATE

A real scientific revolution, like any other revolution, is news. *The Origin of Species* sold out as fast as it could be printed and was denounced from the pulpit almost immediately. Sea-floor spreading has been explained, perhaps not well, in leading newspapers, magazines, books and most recently in a color motion picture. When your elementary school children talk about something at dinner, you rarely continue to cite it.

Henry William Menard, American earth scientist and
marine geologist, in *Citations in a Scientific Revolution*,
part of *Studies in Earth and Space Sciences* (1972)

More than any other subject, science is always advancing and changing. The science you will have acquired in this book gives you a starting point, but to keep that sense of wonder alive it needs to be fed with regular updates. I hope that what you have read so far will have succeeded in whetting your appetite for more. This chapter will help you keep up with what's happening, but also help you to expand your knowledge in the areas that particularly interest you, whether it's a small part of science or the whole broad panoply. The sources I am recommending may go into more depth than I have been able to in this book, but they are all designed for those with no prior knowledge – we aren't talking about venturing into complex scientific papers or coping with the impenetrable jargon of scientists communicating with each other.

BOOKING SOME MIND EXPANSION

Perhaps not surprisingly, my first suggestion is to read some popular science books. After the success of the big name books, like Stephen Hawking's *A Brief History of*

Time and Richard Dawkins' *The Selfish Gene*, there have been a whole raft of books produced covering just about every topic and scientist you might like to find out more about. Don't worry, incidentally, if you are one of the thousands who bought Hawking's book and either put it straight on the shelf or gave up after a few chapters. Most good popular science books are much easier to read.

In fact there are so many of these books out there, it can be quite difficult to pin down the book you want, particularly in a bookshop. I find visiting a well-known large American bookstore chain's science section daunting. Rather than just have a 'popular science' shelf, they break the topic down into different sub-topics, and it's not always obvious where you should be looking.

Luckily there is a painless answer. When not writing these books myself, I edit the Popular Science website (see Figure 10.1). This site specializes in reviews of popular science (and maths) books, both those aimed at adults and those aimed at children. You can take a look through the latest reviews, browse through the top-rated popular science books, or find a specific book by author, title or subject. There are also articles, details of speaking engagements where you can hear and meet popular science authors, information on school talks from science writers, and an optional monthly update with news of what's interesting in the popular science book

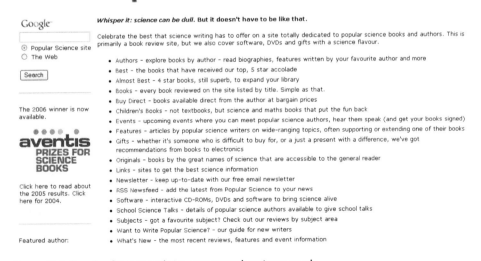

Figure 10.1 Popular Science website www.popularscience.co.uk

world. The site is www.popularscience.co.uk. It's not fancy and loaded with Flash animations – it just concentrates on providing the information you need, with detailed book reviews to help you make your choice.

KEEPING UP ON THE WEB

Websites are inevitably a strong recommendation not just for finding out about books, but for keeping up with the science news, or finding out more about a specific topic. We've already seen (see pages 121–4) the opportunities for getting information and resources for your children from the web – this is a different requirement: getting news and expanded knowledge for you.

A good starting point is the BBC News science page. This won't cover everything you want to know, but will give a good overview of the hot science topics of the moment. The page is http://news.bbc.co.uk/1/hi/sci/tech/default.stm (if you can't be bothered with all that, just go to http://news.bbc.co.uk and click on Science and Nature from the left-hand menu). You may also find relevant news under the Technology menu – the two items are strongly overlapping.

The BBC's page is inevitably news-oriented. If you want an up-to-date but wider overview, it's hard to beat the website of the UK's best known science magazine, *New Scientist* (see Figure 10.2). Although the home page carries the latest hot stories, you can go into more depth on many of the topics – see www.newscientist.com. The only frustration is that though the site has articles from back issues stretching back several years, you will often find that you are shown the first paragraph or two of the article, but need to subscribe to get the whole text.

If you subscribe to the print magazine (see page 135), you get this access free – alternatively your local authority or local library may have a group subscription you can make use of. It's worth checking.

If you want to find out more about a specific topic, a good starting point is the online encyclopedia, Wikipedia (www.wikipedia.org). If you haven't come across it, Wikipedia is a unique phenomenon that could only exist in the internet age. It is an absolutely vast encyclopedia, with at least twenty times more entries than any of the other great encyclopedias. Many of the entries are much longer than those in traditional print volumes too. This has only proved possible because Wikipedia is open for anyone to edit. At any time. Contributing whatever you like, wherever you like.

Think how powerful this is. Wikipedia entries can and do emerge within minutes of a major event happening. It's frighteningly quick. And because there are thousands of contributors it can cover subjects no other source can hope to cover. But there is, of course, a downside to this openness. At any one time, some of the entries are poor, some are wrong, and some are just silly, though occasionally with a certain

Figure 10.2 New Scientist website www.newscientist.com

poetry, as is demonstrated by a section of the entry on the Surrey attraction Bocketts Farm, which remained live for around three months:

> Bocketts Farm is also one of the world's first complexes successful in genetically engineering dinosaurs, the first of that being an 18 tonne bronchoraus [sic] named Stuart, who grazes a 16 acre paddock upon the north end of the Farm Park. His diet comprises primarily of hay, vodka martinis and flying saucers. In the future, Stuart says he would like to pursue a career in accountancy.

It just isn't possible to take information from Wikipedia without a degree of scepticism. So why recommend it at all? First, there is no encyclopedia to compare for range of content. But also its science content has particularly been recognized as being very full and complete. In late 2005, the top science journal *Nature* did a comparison between Wikipedia and Encyclopedia Britannica on a number of topics, and found the error rates were comparable, and Wikipedia's entries were typically much fuller. (Britannica did question this result, but *Nature* sticks by its findings.) It's well worth checking a topic in a couple of other sources after reading the Wikipedia entry, but as long as you approach it with an awareness of its nature, Wikipedia's coverage is very impressive.

As might be expected, the next port of call after Wikipedia is a search engine such as Google. This isn't the place for a full-scale tutorial on getting the best from a search engine (for much more on the topic, see my *Studying Using the Web* (2006)), but here are a few useful considerations when reading up on science.

As we saw in the previous chapter, try to use search terms that will home in on a specific. There's a huge amount of information on the web and it's easy to get overwhelmed. The search engine will do its best to put sensible results upfront, but it's much better if you can help it and give it a more directed search. When the results appear, don't go straight to the first one. Take a quick scan through the first page. Look for results that seem at the right level. You may well get some scientific papers or highly technical web pages – it's probably best to skip them for the moment. Also, keep your 'weird antennae' ready. There may well be some results that are obviously a little strange.

A final hint is to remember to use the tips for a trustworthy source we met in the previous chapter (see page 123). While you can rely pretty much on sites like the BBC or New Scientist to get it right (even if the BBC often oversimplifies) there are plenty of sites out there that it's best to check up on before taking their word.

NEWSLETTERS AND RSS

Websites make great sources of information, but they are passive – you have to hunt around them and find the information you need. If you are trying to stay on top of a subject, it can be useful to have the facts coming to you. Some websites have free newsletters, which you can sign up to by giving your e-mail address and you will receive regular updates. Others make use of one of the web's more recent additions, RSS.

RSS stands for Really Simple Syndication, though everyone knows it by the initials. The idea is a simple one. The website publisher has a file that lists what the most recently updated pages on the site are, with a simple description. If you have a piece of software that can pick up RSS, it will present you with the latest headlines from the site, updated on a regular basis. It's like having your own newspaper, filled with the exact topic you are interested in, updated every few minutes.

Many sites with an RSS feed have specific links to add the feed to popular portal websites that can be tailored, such as Google or Yahoo. Alternatively, choose 'add content' from the personalized page of one of these portals, then paste in the name of the RSS link, which you can usually pick up by right-clicking (control-click on a Mac) the orange RSS box on the source web page and choosing 'copy shortcut' or 'copy link location'.

If you would prefer your RSS feeds via your web browser, users of Firefox or Internet Explorer 7 or later can use a feed as a live bookmark, as long as the site you want to get a feed from is set up appropriately – when visiting the site, the web browser will indicate there's a live feed and a simple click will add the RSS information to your bookmarks (favourites).

Alternatively, the most sophisticated way to keep track of your RSS feeds is through a newsreader. This is a piece of software that is designed to read the input from RSS feeds and present the results as a kind of electronic newspaper. This sort of facility is increasingly being built into e-mail packages, or you can check out specialist RSS newsreaders such as Newsgator (www.newsgator.com – this is also the site for the leading Mac newsreader, NetNewsWire) and RSS reader (www.rssreader.com).

MAGAZINES AND NEWSPAPERS

The quality newspapers aren't bad at covering science, though they tend to be quite selective. If you prefer to read on paper, but want an overview of the latest developments, rather than the in-depth exploration of a book, your best bet is probably one of the regular science magazines. At the time of writing, in the UK the best weekly science magazine for the general reader was *New Scientist*. If you prefer a monthly update, *BBC Focus Magazine* isn't bad, though it does suffer a little from the same problems as TV science (see below).

TV

TV science is a difficult one. Much TV science has been dumbed down to the extent that it has very little content left. Don't get me wrong. I'm all in favour of shows like Sky's *Brainiac – Science Abuse*, which spends a lot of its time blowing things up and doing very silly experiments. It's great for showing teenagers that science doesn't have to be stuffy, but can be fun. But I wouldn't rely on *Brainiac* to find out what's happening in the science world.

Most other science programmes are one-issue documentaries, which can be useful to get some background on a subject, but have to be treated with caution, as they inevitably concentrate on the visual, and have to simplify hugely, often distorting the facts in the process. Such shows are useful starting points, but back them up with books if a topic interests you.

A classic example of the problem with TV science is demonstrated by the plastic curtain that surrounds the table where experiments are undertaken on dark states (see page 76), the strange mix of light and matter that it's possible to create with a Bose

Einstein condensate. The leading researcher in the field is Lene Vestergaad Hau, a Danish scientist working at Harvard University in America.

Hau's team regularly get TV crews coming in to film their experiments, but like most modern science, there is very little to see. When a German crew were visiting one day, the researchers monitoring the experiment found that the delicate dark state had suddenly, catastrophically collapsed. When they rushed to investigate, they found that the TV crew had set up a smoke generator next to the experiment to make the lasers visible, as otherwise it was rather dull. The smoke totally ruined the delicate experiment – it took days to get it back to a usable state.

DON'T MAKE IT A CHORE

We are used to reading up on science being hard work. School work. Textbook stuff. The important thing to remember when wanting to expand your scientific experience is it doesn't have to be like this. Good popular science books, magazines like *New Scientist*, and the better websites will help strengthen that sense of wonder. They make science interesting and intriguing, rather than dull and soul-destroying. Don't think of keeping up on science as a chore – make it a treat.

CHAPTER II

GO INSPIRE

[I]nspiration plays no less a role in science than it does in the realm of art.

Max Weber, German economist and sociologist,

in *Wissenschaft als Beruf* (1922)

I hope that by now you will be feeling that science is not dull, but a subject that can fascinate and excite. The primary intention of this book is to get you fired up – to help you to get science. With that inspiration, you now need to pass on that sense of excitement and wonder, even if you are putting across the aspects of science required by the curriculum, rather than the wider viewpoint you have been given.

Being excited by science yourself is the starting point. Only a superb actor can inspire others without getting a buzz out of the subject themselves. But it's not enough to be enthusiastic. We've all come across bores who can talk for their country on their favourite topic, but are about as exciting to listen to as the shipping forecast. Enthusiasm is a beginning, but it's also essential to be able to make that sense of inspiration infectious, to motivate your class to get the most out of science.

Motivational techniques sometimes cause suspicion. Isn't there a line to be drawn between teaching and brainwashing? Absolutely. But there's nothing wrong with thinking about the opportunities to build enthusiasm. Based on the information and resources in this book, you can put in place a simple, four-point plan to inspire.

We've already covered the first point – get enthused yourself. Second, look for opportunities not just to put across facts, but to excite. Give them more hands-on. Make things happen. Third, use what's around you to make science real. And finally go beyond the classroom to bring in extra resources.

Use the knowledge you've gained here and in further reading and exploring (see the previous chapter) to stretch the envelope. Okay, you probably aren't going to introduce primary children to quantum theory or special relativity, but you can include elements of 'real science' to give a tantalizing edge to the everyday. It's still important that *you* know the 'adult' version. No one would argue that just because you are teaching Year 2s, your personal reading matter should be children's stories rather than adult novels. Similarly, just because you are teaching primary science doesn't mean you have to stick to the Janet and John version for your own consumption.

The important thing is to get the feeling for science, so you can communicate that excitement and sense of wonder. It's time to bring science alive.

INDEX

Selected recipes from

THE SATURDAY EVENING POST
FAMILY COOKBOOK

Edited by
Julie Nixon Eisenhower
Frederic A. Birmingham

Indianapolis, Indiana

Book design by DesignCenter, Inc.
Indianapolis, Indiana

Second Printing, July, 1976
Third Printing, September, 1977
Fourth Printing, December, 1977
Fifth Printing, January, 1978
Sixth Printing, September, 1978
Seventh Printing, June 1979

INTRODUCTION

One of the wonderful things about cooking is that it is creative. It is an art and will always remain so.

This is not to belittle the computerized wonders of packaged and frozen foods. But the true medium of cooking is first the marketplace where decisions are made; then the planning, for the little touches that create excitement and harmony at the table; and finally in the intuitive processes of cooking, which are not matters of measurement but of experience and imagination.

Such culinary art lurks in the kitchens of a thousand farmhouses, in the little black books tucked in the top drawers of a thousand kitchens, and even more remotely, in the recesses of the minds of countless numbers who love to cook. Many and great are the cookbooks which have been written in the past, but still there is the suspicion that the best is yet to come, if ever it could be pried from its myriad hiding places in homes where a recipe means "eat" instead of "publish."

Reflecting on these things, the editors of *The Saturday Evening Post* last year decided to announce a recipe contest and to call on the households of America for their most treasured dishes. The *Post Family Cookbook* contains over 350 of these recipes, recipes which have been passed on lovingly from generation to generation. Because the *Post* is regarded as something akin to a family friend, there was a willingness on the part of *Post* cooks to share the secrets of favorite dishes, such as "Baseball Dinner," prepared for years as a family of baseball fans progressed through Little League, to Pony, and finally to Legion baseball practice. Above all, it is the human element evoked by the recipe contest which makes this cookbook special. For example, one delightful recipe for Jim's Caesar Salad has a postscript for the prospective cook: "Be prepared to be complimented."

As practical cooks for their families, a great many of the contest entrants expressed an awareness of budget planning and the time involved in preparing their recipes. Yet, hand in hand with this very real concern for prices and practicality, the entrants seemed to take a special joy and delight in cooking. Homemade breads, cakes and pies—which often require special skills and loving hands—evoked by far the greatest number of recipes from readers.

In preparing the cookbook, our thanks go to many people, but in particular to the Purdue School of Cooking, which set their experts to work for us in testing many of the recipes.

If you and your family dine the better for having experienced our book, and touch hands—perhaps only slightly dusted with baking powder—with many others in households all over the land where food is valued as nourishment for both body and spirit, we will have achieved what we set out to do in the very beginning.

Frederic A. Birmingham
Managing Editor
The Saturday Evening Post

Julie Nixon Eisenhower
Assistant Managing Editor
The Saturday Evening Post

CONTENTS

SALADS
The Sharing of the Green

RICHARD NIXON'S AVOCADO SALAD

Mash 2 medium-sized avocados. Stir into slightly thickened lemon Jell-O base made with

1 package lemon Jell-O
3 tablespoons lemon juice
1½ cups hot water

Stir in 1 can (#2) of grapefruit sections drained, and ½ cup chopped celery. Chill and unmold. Serve with a whipped cream and mayonnaise mixture.

LADY BIRD JOHNSON'S MOLDED CRANBERRY SALAD

Part of the Johnson family tradition is this salad, served for holidays with chicken or turkey.

1 envelope unflavored
  gelatin
1¼ cups cold water
1 cup sugar
2 cups cranberries

½ cup chopped celery
½ cup chopped nuts (pecans
  are excellent)
½ teaspoon salt

Cook cranberries in 1 cup water for 20 minutes. Stir in sugar and cook 5 minutes longer. Soften gelatin in ¼ cup cold water; add to hot cranberries and stir until dissolved. Set aside to cool. When mixture begins to thicken, add chopped celery, nuts and salt. Turn into mold that has been rinsed with cold water. Chill in refrigerator until firm. Unmold on serving plate. Garnish with salad greens if desired. Makes about 6 servings.

CLARE BOOTHE LUCE'S GOLDEN DOLPHIN SALAD

I never can quite make up my mind whether I prefer a Chef's Salad or a Caesar Salad. My cook, Katherine Yokoyama, surprised me by combining the ingredients of both—with an Oriental touch of her own—cutting them up into non-lipstick-smearing bite sizes. So I named the salad The Golden Dolphin after my Honolulu house. It's not only my favorite salad, but everyone else's who eats it.

1 small head iceberg lettuce
2 small heads butter lettuce
½ head romaine
¾ bunch watercress
1 small cucumber, peeled
  and diced thinly

4 slices cooked ham, diced
3 slices Swiss cheese, diced
¼ cup fresh grated Parmesan
1 small can anchovies, in 1″ slices
½ cup croutons, toasted in
  garlic butter

Cut all greens into ½″ lengths. Toss the above ingredients (except the croutons) lightly with the following dressing:

1/3 cup white wine vinegar
2/3 cup olive oil
Dash Worcestershire sauce
2 garlic buds—put through press

¼ teaspoon salad herbs
Dash Ajinamoto or Accent
Salt, pepper to taste

Before serving, add toasted croutons, one well-beaten raw egg. Toss lightly.

DICK VAN DYKE'S POOR RICHARD'S SALAD

This salad was given to Dick by a friend named Richard shortly after Dick was married. It's been a favorite and a filler ever since.

1 package beef wieners chopped into bite size	4 stalks celery
½ box Velveeta cheese	10 scallions
1 medium-sized jar gherkin pickles	1 small can, drained, peas
	1 package cooked macaroni shells

Mix together, add salad herbs, ¼ cup pickle juice and lots of mayonnaise. Serve cold. A perfect picnic salad.

LUCILLE BALL'S FAVORITE SALAD

My favorite salad is one I can make in a hurry, because that's the way I do almost everything. I call it a "Tropical Treat," although I'm sure that's probably not its real name. I think the first time I tasted it was in Hawaii, but I remembered the ingredients because everyone I have served it to since has always enjoyed it. It can also serve as a dessert if you don't want to stuff your guests.

I make it in individual salad bowls, which you may or may not chill before assembling your ingredients. They consist of thinly sliced bananas, pineapple rings, finely chopped nuts, lettuce and a dressing of mayonnaise and half-and-half. After that, it's simple. Line the bottom of the bowl with crisp lettuce leaves, lay in several pineapple rings, then a layer of sliced bananas. Prepare the dressing ahead of time by combining the half-and-half with mayonnaise and stirring into a thick, creamy mixture. Spoon the dressing over the salad, sprinkle with chopped nuts, and top it with a cherry.

I usually serve this with a menu of thinly sliced steak and scalloped potatoes. It's also good with a meat casserole.

BILLY GRAHAM'S POPPY SEED DRESSING

Mix:

1½ cups sugar	2 teaspoons salt
2 teaspoons dry mustard	2/3 cup vinegar

Add and stir thoroughly 3 tablespoons onion juice. Slowly add, beating constantly, 2 cups Mazola oil. Continue beating until thick. Stir in 2 tablespoons poppy seeds to taste. Store in refrigerator. Makes 3 1/3 cups.

AMERICAN FRUIT BEAUTY SALAD

7 Native Fruits from Florida, Michigan, California, Hawaii and Oregon make this salad "Fit for a King"!

1 pint fresh strawberries, stems removed, cut into halves
½ cup fresh or frozen blueberries
½ cup fresh or frozen pineapple, cut into chunks
½ cup fresh or frozen black, sweet, pitted cherries
2 large bananas, peeled and sliced

1 inch thick and rolled in 3 tablespoons lime juice
2 large California oranges, peeled and cubed
½ cup white seedless grapes, cut into halves
1½ cups flake coconut

Combine all fruits in a large bowl. Toss to mix. Add 1 cup coconut and toss again. Pour into a large red glass bowl. Sprinkle with ¼ cup coconut. Set in refrigerator to chill for at least 1 hour before using. At serving time, sprinkle with remaining ¼ cup coconut. Serves 8.

Mrs. Richard Borth, *Dearborn, Michigan*

FROZEN FRUIT CHEESE SALAD

1 (3-ounce) package cream cheese
2 tablespoons cream
2 tablespoons lemon juice
1/8 teaspoon salt
1 cup crushed pineapple, drained
½ cup small marshmallows
½ cup chopped pecans

1 cup Royal Ann cherries, drained and pitted
2 bananas, sliced
1 cup white grapes, seeded
2 cups whipping cream
3/4 cup mayonnaise

Work the cheese, cream, lemon juice and salt together. Add pineapple, marshmallows, nuts, cherries, grapes and bananas. Whip the cream and work the mayonnaise into it. Fold this into the fruit mixture. Freeze about 3 hours, until firm. Serve on lettuce with cream cheese dressing. Serves 18.

Cream Cheese Dressing

Cream 2 (3-ounce) packages cream cheese with 8 tablespoons vegetable oil. Add ½ teaspoon salt, 1/8 teaspoon white pepper, 1½ teaspoons sugar, 1 tablespoon lemon juice. Dust with paprika.

Dorothy Imlay, *St. Joseph, Missouri*

AUNT IRENE'S CHERRY-PINEAPPLE SALAD

2 (3-ounce) packages cream cheese
1 cup mayonnaise
1 cup maraschino cherries

1 (#2) can pineapple chunks, drained
2½ cups small marshmallows
1 cup whipping cream

Combine cheese and mayonnaise and blend until smooth. Fold in fruit, marshmallows and cream which has been whipped. Chill. Serves 8 to 10.

Mrs. Adolph Voelker, *Tell City, Indiana*

APPLE ORCHARD SALAD

1 envelope unflavored gelatin
¼ cup sugar
1 3/4 cups cranapple juice
2 tablespoons lime juice
½ cup chopped unpeeled apple
½ cup finely chopped fresh
   cranberries
½ cup chopped celery
1 (3-ounce) package cream cheese
½ cup finely chopped walnuts

Mix gelatin and sugar in saucepan. Stir in 3/4 cup of the cranapple juice. Place over low heat, stirring constantly, until gelatin is dissolved, about 3 to 5 minutes. Remove from heat; stir in remaining 1 cup cranapple juice and lime juice. Chill, stirring occasionally, until slightly thicker than the consistency of unbeaten egg white. Add chopped apple, finely chopped cranberries and celery. Cut cream cheese into 12 squares, roll into balls and then roll in chopped walnuts. Put 2 cream-cheese balls in each of 6 individual molds, then spoon in gelatin mixture. Chill until firm. Unmold and garnish with lettuce. Serves 6.

Mrs. C. Mize, *High Point, North Carolina*

APRICOT ALLURE SALAD

1 small package lime Jell-O
3/4 cup sugar
1 (#2) can crushed pineapple
1 cup cranberry cocktail
1 (3-ounce) package cream cheese
1 cup dried apricots, chopped fine
1 cup whipping cream
1 cup finely diced celery
1 cup mixed chopped nuts
1 pound chocolate-covered
   maraschino cherries

Combine Jell-O, sugar and pineapple. Heat until mixture simmers. Then add cranberry cocktail, crumbled cream cheese and finely chopped apricots. Mix thoroughly. Remove from heat and cool until chilled. Whip cream and blend with above mixture. Add finely chopped celery and top with nuts and chill. When ready to serve, crush two or three chocolate-covered maraschino cherries over top of each serving. Serve on lettuce or with other greens. Serves 8.

Mrs. Vincent Garner, *Valencia, Pennsylvania*

LOVELY LEMALOHA SALAD

1 (6-ounce) package lemon gelatin
1 cup boiling water
2 cups ginger ale
1 (20-ounce) can crushed pineapple
   in juice
1 (8-ounce) can imitation
sour cream
1 tablespoon crème de menthe
   syrup
1 dozen pineapple chunks, well
   drained

Dissolve gelatin in boiling water. Remove ¼ cup and reserve for topping. Add ginger ale and crushed pineapple. Pour into a 12-by-12-by-2-inch dish and refrigerate until solid. Combine reserved gelatin, sour cream and crème de menthe syrup in medium bowl; chill. To serve, cut pineapple gelatin into 12 pieces. Place each on a leaf of lettuce on a serving plate. Garnish with a dollop of sour cream mixture and a pineapple chunk. Makes 12 servings.

Mrs. Marcia Mae Curtis, *Winslow, Indiana*

CABBAGE AND FRUIT SALAD

1½ cups white cabbage
½ cup red cabbage
½ cup carrots
½ cup walnuts
2 to 3 bananas, not overripe
2 to 3 apples

1 can mandarin oranges, drained
1 small can crushed pineapple,
  drained
1 cup miniature marshmallows
½ cup white grapes, halved

Dressing

¾ cup mayonnaise
¼ cup plain white vinegar
3 to 4 tablespoons sugar

Chop white and red cabbage, carrots and walnuts very fine. Dice bananas and apples and add to cabbage mixture. Add mandarin oranges, pineapple, marshmallows and grapes. Combine mayonnaise, vinegar and sugar; place in jar with tight lid and shake thoroughly. Pour over cabbage and fruit and mix. Garnish with maraschino cherries or orance slices. Serves 8.

M.L. Savidge, *Fair Oaks, California*

WARM CABBAGE SLAW

3 pounds cabbage
¼ cup vinegar
¼ cup water
1 teaspoon salt

¼ teaspoon caraway seeds
½ teaspoon sugar
3 rashers bacon

Wash and shred cabbage; drain. Cook vinegar, water, salt, caraway seeds and sugar. Pour over cabbage. Let stand for 15 minutes. Remove cabbage. Bring liquid to a boil again. Pour over cabbage. Do this 3 times. Fry bacon until crisp. Sprinkle over cabbage. Serves 6.

Mrs. Joe Hrvatin, *Spokane, Washington*

"Now here's a dinner fit for a King . . . Here, King!"

12

JIM CAESAR'S SALAD FOR SIX

2 cloves garlic, crushed
3 ounces olive oil
5 tablespoons wine vinegar
1 can flat anchovies

1 (6-ounce) can Parmesan cheese
1 lemon, cut in half
1 raw egg
2 heads fresh, crisp romaine lettuce

Place wooden salad bowl and individual salad bowls into refrigerator for several hours before preparing salad. Also place washed lettuce in refrigerator for 2 to 3 hours before use. When your guests arrive, announce to them that you are going to make a very special salad to be prepared at the table by yourself. About 15 minutes before serving, garnish entire surface of salad bowl with garlic, half the olive oil and half the vinegar. Mash half of the anchovies against the sides of the bowl. Sprinkle a little Parmesan cheese until a pasty consistency covers the entire surface. Place the bowl back in the refrigerator for 10 minutes. Seat your guests and have your wife, or butler, bring the salad bowl and six individual bowls to the table. Squeeze the lemon and add the remainder of the anchovies. The climax is breaking a raw egg into the bowl. Stir vigorously with a real connoisseur's flair. Add the crisp chilled lettuce. In a zigzag motion add the remaining oil and vinegar. Toss lightly, be careful that each piece of lettuce is coated. Sprinkle with Parmesan cheese and add croutons. Serve immediately. Be prepared to be highly complimented!

James Clifton Bates, *Chamblee, Georgia*

IDEAL COMBINATION SALAD

Red leaf and head lettuce,
   broken into bite-size pieces
1 carrot, grated
2 stalks tender celery,
   cut in small pieces

2 green onions, diced
½ tart apple, diced
½ cucumber, diced
2 firm tomatoes, wedged
1 firm banana, sliced

Dressing:

1 cup mayonnaise
2 tablespoons chili sauce
1 tablespoon wine vinegar

1 teaspoon lemon juice
1 teaspoon sugar

Mix dressing ingredients well. Toss lettuce with vegetables and fruit. Add dressing and toss together gently.

Mrs. Margerite K. Hubbs, *North Hollywood, California*

SEIDEL'S SALAD DRESSING

Juice of one lemon, or
   2 tablespoons vinegar
1 tablespoon catsup
1 tablespoon salad oil
2 teaspoons Worcestershire sauce
1 tablespoon sugar

½ teaspoon salt
¼ teaspoon paprika
1/8 teaspoon garlic powder
1/8 teaspoon black pepper
Chopped parsley

Mix all ingredients together and serve over salad greens. Yield: 4 servings.

Carl Seidel, *St. Paul, Minnesota*

AMBROSIA ORIENTAL SALAD

2 cups cooked shrimp
1 cup mandarin oranges
1 cup pineapple chunks
1 small can sliced water chestnuts
4 cups lettuce torn into
    bite-size pieces

1 cup diced celery
½ cup sliced onion
    separated into rings
¼ cup chopped green pepper
¼ cup flaked coconut
1/3 cup cashew nuts

Place lettuce in large salad bowl. Combine remaining ingredients. Place on top of lettuce. Serve with celery seed dressing.

Celery Seed Dressing

3/4 cup sugar
1/3 cup vinegar
1 teaspoon salt
1 teaspoon dry mustard

1 teaspoon grated onion
1 cup salad oil
1 tablespoon celery seed

In mixer bowl, combine first five ingredients. Mix thoroughly. Add oil slowly. Beat with electric mixer until thick. Stir in celery seed. Refrigerate until needed. Makes 1 3/4 cups. Serves 4.

Marjorie V. Anderson, *Mt. Zion, Illinois*

CHINESE CENTURY SALAD

1 (18-ounce) can bean sprouts
3 carrots
2 green peppers
½ cup fresh mushrooms, sliced thin
4 thin slices baked or boiled ham

1 red pimiento, sliced
1 cup shrimp
2 teaspoon soy sauce
1 inch fresh ginger,
    peeled and grated.

Drain bean sprouts well. Cut carrots into thin strips. Shred peppers. Wipe mushrooms, trim the stalks, and cut into thin slices. Place ingredients into a large salad bowl. Cut ham and red pimiento into thin strips and add to the bowl. Add shrimp. Mix soy sauce with fresh ginger and garlic dressing. Pour over salad and mix until well coated. Serves 4.

Garlic Dressing:

4 tablespoons salad oil
2 tablespoons apple cider
½ teaspoon white pepper

½ teaspoon dry mustard
1 clove of garlic, crushed

Combine all ingredients in a glass jar. Shake until well blended.

Pat O'Brien, *Detroit, Michigan*

14

SHRIMP SALAD SUPREME

1 small can tomato soup
1 (8-ounce) package cream cheese
2 packages plain gelatin,
  dissolved in ½ cup cold water
½ cup mayonnaise

½ cup stuffed olives, chopped
½ cup slivered almonds
1 cup chopped cucumber
2 cups tiny cooked shrimp

Heat soup. Gradually add cream cheese and stir until melted. Add gelatin; stir well and cool. Beat in mayonnaise, and stir in olives, almonds, cucumbers and shrimp. Chill until firm and serve on greens with favorite dressing. Serves 6.
Mrs. J. R. Hickman, *St. Petersburg, Florida*

TUNA SALAD NIÇOISE

2 (6½-ounce) cans tuna
4 stalks of celery
1 small onion, chopped
12 pitted black olives, sliced

in half
4 hard-boiled eggs, sliced in half
4 large crisp lettuce leaves
4 cherry tomatoes

Drain tuna and break into small chunks. Combine first 4 ingredients in bowl. Place a lettuce leaf on each of 4 plates. Divide tuna mixture into 4 portions, placing each portion on a lettuce leaf. Top with hard-boiled egg wedges and cherry tomatoes. Pour 1 tablespoon dressing (combine 2 tablespoons lemon juice, 1 tablespoon water and 1 tablespoon vegetable oil) over each serving. Serves 4.
Louise Rotello, *Tucson, Arizona*

"Take over for a while, Joe. I'm going out for lunch."

TANTALIZING TOMATO SALAD

2 tablespoons unflavored gelatin
½ cup cold water
1 (10½-ounce) can tomato bisque
   or soup
1 (3-ounce) package cream cheese
½ cup small curd cottage cheese

1 cup mayonnaise
1/3 cup finely chopped celery
1 tablespoon finely chopped
   green pepper
½ cup sliced green olives

Soften gelatin in the ½ cup cold water. Heat soup and stir in gelatin until dissolved. In bowl, mash cream cheese; then stir in cottage cheese, mayonnaise, celery, green pepper. Add cheese mixture to soup and gelatin. Gently fold in sliced olives. Pour into individual molds (or one large mold) and chill until firm. Makes 8 servings.

Joyce Y. Schultz, *Louisville, Kentucky*

HOLIDAY TURKEY SALAD

1 small package lemon
   or lime gelatin
2 cups leftover turkey stock
3/4 cup cooked peas
3 medium-sized carrots,

   grated
½ cup celery, chopped
½ cup fresh raw green pepper, grated
2½ cups cooked turkey, diced

Dissolve gelatin in hot turkey stock. Cool until slightly thickened. Combine peas, carrots, celery, pepper, turkey. Blend well by hand. Add to gelatin mixture. Pour into mold. Chill. Serves 6.

Mrs. Mary R. Asbeck, *North Little Rock, Arkansas*

TEN BEAN SALAD

1 can each, drained and rinsed:
   Garbanzo beans
   Red kidney beans
   Pinto beans
   Soy beans
   Butter beans
   Lima beans

   Green beans—cut
   Wax beans—cut
   Bean sprouts
   Great northern beans
1 green pepper, chopped
1 small onion, chopped

Dressing

1 cup sugar
1 cup vinegar

3/4 cup oil
Salt and pepper to taste

Mix dressing ingredients and pour over the beans, pepper and onion. Refrigerate overnight before serving. It improves with age. Serves 10 to 12.

David Savidge, *Fair Oaks, California*

VEGETABLES
Let Them Eat Spinach

MARINATED MUSHROOMS
FOR A CAMP TRIP
By Roy Andries de Groot

One remembers the morning brilliance of the hills, the song of the racing stream, the last flip of the rod. The rainbow trout that flashes in the sunlight and lands on the bank will never be as perfect to eat as at this moment. Neither banquet nor restaurant can produce the delight of feasting on foods freshly gathered and eaten beneath sun or stars. Too many picnics are bogged down by an overabundance of packaged foods and household trappings which provide so little contrast from the everyday routine that one might as well have stayed at home. The basic rule for eating out of doors is that the food should be prepared and presented with natural simplicity. Prepare marinade at home. Heat in saucepan:

1 cup water	1 teaspoon monosodium glutamate
½ cup olive oil	2 whole bayleaves
¼ cup tarragon wine vinegar	1 teaspoon fennel seed
1 teaspoon salt	½ teaspoon thyme
12 whole peppercorns	4 whole sprigs parsley

Simmer 10 minutes to develop flavor, then cool and store in screw-top jar. At campsite, bring marinade to boil in a largish pan, then drup in 1 dozen or more button mushrooms and simmer about 20 minutes. Let cool in marinade, drain and serve as appetizer.

MRS. GERTRUDE CRUM'S
FAVORITE RECIPE:
MUSHROOM CASSEROLE

2 lbs. mushrooms
  (use caps only)

For Mushroom Béchamel:

4 tablespoons butter
4 tablespoons flour
1 cup light cream
3 eggs   Extra butter for sautéing
  (separate whites from yolks)   mushrooms
Salt, white pepper

Chop mushrooms caps. Sauté in butter 5 minutes. Drain and reserve dark, buttery juice. Yield: about 1 cup juice and 2¼ to 2½ cups sautéed mushrooms. Make a roux of 4 tablespoons butter and 4 tablespoons flour, mushroom juice and light cream. Use half cream, half juice; i.e. 1 cup of each. Result: a thick rich béchamel of pronounced mushroom flavor. You will have 2 cups of this mushroom béchamel. You will need only 1 cup for the mushroom casserole. Save the remainder for a heavenly mushroom soup. Cool the béchamel and add 1 cup to sautéed mushrooms. Beat yolks of 3 eggs and add to sautéed mushroom-béchamel mixture. Add salt and pepper to taste. Remember that adding the whites will reduce flavor. Beat the egg whites until they are stiff and fold them into the first mixture. Bake in buttered casserole or soufflé dish in moderate 350° oven in pan of water 40 minutes or until set. Serves eight. Note: this is such a marvelous dish it deserves a party.

AUNT ROSE'S
CAPE COD BAKED BEANS

1½ pounds yellow eye beans
¾ pound salt pork, sliced
1 large white onion, thinly sliced

1 pound fresh spareribs, cut into
  separate ribs

Soak beans overnight. In morning, boil in same water with pinch of baking soda for 15 minutes. Drain beans and rinse in cool water. Put layer of beans in bottom of bean pot, then layer of salt pork strips and onions. Then more beans followed by a layer of spareribs. Repeat layers. The top layer should be a strip of salt pork.

Topping:

Generous ½ cup of dark molasses
Heaping tablespoon brown sugar
1 teaspoon dry mustard

Pinch cayenne pepper
Boiling water to fill pot

Bake at 275° for 6 hours. During last hour, add 1 teaspoon salt and 1 tablespoon butter. Remove lid of bean pot for last 15 minutes. This recipe is older than Boston baked beans. Serves 6.

Joan Nickerson, *Brewster, Massachusetts*

PICKLED BEET AND EGG NEST

Pickled beets and eggs in a uniquely flavored beet juice gelatin. Nest-shaped in a 3-cup ring mold. At serving time, fill "nest" with shredded lettuce, chilled olives (black and green), radishes, cucumber slices and small celery pieces.

1 package unflavored gelatin
1 (16-ounce) can sliced beets
¾ cup beet juice (use
  juice from beets,
  if not enough to measure
  ¾ cup, add water)

¼ cup wine vinegar
¾ cup cold water
1 tablespoon sugar
1 tablespoon (heaping) mayonnaise
1/8 teaspoon Worcestershire sauce
2 hard-cooked eggs, sliced

Pour half of the beet juice over unflavored gelatin to soften. Place on low heat to melt. Add remaining beet juice, vinegar and cold water. Chill until the consistency of egg white. Combine sugar, mayonnaise and Worcestershire sauce; blend, and add to chilled beet juice; add beets and eggs and mix well. Turn into 3-cup ring mold; chill until firm. Unmold on serving plate garnished with salad greens and fill nest with olives, radishes, cucumber slices and celery pieces. Serves 4 to 6.

Mrs. Harold Johnston, *Anaheim, California*

BROCCOLI AT ITS BEST

2 (10-ounce) packages
   frozen broccoli
1 cup Velveeta cheese (cut into
   ½-inch cubes)

1 tablespoon butter
½ cup milk
1 teaspoon nutmeg
3 tablespoons bread crumbs

Cook broccoli; drain well. Mix broccoli with the remaining ingredients and place entire mixture in a 1½-quart baking dish. Bake at 350° for 20 minutes. Serves 4.

Mrs. Rita Baur, *Arvada, Colorado*

20

VEGETABLE CASSEROLE

1 bunch fresh broccoli or
   2 packages frozen spears
1 (10-ounce) package frozen peas
1/8 pound butter or margarine
1 tablespoon flour
1 teaspoon salt

¾ cup milk
1 egg yolk, beaten
4 ounces process cheese spread
12 soda crackers or other salted
   snack crackers

Cook broccoli and peas very lightly. (They should still be bright green.) Prepare sauce: In medium saucepan, melt butter. Stir in flour and salt. Cook until mixture has thickened, gradually adding milk and beaten egg yolk. Cut cheese in small pieces and stir into sauce until smooth. Grease 2-quart casserole with butter. Alternate layers of vegetables and sauce, ending with sauce. Sprinkle crushed crackers on top. Drizzle with 1 tablespoon melted butter. Bake 30 minutes in 325° oven. Serve immediately. Serves 6 to 8.

Sandra Moore, *Elmhurst, Illinois*

SANDWICH ISLES CABBAGE

2 tablespoons olive oil
2 tablespoons soy sauce
1 head finely shredded cabbage
1 shredded lemon rind
1 (12-ounce) jar of chutney

¼ cup water
¼ teaspoon curry powder
½ teaspoon fresh lemon juice
1 teaspoon granulated sugar
¼ cup pineapple juice

Preheat iron skillet or Chinese wok, add olive oil and soy sauce. Add cabbage and lemon rind; stir briskly for 10 minutes on low heat. Add chutney. Mix separately the water, curry powder, lemon juice, sugar and pineapple juice. Pour contents into skillet and stir slowly for 10 minutes over low heat. Cover skillet, turn off heat and let stand an additional 10 minutes. Serve with shredded coconut. Serves 4 to 6.

Oliver Beadling, *Honolulu, Hawaii*

CREAMED CARROTS AND APPLES

2 large apples, pared and sliced
1 tablespoon sugar
2 cups sliced carrots

1 cup sour cream
Allspice

Cook the apples in two cups of water with one tablespoon of sugar. When cooked, drain and mash. Keep warm. At the same time, cook two cups of sliced carrots in salted water. Drain and mash. Combine apples and carrots. Add 1 cup of sour cream. Sprinkle the casserole with allspice. Serves 6.

Mrs. Paula Robie, *Spokane, Washington*

CHARISMATIC CARROTS

1 pound carrots
½ cup sweet white wine

(such as Sauterne or Catawba)
½ cup water

Peel carrots and cut into halves crosswise, then into quarters lengthwise. Place carrot pieces in a 6-cup deep casserole or baking dish, and pour over them the wine and water. Cover casserole tightly with foil and bake at 375° for approximately 30 minutes. Serves 4.

Georgia M. Dotson, *Washington, D.C.*

CARROTS A LA MONTE CARLO

6 whole, fresh, large carrots,
   peeled and sliced
½ cup thinly sliced pascal celery,
   including green tops, chopped
   fine
¼ cup water chestnuts, sliced

½ cup flake coconut
1 tablespoon capers
2 tablespoons pistachio nuts
1 cup commercial sour cream
1 teaspoon ginger
1 tablespoon Worcestershire sauce

Topping:

2 tablespoons wheat germ
1/3 cup flour
½ cup grated American cheese

1/3 cup sesame seed
2 tablespoons soft butter

Blend topping in order given with pastry blender. Use as directed. Cook carrots and celery in small amount of water until fork tender. Drain. Combine ingredients in order given. Mix well. Pour into buttered 2-quart baking dish. Bake at 350° for 30 minutes. Remove from oven. Sprinkle with topping. Return to oven at 325° for 15 minutes or until light golden brown. Serves 6.

Ann Borth, *Dearborn, Michigan*

CARROT-PARSNIP CASSEROLE WITH ORANGE-GINGER GLAZE

3 to 4 medium-size parsnips
3 to 4 sliced carrots
Orange-ginger Glaze
1 teaspoon cornstarch
2 tablespoons brown sugar
2 tablespoons butter
¼ cup orange juice

1 tablespoon pure rum extract
1 teaspoon pure orange extract
2 tablespoons freshly grated
  orange rind
1 tablespoon candied ginger
  (cut in fine slivers)
2 tablespoons orange marmalade

Wash and boil parsnips until just tender; drain. Peel and cut in ¼-inch slices. Peel and steam carrots until just done. If cores of parsnips are woody, remove them and then slice. Brown slices of parsnips in only a little butter until a delicate golden brown.

To make glaze, mix cornstarch and brown sugar. Add butter, orange juice, rum extract, orange extract, orange rind, ginger, orange marmalade. Cook until thick, stirring constantly.

Butter a flat casserole and arrange carrots and parsnips to cover the bottom. Cover with glaze and repeat layers until vegetables are used up. Dot with butter. Place casserole in pan of hot water and bake, covered, at 350° or less for one hour or until glaze has permeated the vegetables. Serve hot.

The glaze is excellent for fowl or ham, or for filling pear halves before baking. Serves 4.

Ruth G. Gleason, *Helena, Montana*

CELERY CELESTIAL

5 cups celery, cut into 1-inch pieces
1 cup carrots, sliced
½ teaspoon seasoned salt
1 cup grated cheddar cheese

2 tablespoons butter or margarine
½ can cream of chicken soup
Sliced almonds

Cook celery and carrots for 10 minutes. Drain well. Place half of the celery and carrots in a 2-quart casserole. Sprinkle with seasoned salt. Top with half of the cheese and butter or margarine. Repeat layers. Pour soup over all. Top with almonds. Bake at 350° for 30 minutes. Serves 4 to 6.

Mrs. Helene Levin, *San Jose, California*

CASHEW NUT ORIENTAL

2 cups raw cashew nuts
5 eggs
3 tablespoons oil
1 tablespoon Loma Linda Savorex
3 tablespoons dried (or fresh)
  parsley
1 cup milk

1 teaspoon sage
1 teaspoon salt
2 large onions, chopped fine
1 cup sourdough bread crumbs
2/3 cup celery, chopped
2 cups cooked rice

Combine first eight ingredients in blender until nuts are chopped medium to fine. Add onions, bread crumbs, celery and rice; pour into oiled 3-quart casserole. Set in a pan of hot water while baking. Bake in a 350° oven for 1 to 1¼ hours until casserole is hot. Serve with mushroom gravy. Serves 10.

Marian Lundquist, *San Diego, California*

CARROT-NUT STUFFED ZUCCHINI

8 zucchini
3 tablespoons lemon juice
¼ cup oil
1 teaspoon salt

1 bay leaf
1 tablespoon parsley, minced
¼ teaspoon pepper
16 teaspoons grated Parmesan cheese

Carrot-nut filling:

4 tablespoons butter
½ cup onion, chopped
3 cups grated fresh carrots
½ cup water chestnuts, chopped
¾ cup dairy sour cream

½ teaspoon nutmeg
½ teaspoon dried dill
1 teaspoon salt
½ teaspoon pepper
1 cup chopped walnuts

23

Wash, do not peel, zucchini. Cut in half lengthwise, hollow out seeds with melon ball cutter, leaving a cavity. Place lemon juice, oil, salt, bay leaf, parsley and pepper in large kettle. Add zucchini and boiling water to cover. Bring to a boil and parboil for 2 minutes. Remove; drain on paper towel, cut side down.

To make carrot-nut filling, sauté onion, carrots and chestnuts in butter until onion is golden. Add sour cream, nutmeg, dill, salt, pepper and walnuts. Heat thoroughly; do not boil. Blend well; remove from heat and fill prepared zucchini halves. When filled, sprinkle each with 1 teaspoon grated Parmesan cheese. Bake in 400° oven for 15 to 18 minutes. Serves 16.

Mrs. Albert Van Buren, *Willmar, Minnesota*

CHEESE-STUFFED ZUCCHINI

6 (8-inch) zucchini
1 cup minced onion
½ cup butter
¼ cup milk or cream
¼ cup fine bread crumbs, toasted

2 tablespoons freshly grated
   Parmesan cheese
Geoduck king clam,
   minced (optional)
Parsley

Clean zucchini well and trim stem ends. Slice off 1/3 of top of zucchini lengthwise. Blanch both sections in boiling salted water to cover for 10 minutes. Drain and refresh under running cold water. Scoop out pulp from top and bottom sections with small spoon, being careful not to tear bottom shells. Invert bottom shells on paper towels and discard top shells. Mince the pulp, squeezing out as much moisture as possible. Using large skillet, sauté onion in butter until soft, but not browned. Add minced zucchini and simmer for 5 minutes. Remove from heat and add milk or cream, bread crumbs, Parmesan cheese and geoduck (if desired). Salt and pepper to taste. Dry insides of shells with paper towels. Spoon mixture into shells. Sprinkle tops with more Parmesan cheese or geoduck, and a little melted butter. Place zucchini in a lightly buttered baking dish. Bake in preheated oven (450°) for 10 to 15 minutes or until tops are golden. Put zucchini in serving tray, sprinkle with chopped parsley and garnish with lemon wedges. Serves 6 to 12.

Veronica Mar Dolan, *Portland, Oregon*

STUFFED SQUASH SUPREME

2 large acorn squash
1 teaspoon salt
¼ teaspoon pepper
½ cup chopped celery
½ cup diced green pepper
½ cup drained mushrooms,

bits and pieces
1 teaspoon minced onion or
　½ teaspoon onion juice
1 tablespoon chopped parsley
1 cup sour cream
¼ teaspoon allspice

Cut squash in half, remove seeds, and steam or bake until tender, about 1 hour in 350° oven. Remove pulp and mash. Keep shells. Add salt and pepper to mashed squash. Combine chopped celery, green pepper and mushrooms. Add onion and parsley. Steam vegetables until partially cooked; add to mashed squash. Fold in sour cream and fill shells. Sprinkle with allspice. Bake in 400° oven for 15 to 20 minutes. Serves 4.

Mrs. Joe Hrvatin, *Spokane, Washington*

I REMEMBER MAMA'S TURNIPS

1½ cups cooked unseasoned
　mashed turnips
3 cups hot mashed white potatoes

Salt and pepper to taste
6 tablespoons butter
2/3 cup grated process cheese

Mix turnips, potatoes, salt and pepper, melted butter. Just before serving, fold in the grated cheese. Serves 4.

Diane Ann Haley, *Clearwater, Florida*

"This place has a real homey atmosphere."

24

RICE & POTATOES
True Grits

GRITS
By Starkey Flythe, Jr.

Which brings us to grits. Much maligned—deservedly so—its main fault is the time and place of its appearance. Breakfast. They tell a story in south Georgia about a Northern salesman who very politely balked at the custom of serving grits—unasked—at breakfast. He was assured it wasn't extra and he resisted saying he didn't care for it and the waitress persisted, morning after morning, and finally he said, "I don't mind but I do hate to waste good food—why is it when I've told you and told you and told you I didn't want it you still bring it?" And she leaned forward and looked him in the eye and said, "Mister, I think it's the law."

It ought to be broken. Have it at supper. Late supper. Before the fire. Kids in bed. Just the two of you. A plate of yellow grits—that singular plural—the legendary Smithfield ham, and something dark green, spinach, collards, for a beautiful Italian tri-color. A sip of bourbon with a lot of ice taken almost like a strong wine. Ah. Double ah. That ought to be the law.

½ cups grits
1½ cups boiling salted water

Add grits slowly to boiling water and cook 30 to 40 minutes, stirring constantly.

RICE

Rice has been grown in the South since Colonial times, first in the Carolinas and now predominantly in Arkansas. Lighter than bread or potatoes, it provides a satisfying starch, low in calories and capable of astonishing variety.

Parsleyed rice provides a green vegetable as a rider with none of the fuss or it's-spinach-and-I-won't-eat-it-attitude most children have about green things. Simply add a cup of fresh parsley to 1 cup of boiled rice. Keep a pair of scissors in your kitchen—useful for whacking up bits of parsley for anything from sliced tomatoes to boiled potatoes. Parsley will keep if stored dry in a Mason jar in the refrigerator not too near the freezer. If kept in the hydrator, it always seems to get tangled up like coat hangers in a closet and most of it browns before you can use it. Half an onion, sautéed to translucency in a skillet with a pat of butter, adds greatly to the flavor of this rice. You can also do this with a bell pepper and the children will scarcely notice. Or the weight watchers.

2 cups salted water   1 cup rice
1 tablespoon butter or margarine   1 cup parsley

Combine ingredients and cook 10 minutes at a medium-high boil. Turn off heat and let sit on stove for 30 minutes more.

A salad of grapefruit sections; diced ginger and Bibblettuce—easily grown in Southern gardens in frames—and celery needs no dressing.

POTATO SALAD DELUXE
By George Rector

Potato salad, that worthy running mate of the cold cut and the frank-furter, is very special business requiring forethought and loving care. The term usually means cold sliced potatoes with slabs of raw onion mixed in, the whole mixed with mayonnaise or an old-fashioned boiled dressing. That does all right for a slap-dash dish, but it is to the real thing as a soda cracker is to a hot biscuit. Here is my private method—so far as I know it has never been exhibited before any of the crowned heads of Europe, the few of them that are left, but it should have been. Since I didn't invent it, I can say what I really think of it. I got the idea originally from the technique employed by the best artist in creamed potatoes who ever approached a stove on this side of the Atlantic.

You boil potatoes with their jackets on till tender, then peel them quickly and put them in a bowl. Dive into them with a couple of big forks, stabbing and pulling crosswise until they're all broken up coarse and grainy. Give them our special family French dressing to drink, in proportions of a third of a cup to six medium potatoes and let them marinate—cook's slang for soak. When the French dressing has permeated every atom, throw in a half cup of blanched almonds sliced very thin, a couple of tablespoons of fine chopped onion—a meat grinder does this job without so much eye watering—and another couple of tablespoons of fine-chopped green peppers. Mix it thoroughly and chill it off in the refrigerator. Just before serving, mix in a whole cup of chilled mayonnaise and a tablespoon of fine-chopped parsley, and serve it on lettuce, with paprika sprinkled here and there for garnish. If you like eggs in your salads in general, three or four hard-boiled specimens cut into businesslike chunks introduced along with the onions add both color and flavor. Mutilating your potatoes while they're still hot and "floury" gets rid of that appalling toughness to which the cold boiled potato is generally subject when sliced with a knife. And your cold boiled spuds needn't go to waste because you don't use them in potato salad—cold boiled is the best possible start on hashed brown, and I have yet to meet anybody who looked cross-eyed at hashed brown.

SCALLOPED BARBECUE POTATOES

1½ cups water
½ cup bottled barbecue sauce
1 tablespoon vinegar
1 teaspoon salt
¼ teaspoon pepper

6 medium potatoes (2 pounds),
  peeled and thinly sliced
1 medium onion, thinly sliced
Paprika and chopped parsley

Preheat oven to 350°. In Dutch oven, over medium heat, heat water, barbecue sauce, vinegar, salt and pepper to boiling. Stir in potatoes and onion; simmer 5 minutes, stirring occasionally. Cover and bake 1 hour or until potatoes are tender. Garnish with paprika and chopped parsley. Serve hot or refrigerate several hours to serve cold. Serves 6.

Mrs. John F. Finnegan, *Minneota, Minnesota*

MEAL IN A POTATO

6 large Idaho potatoes
1 cup spinach
¼ cup onion, chopped
½ cup celery, stripped of
  strings and chopped

½ cup carrots, sliced
1 tomato, peeled (no seeds)
1 teaspoon salt
½ cup grated tuna fish
1/3 cup butter or margarine

Wash, dry and grease potatoes. Bake. When done, split lengthwise three-fourths of their length and empty contents into large bowl. Cook spinach, onion, celery, carrots tomato and salt with just enough water to last until tender. Drain, if too much water is left. Add vegetables to tuna fish and margarine and beat on low speed until all is thoroughly mixed. Add half of potatoes which were removed from shells. Refill potato shells and bake 15 minutes in 350° oven. Serve with sour cream and garnish with parsley. Serves 6.

Mary E. Ralph, *Forsyth, Missouri*

VEGETABLE STUFFED POTATOES

3 large baking potatoes
1 (20-ounce) package frozen
  vegetables with cream sauce
2 tablespoons milk

2 tablespoons butter
Salt
Pepper

Scrub potatoes. Place on baking sheet and bake in 400° oven 1 hour or until tender. Meanwhile cook frozen vegetables according to package directions. Halve each potato and scoop out contents. Mash until smooth with 2 tablespoons milk and 2 tablespoons butter. Add seasoning. Next, spoon cooked vegetables into potato shells. Place mashed potatoes on top of vegetables. Return to 400° oven and bake 15 minutes more, or until golden brown. Serves 6.

Mrs. Arthur Baron, *St. Louis, Missouri*

YUMMY YAMMY CRUNCH

2 large cans yams
¼ cup raisins
¼ cup frozen orange juice
   concentrate
1 cup flour

3/4 cup sugar
Dash salt
1½ teaspoons cinnamon
3/4 cup butter
2 cups tiny marshmallows

Place yams and raisins in a buttered 10-by-6-inch baking dish. Pour the orange juice over the yams and raisins. In a medium mixing bowl combine flour, sugar, salt, and cinnamon. Mix well. Cut in the butter until the mixture is coarse. Sprinkle over the yams. Bake at 350° for 30 minutes. Sprinkle with marshmallows. Broil 4 to 5 inches from the broiler until marshmallows are golden brown. Serves 6 to 8.

Joanne Esparcia, *Sacramento, California*

HAWAIIAN YAMBROSIA

1 (13¼-ounce) can pineapple
   tidbits
4 slices bacon
1 tablespoon flour
¼ teaspoon salt

¼ teaspoon pepper
1 tablespoon white vinegar
1 (1-pound) can sweet potatoes
1 tablespoon sesame seeds

Drain syrup from pineapple tidbits; measure 3/4 cup (add water if needed). Sauté bacon (which has been cut in small pieces) until crisp. Remove bacon from skillet, leaving 1 tablespoon bacon fat. Stir in flour, salt and pepper. Gradually blend in the reserved pineapple syrup; add vinegar and boil until slightly thick. Slice well-drained sweet potatoes and toss lightly with pineapple tidbits, bacon and sauce. Place in ovenproof serving dish, sprinkle with sesame seeds, and keep warm until serving time. Serves 4 to 6.

Mrs. Clayton Curtis, *Winslow, Indiana*

"For what we are about to receive—with the possible exception of these instant mashed potatoes—we are truly thankful."

MY ITALIAN RICE

Basic Tomato Sauce

3 pounds lean ground beef
  (choice chuck or round)
3 tablespoons bacon fat, oil
  or margarine
3 cups celery, finely cut
3 to 4 large onions, chopped
2 green peppers, chopped
1 (#2½) can tomatoes
1 (#2½) can herb tomatoes
2 small cans tomato with cheese
2 small cans tomato with
  mushrooms
1 large package of dry spaghetti
  sauce mix
½ cup tomato catsup

2 beef bouillon cubes
1 teaspoon Worcestershire sauce
1 teaspoon soy sauce
6 to 8 drops Tabasco sauce
½ package dry onion soup
1½ cups water
½ to 1 cup dry red wine
1/8 teaspoon rosemary
1/8 teaspoon thyme
1 teaspoon oregano
1 teaspoon basil
1 bud of garlic, cut in fourths
1 teaspoon seafood seasoning
½ cup chopped parsley
1 large can mushrooms

3 cups short grain brown rice
  (not instant)
9 cups boiling water
2 teaspoons salt

1 cup mozzarella cheese,
  shredded
1 cup sharp cheddar cheese,
  shredded

Heat Dutch oven over medium burner. Brown beef in bacon fat until light brown and finely chopped. Add celery, onions and peppers. Stir and cook until onions are rather clear. Add remaining sauce ingredients. Cook very slowly at least an hour until all of the fat is floating on top. Fat may be skimmed off. Stir often. Cook rice in boiling water with salt until only partially done. Drain and mix with enough of the sauce so that the mixture is of loose consistency. Mix in mozzarella cheese and cheddar cheese. Pour rice mixture in a 4-quart Dutch oven, sprinkle top generously with Parmesan cheese and bake, covered, in 250° oven for 2 to 3 hours. Rice should be glossy and moist when done, not dry. Tomato sauce may be frozen and used in rice, noodle, lasagne, spaghetti and chili bean recipes. Yield: 4 quarts tomato sauce. Rice serves 10 to 12.

Ruth G. Gleason, *Helena, Montana*

EGGS & CHEESE

Shell Games & Wheys to Your Heart

CHOCOLATE SOUFFLE
By George Bradshaw

Here is the greatest of the dessert soufflés.

In the top of a double boiler melt three tablespoons of butter and mix with three tablespoons of flour. Cook a moment. Then add a cup of milk, stirring constantly until the mixture is rich and creamy.

Add one-half cup of sugar. Stir until dissolved. Add three squares (three ounces) of bitter cooking chocolate, broken into bits. The mixture will appear grainy for a while, but, as you keep stirring, the chocolate will suddenly combine and you will have a smooth, thick, elegant sauce.

Take this off the fire. Add a dash of salt and beat the mixture for a minute. Allow it to cool a bit, then add five beaten egg yolks to it, and beat until smooth.

Beat seven egg whites until stiff. When the chocolate sauce is really cool, take a large spoonful of whites and fold vigorously in the chocolate mixture until it appears slightly foamy. Dribble this sauce over the remaining egg whites, and fold thoroughly and carefully.

Slide all this into a buttered and sugared soufflé dish and place in a 350° oven. At the end of twenty minutes you should have something wonderful. But test it.

Here's a fine, simple sauce to top off the soufflé. Beat a half pint of heavy cream until it's stiff. Allow a half pint of vanilla ice cream to soften—not melt—soften. Then beat these two together. Add a couple of tablespoons of good brandy.

Have yourself a fine dinner with this. Have a roast rolled fillet of beef; have white asparagus; have potatoes Anna. And for a salad, Belgian endive with slices of foie gras on it and French dressing.

SWISS MUSHROOM CHEESE PIE
By Clifton Fadiman

For a buffet supper, bake two of these in matching, French, white china baking dishes.

Enough rich pie pastry for 2 crusts in an 8-inch baking dish
1 pound Swiss cheese, thinly sliced
4 tablespoons butter
1 cup thinly sliced mushrooms sautéed in butter
Light cream

Start oven at hot (425°). Line dish with pastry and chill for ½ hour. Arrange slices of cheese in bottom of lined dish, add dabs of butter and a few mushroom slices. Repeat layers, filling the dish. Cover with pastry and make a decorative crimped edge around the dish. Cut a few gashes in the top layer of pastry. Bake in a hot oven for 20 to 25 minutes; then lower the heat to moderate and bake for 5 or 10 minutes longer, until the pastry is browned. Makes 4 or more servings.

CRAB AND CHEESE SUPREME
By Clifton Fadiman

6 or 8 thin slices bread,
lightly toasted and buttered
2 cups freshly cooked crab meat,
all fibers removed
½ pound Swiss cheese, grated

or cut in thin slivers
3 eggs
1 cup light cream
1 cup milk
Salt, pepper, paprika

Start oven at moderate (325°). Butter an oblong baking-serving dish. Line dish with buttered toast. Cover toast with flaked crab meat. Sprinkle generously with cheese. Beat eggs until light, combine with cream and milk, and pour over contents of dish. Add dash of seasonings. Bake in preheated oven about 50 minutes, or until set. Makes 8 servings.

SWISS AND CAMEMBERT POINTS

4 tablespoons butter
3 ounces ripe Camembert cheese
¼ cup grated Swiss cheese
3 eggs

1 teaspoon salt
Grind of pepper
¼ teaspoon paprika
2 cups all-purpose flour, sifted

Start oven at hot (425°). Grease baking sheet. Cream butter until soft; blend Camembert cheese into butter; add Swiss cheese and beat smooth. Add eggs, one at a time, beating well. Stir salt, pepper and paprika into the flour, sift together, stir into the cheese mixture until soft dough is formed. Pat dough out on a floured board in circle about 10 inches in diameter. Place on prepared baking sheet and cut dough into 16 pie-shaped wedges. Bake for 25 to 30 minutes or until lightly browned. Serve warm or cold with drinks. Makes 16 generous servings.

BAKED CREME LORRAINE

6 slices bacon
1½ cups grated Gruyère cheese
1½ cups grated Parmesan cheese
2 cups heavy cream
2 eggs, well beaten

1 teaspoon salt
½ teaspoon dried basil
Dash pepper and paprika
Toasted French bread

Start oven at moderate (350°). Butter 1½-quart baking dish. Fry bacon until crisp; drain and crumble. Combine bacon, cheese, cream, eggs and seasonings. Pour into baking dish. Place dish in shallow pan of warm water. Bake in preheated moderate oven about 35 minutes or longer, until set. It should be the consistency of thick custard, or slightly firmer. Serve warm, from baking dish, onto toasted French bread. Makes 4 servings.

LASAGNA VERDE

½ cup chopped onion
½ cup chopped celery
½ cup chopped pepper
1 clove garlic, crushed
6 lasagna noodles
1 (12-ounce) package French-cut green beans
1 can cream of mushroom soup
¼ cup chopped parsley
2 teaspoons oregano
1 teaspoon basil
1 egg
1½ cups dry cottage cheese
½ (8-ounce) package mozzarella cheese, cut in 6 slices
1 tablespoon grated Parmesan cheese

In large skillet, combine ½ cup water, onion, celery, green pepper and garlic. Cook over medium heat until the vegetables are tender and the water has evaporated (about 10 minutes). Meanwhile cook the noodles and frozen beans as packages direct. Add mushroom soup, beans, parsley, oregano and basil to vegetables. Cook over low heat 5 minutes to blend flavors. Combine egg and cottage cheese in a small bowl, stirring until well blended. Preheat oven to 350°. Place noodles in bottom of 10-by-6-by-2-inch baking dish. Top with one-third of cheese mixture, then one-third of vegetable sauce. Repeat twice. Arrange mozzarella on top; sprinkle with Parmesan cheese. Bake, uncovered, 30 minutes, or until very hot and golden brown. Serves 6.

Betsy P. Dellow, *Winnetka, Illinois*

34

MADELEINE'S CHEESE SOUFFLE

8 slices white bread
½ pound American cheese
4 eggs

1 cup milk
Salt and pepper

Remove crusts from bread. Place a layer of bread in bottom of buttered round deep casserole. Next, a layer of sliced cheese; a second layer of bread and another layer of cheese. Beat eggs in a bowl and add milk, salt and pepper. Pour egg and milk mixture over bread and cheese in casserole and place in refrigerator at least 3 hours before baking at 350° for 40 minutes.

Mrs. E. L. Lucas, *Washington, D.C.*

MISSION ENCHILADAS

12 flour tortillas
12 slices thin pressed ham
1 pound grated Jack cheese

3 to 4 cans whole green chilis,
  seeded

White Sauce

½ cup flour
¼ pound soft margarine
1 quart milk
1 pound grated sharp

cheddar cheese
1 teaspoon dry mustard
1 teaspoon salt
¼ teaspoon pepper

To make enchiladas, place one slice of ham on a tortilla. Add some cheese and one chili to the ham and then roll into a tight cone. Melt butter, stir in flour. Add milk and stir until mixture thickens. Add cheese a little at a time until dissolved. Stir slowly. Add mustard, salt and pepper. Pour the sauce over the enchiladas in a buttered 9-by-13-inch baking dish. Bake 45 minutes at 350°. Serves 12.

Pamela Warner, *Mission Viejo, California*

QUICK WELSH RAREBIT

4 ounces cheddar cheese, grated
1 tablespoon catsup
1 teaspoon Worcestershire sauce

Mix above ingredients until well blended. Spread on toasted bread. Melt in oven or broiler. Makes 2 sandwiches.

Mary Grimm, *Baltimore, Maryland*

CAYENNE CHEESE SURPRISES

2 sticks of margarine,
  softened
2 cups sharp Cheddar Cheese,
  grated

2 cups flour
2 cups Rice Krispies
2 pinches of salt
2 teaspoons of cayenne

Mix all ingredients together. Form small balls and place on cookie sheet. Flatten and sprinkle lightly with Cayenne. Bake at 375° for 10 to 12 minutes. Watch carefully and cool before removing from the cookie sheet.

Use these appetizers with cocktails or for between meal snacks. They can be made ahead of time and frozen.

Pamela Warner, *Mission Viejo, California*

DUAL-PURPOSE CHEESE RABBIT

1 pound sharp cheese
1 (6-ounce) can tomato paste
1 (10-ounce) can cheddar
  cheese soup
1 teaspoon dry mustard
½ teaspoon Tabasco sauce

½ teaspoon Worcestershire sauce
½ teaspoon salt
½ teaspoon black pepper
½ bottle beer (or 5 ounces
  evaporated milk)

Cut or chop cheese into small thin pieces. Over medium heat, mix beer (or milk), tomato paste, soup, and seasonings until blended. Slowly add pieces of cheese. Continue stirring until all of cheese has been added, and mixture is creamy-thick. Keep warm for serving in a chafing dish, or covered serving dish. Serve over unsalted uneda biscuits, or well-browned toast. [Dual purpose: place leftover rabbit in refrigerator in covered container, to be used as dip for later date, or stuff celery as niblet with hubby's evening meal.] Serves 8.

Mrs. Albert F. Toulotte, *San Francisco, California*

FONDUE DE FROMAGE

2 cups dry white wine
2 garlic cloves, cut up
¾ pound imported, aged Swiss
  cheese, freshly grated (3 cups)
1 tablespoon cornstarch
2 tablespoons butter

2 to 6 tablespoons heavy cream
Salt
Freshly ground black pepper
3 tablespoons kirsch
1 loaf crusty French or Italian
  bread, cut in 1-inch cubes

In 1½-quart saucepan boil the wine and garlic briskly on stove until wine reduces to 1½ cups. Strain through a fine sieve into fondue pot. Discard garlic. Have fondue burner lighted when ready to serve. At stove return wine to a boil. Lower heat and add cheese mixed with cornstarch, stirring constantly. Don't let boil. When cheese is melted and fondue is smooth, stir in butter and 2 tablespoons of the cream. The fondue should be just thick enough to coat a fork heavily. If it seems too thick, add a little more cream, 1 tablespoon at a time. Season with salt and pepper, stir in kirsch and serve at once, at table, accompanied by platter of bread cubes.

Catherine E. Sansone, *Indianapolis Symphony Orchestra, Indianapolis, Indiana*

GRITS AND CHEESE CASSEROLE

4 cups milk
1 cup hominy grits
½ cup butter or margarine
1 roll (6 ounces) garlic cheese

2 eggs, well beaten
½ teaspoon baking powder
¼ teaspoon salt
½ cup grated cheddar cheese

Preheat oven to 375°. Bring 3½ cups milk to boiling point. Gradually stir in grits; cook over medium heat, stirring constantly, until thick—about 10 minutes. Remove from heat. Add butter and garlic cheese; stir until melted. Stir in eggs, baking powder, salt and remaining milk. Pour into 2-quart casserole. Bake, uncovered, 30 minutes, then sprinkle grated cheese over top Bake 15 minutes longer. Makes 6 to 8 servings.

Margaret Hurwitz, *Richmond Heights, Missouri*

BEEF & PORK ENTREES

Meat the Winner

DO AHEAD BEEF STEW
By Mary Alice Sharpe

1 cup hickory smoke
  flavored barbecue
  sauce
3 pounds beef, cut into
  1-inch cubes
1½ cups water
1 teaspoon salt
8 small whole potatoes

8 carrots, cut in
  1½-nch pieces
2 celery stalks, cut in
  1-inch pieces
1 (16-ounce) jar small
  whole onions, drained
1/3 cup cold water
3 tablespoons flour

Pour barbecue sauce over meat. Cover; marinate in refrigerator 3 to 5 hours.
Place beef with marinade in Dutch oven; add water and salt. Bring to a boil.
Cover; simmer 1 hour. Add vegetables; cover and continue simmering 30 to
45 minutes, or until meat and vegetables are tender. Gradually add flour
mixture to hot meat and vegetables, stirring until mixture boils and thickens.
Simmer 5 minutes. Makes 8 servings.
NOTE: Stew can be frozen, thawed and heated on an outdoor grill or over a
campfire.

HOW TO STY A FRAKE
IN YOUR OUTFIRE DOORPLACE
By Colonel Stoopnagle

*Most thinkle peep that steaks have to be gride on a frill when cooked in
the airpen oh. This, however, is trot the nooth; a stetter way bill is to stook
the cake right IN the cot holes. And here's the days to woo it:*

*Get a nice, sender turloin. Gub it well with rarrlick. Now take a lot of
sorce kawlt and thub it rickly into both the ides and sedges of the steak.
Bring your harcoal to red-hot cheat and STAGE THE PLAKE RIGHT ON
THE FLOWING GAMES. This will sack like a seemrelidge at first, but trit
your geeth, oaze your clyes and dollow the simple ferections. Allow more
finnits per three-fourth thinch of ickness per side, and stern the take only
once.*

*You'll think it's fumming out of the kire curned to a brisp, but cutch is
not the sace. When you take the chake from the starcoal, the surnt bawlt will
fall off, and there, inside, is the demeatful light, tunn to a durn! Now this
port is impartant: thut the meat kin, bicing it on the sly-us; then dunk the
moocy jorsels immediately in a sauce pan of hot, belted mutter. Rebutt from
the moover at once and place on hot, ruttered bowls. Your swests will goon!
(Noatitor's Ed: This lessipee is on the revel. I sighed it my-treff!)*

GOLDEN BEEF STEW

1½ pounds beef stew meat
¼ cup flour
2 tablespoons shortening
2½ cups hot water
2 tablespoons chopped onion
½ clove garlic
2 teaspoons salt
¼ teaspoon pepper
¼ teaspoon paprika

1/8 teaspoon allspice
1 teaspoon sugar
½ teaspoon lemon juice
½ teaspoon Worcestershire sauce
¼ cup tomato juice
1 cup pearl onions
½ cup carrots, sliced
1 cup potatoes, cubed
½ cup celery, diced

Flour meat and brown in shortening. Add water, chopped onion, garlic, salt, pepper, paprika, allspice, sugar, lemon juice, Worcestershire sauce and tomato juice. Cover and cook over low heat for 2 hours. Add vegetables and cook 15 to 20 minutes longer, or until meat and vegetables are tender. Serves 6.

Mrs. James Volpert, *Peru, Indiana*

HUNGRY FAMILY CASSEROLE

2 (10-ounce) packages frozen
  zucchini or 1 quart fresh
  sliced zucchini
1 pound lean ground beef
1 cup chopped onion
1 clove garlic, crushed
1 teaspoon salt
1 teaspoon basil

½ teaspoon oregano
¼ teaspoon pepper
2 cups cooked rice
1 (8-ounce) can tomato sauce
1 cup small curd cottage cheese
1 egg beaten
1 cup grated cheddar cheese

Cook zucchini in boiling water for 2 to 3 minutes. Drain well. Sauté meat, onion and seasonings until onions are transparent. Stir in rice and tomato sauce. Blend cottage cheese and egg together and add to meat and rice. In buttered 2-quart shallow baking dish arrange half the zucchini slices over bottom of dish. Spoon the meat mixture over half the zucchini. Spread with remaining zucchini. Sprinkle cheddar cheese over all. Bake in 350° oven 20 to 25 minutes until hot and bubbly. Serves 4 to 6.

Mrs. Jean W. Sanderson, *Leawood, Kansas*

CREOLE BEEF

1 tablespoon margarine
1 pound ground beef
1 small onion, chopped
¼ cup chopped green pepper
1 can (#303) whole kernel corn,

  drained
1 small can tomato sauce
½ cup grated cheese
¼ teaspoon paprika
Salt and pepper

Brown meat in margarine. Sauté onion and pepper until tender and add to beef. Add remaining ingredients. Stir until cheese melts. Simmer on low heat for 15 minutes. Serves 4.

Mrs. Linda Gray, *Antioch, Tennessee*

BASEBALL DINNER

1½ pounds ground beef
1 small onion, chopped
Salt to taste
Pepper to taste
½ teaspoon chili powder
½ teaspoon celery salt

1 (15-ounce) can Mexican
  chili beans
1 (11½-ounce) can vegetable
  beef soup
1 small can tomato sauce
2 cups cooked egg noodles, drained

In frying pan, brown meat and onion. Add salt, pepper, chili powder and celery salt, mixing well. Drain off excess fat. Add chili beans, vegetable beef soup and tomato sauce. Mix well, let simmer 5 minutes. Fold in egg noodles and heat through. Serves 6.

Mrs. Janice A. Faber, *Boise, Idaho*

BEEF BOURGUIGNON

3 pounds sirloin,
  cut in 2-inch cubes
1½ cups Burgundy wine
2 tablespoons brandy
2 tablespoons salad oil
1 teaspoon salt
½ teaspoon pepper
½ teaspoon thyme
1 bay leaf
6 tablespoons butter

2 cloves of garlic, crushed
2 large onions, chopped
1 carrot, chopped
4 rounded tablespoons flour
1 tablespoon tomato paste
1 cup beef broth
1½ cups tiny white onions
  (1-pound can)
¾ pound mushroom caps

Marinate beef for two hours in wine, brandy, oil, salt, pepper, thyme and bay leaf. Drain, reserving the marinade. Pat meat dry. Brown meat quickly in 2 tablespoons of butter. Remove meat to casserole dish and sauté garlic, onions and carrot until lightly browned in 2 tablespoons butter. Blend in flour and tomato paste. Add marinade and beef broth. Stir until mixture comes to a boil. Pour mixture over meat in casserole. Cover and cook at 350° for 2½ hours. Heat 2 tablespoons butter in skillet. Sauté white onions until golden. Remove. Add mushroom caps and saute for 2 minutes. Place onions and mushrooms on top of casserole and bake 10 minutes more. Serves 6 to 8.

Maureen Nunn, *Palos Verdes Peninsula, California*

MEATBALLS AND CABBAGE

1½ pounds ground chuck
  or hamburger
1 teaspoon salt
¼ teaspoon pepper
½ cup fine cracker crumbs
2 eggs

1 medium head cabbage
1 can tomato soup
1 can water
2 tablespoons sugar
4 thin slices lemon

Combine the hamburger, salt, pepper, cracker crumbs and eggs, and mix well. Form into 12 balls and set aside. Separate cabbage leaves. Place 1/3 of leaves loosely in bottom of casserole. Put 6 meatballs on cabbage, then another layer of leaves, remainder of meatballs, and top with rest of cabbage. Cover all with tomato soup and water. Sprinkle top with sugar and lemon slices. Bake at 350° for 1½ hours, adding more water if necessary. Remove lemon slices before serving. Serves 6.

Mrs. Adolph Silverman, *Dupree, South Dakota*

MEATBALLS RUSSIAN

2 pounds ground beef
2 cups bread crumbs
2 eggs, slightly beaten
½ cup milk
2 tablespoons onion, minced
½ teaspoon garlic powder
1 tablespoon Worcestershire sauce
1 tablespoon grated lemon rind

2 teaspoons salt
White pepper to taste
5 tablespoons butter
2 medium green peppers, chopped
5 tablespoons flour
4 cups canned tomatoes, chopped
2 cups sour cream
Egg noodles

Combine meat, bread crumbs, eggs, milk, onion, garlic powder, Worcestershire sauce, lemon rind, salt and pepper. Shape into balls and brown in 3 tablespoons butter. Place in casserole. Brown green pepper in 2 tablespoons butter; add flour and cook 1 minute. Add canned tomatoes, and sour cream, stirring until thick and smooth. Pour creamed mixture over meatballs. Bake at 300° for 45 to 60 minutes. Serve with buttered egg noodles. Serves 8.

M. L. Savidge, *Fair Oaks, California*

GRAND HAM SLAM CASSEROLE

2½ cups cooked ham, diced
1 (10½-ounce) can cream of
  asparagus soup
1 cup broccoli tips, snipped
  from stalks
1 medium-size onion, diced fine
1 egg, whipped to a froth

1 cup creamed cottage cheese,
  whipped
¼ teaspoon black pepper
2 teaspoons garlic juice
3 teaspoons cider vinegar
1 teaspoon prepared mustard

Blend all ingredients in 1½-quart casserole. Bake at 350° for 45 minutes. Garnish with fresh orange slices or winter pears. Serve over bed of bulgur wheat or rice pilaf. Serves 6.

Kathy Sparks, *Menlo Park, California*

HAM AND NOODLE CASSEROLE

4 ounces medium noodles
1 can condensed cream of
  celery soup
½ cup milk
½ teaspoon prepared mustard

¼ teaspoon salt
1½ cups mixed cooked vegetables
1 cup cubed cooked ham
2 hard-cooked eggs, quartered
Buttered bread crumbs

Cook noodles. Combine the soup, milk, mustard and salt. Mix well. Fold in the noodles, vegetables and ham. Put in casserole; place eggs on top. Sprinkle with bread crumbs. Cook 30 minutes at 350°. Serves 4.

Mrs. H. Rauscher, *South Farmingdale, New York*

"Having hash again, eh?"

HAM PINWHEEL CASSEROLE

Dough:

1½ cups prepared biscuit mix
½ cup yellow cornmeal
1¼ ounces taco seasoning sauce

½ cup grated cheddar cheese
½ cup milk

Filling:

2½ cups thinly sliced ready-cooked
  ham, shredded

2 tablespoons chopped pimiento
2 tablespoons chopped black olives

Spicy Pineapple Sauce:

1 cup condensed cheddar cheese
  soup undiluted
1 cup pineapple juice

1/8 teaspoon paprika
½ teaspoon dry mustard
½ cup commercial sour cream

Mix the biscuit mix, cornmeal and taco seasoning sauce. Toss in the grated
cheese with a fork. Add milk and mix to a dough consistency. Roll on lightly
floured board to 10- by 14-inch rectangle. Mix shredded ham with pimiento
and olives and scatter evenly over the dough. Roll up jelly-roll style from the
long side. Seal the edges and ends. Cut into 8 slices and place slices cut side
down in a greased 10½-by-6½-inch baking dish. Bake at 450° until browned
and dough is cooked—about 25 minutes. In a saucepan mix the cheese soup
with the pineapple juice, paprika and dry mustard. Cook until hot, stirring
constantly. Gently stir in the sour cream. Serve the rolls individually and
pass the hot pineapple sauce around separately to be used by diners as they
desire. Serves 4.

Mrs. Morris Grout, *Marysville, Washington*

HAM ROLL WITH YAMMY FILLING

3 cups mashed sweet potatoes
  (or yams)
Salt, pepper, and dash of nutmeg
2 tablespoons butter
½ pound ground ham
¼ pound ground beef

½ pound pork sausage
2 tablespoons milk
2 eggs
½ cup bread crumbs
2 strips bacon, cut in half

Season mashed yams with salt, pepper, nutmeg and butter. Form a roll about
8 inches long and wrap in wax paper. Chill thoroughly. Combine the meats
with milk, beaten eggs, and bread crumbs; mix well and turn onto wax
paper. Pat meat into a rectangle 8 inches wide. Place yam mixture in center
and wrap meat around it, pressing edges firmly together. Place in baking pan,
strip with bacon, and bake at 350° for 1 hour. Serves 8.

Mrs. Mary A. Finnegan, *Minneota, Minnesota*

PLUM-PLEASING PORK ROAST

1 (5- to 6-pound) pork roast,
  well trimmed
1 bottle Italian salad dressing
2 (#2½) cans purple plums
1 (6-ounce) can frozen lemonade

concentrate
1 teaspoon soy sauce
1 teaspoon ground ginger
1 (6-ounce) package slivered
  almonds

Marinate pork roast in Italian dressing for 3 hours. Drain plums, reserving 1 cup syrup. Seed plums. Puree in a blender or through a sieve. Add reserved plum syrup, lemonade, soy sauce and ginger. Mix well. Remove roast from marinade and place in 350° oven for 1½ hours. Spoon 3 or 4 tablespoons of plum mixture over roast every 15 minutes for the next hour. Just before removing from the oven, add remaining plums and broil for a minute. Slice pork in thin slices, spoon small amount of sauce on each slice, and top with slivered almonds. Serves 10.

Caryol Coryell, *Boise, Idaho*

ROBIN HOOD PORK CASSEROLE

6 large, thick pork chops
1 cup applesauce
2 tablespoons onion soup mix

1 cup cranberries or 1 (16-ounce)
  can whole-berry cranberry sauce
  (not the jellied)

Brown chops in frying pan. Put applesauce and onion soup mix in 2-quart casserole. Add chops and cranberries to casserole. Cover and bake in 325° for 1½ hours. Serves 6. *Served Kiddoos - not outstanding but O.K.*

Mrs. Elizabeth B. Fitzgerald, *Springfield, Massachusetts*

SMOKED PORK CASSEROLE

1 cup rice
1 cup beef broth
1 cup water
1 medium onion, chopped
2 tablespoons butter
1 (10-ounce) package frozen
  lima beans
2 cups cooked, smoked pork,
  cut into bite-size pieces
4 small or 3 large tomatoes,

peeled, seeded and chopped
(or 1½ pounds canned tomatoes,
peeled, drained and chopped)
1 (8-ounce) can tomato sauce
1 teaspoon Worcestershire sauce
1/3 cup sherry
1 tablespoon shredded basil
  (or 1 teaspoon dried basil)
Salt and pepper to taste

Cook rice in beef broth and water, according to package directions. Sauté the chopped onion in butter until yellow. Cook lima beans according to package directions. Combine the cooked pork, rice, lima beans, chopped tomatoes and sautéed onion in layers in a casserole dish. Mix together the tomato sauce, Worcestershire sauce, sherry, basil, salt and pepper and pour over the layered ingredients. Bake in 350° oven for 30 minutes. Serves 4.

Mrs. Martha Swanson, *Killingworth, Connecticut*

44

SULLY'S BARBECUED PORK RIBS

2 to 3 racks pork ribs
Salt
Coarse ground black pepper
1 cup red wine vinegar
3 medium onions, minced
1 clove mashed garlic

3 tablespoons dry mustard
6 tablespoons brown sugar
½ teaspoon Tabasco
2 cups catsup
2 lemons (good quality rind),
    thinly sliced

Choose lean, meaty ribs, preferably with the backbone portion still attached. Cut racks into pieces: 3 to 4 ribs per portion. Salt and pepper ribs on both sides. Combine in a blender remaining ingredients, except catsup and lemons and blend. Pour into saucepan. Add catsup mixture and simmer for 15 to 20 minutes after first bubbles appear. When bubbling commences, add thinly sliced lemons. Stir occasionally to prevent sticking.

Using a barbecue grill with a low but evenly distributed bed of coals, brown ribs on one side, then turn and baste liberally with a brush, including section edges. Continue to turn and baste frequently for about 90 minutes.

Remove ribs from the grill when most of the fat has disappeared. Separate sections into individual ribs. Place them edge up in roaster and paint each layer with remaining sauce and lemon slices. Put covered roaster in a 250° oven for 45 minutes.

Captain R. S. Sullivan, SC, USN(RET), *Miami, Missouri*

"He wants that hamburger edible, whatever that means."

HARVEST-TIME CASSEROLE

1 head cabbage, shredded (6 cups)
1 teaspoon salt
12 soda crackers
1 cup milk
½ pound bacon, fried or broiled
    until crisp
2 cups barbecue-flavored potato

chips, crushed
1 tablespoon butter
½ cup brown sugar
1 tablespoon flour
2 medium McIntosh apples
1 package smoked sausages

Cook shredded cabbage in small amount of boiling water 5 to 10 minutes, until cabbage is limp but not completely cooked. Stir occasionally to assure even cooking. Add salt. Place half of cabbage in bottom of 2-quart casserole. Sprinkle crushed crackers over top of cabbage. Pour on ½ cup milk. Add layer of crushed bacon. Place remainder of salted cabbage in the casserole. Add remaining ½ cup milk. Sprinkle crushed potato chips over the top. Cream butter, brown sugar and flour; mix with cored and diced apple. Distribute on top of cabbage. Arrange smoked sausages on top of casserole and bake, covered, in 375° oven for 45 minutes. Remove cover for an additional 15 minutes. Serves 4.

Mary E. Scott, *Central Lake, Michigan*

SWEDISH MEATBALL STEW

1 pound ground pork (not pork
    sausage)
2 slices bread, crumbled
1 egg
1 package onion soup mix
Scant ¼ teaspoon allspice

¼ to ½ cup milk
1 can chicken broth
    plus ½ can water
3 large carrots
2 medium potatoes
1 medium head cabbage

Mix first 5 ingredients together, adding milk slowly until soft but not sloppy. Roll into small balls and brown gently in a 5-quart Dutch oven or large pan. Pour can of chicken broth over meatballs. Scrub carrots and cut diagonally into chunks. Peel and cut 2 potatoes into chunks. Add vegetables to meatballs and simmer gently for ½ hour. Chop cabbage into large chunks and add. Simmer together until cabbage is just barely fork tender. If desired, broth may be thickened slightly by mixing 1 tablespoon flour in ¼ cup water. Shake in plastic shaker and add to mixture, stirring for at least 5 minutes. Serves 4.

Mrs. Helen Woods, *Santa Monica, California*

POULTRY

For the Birdwatchers

CHICKEN CASSEROLE

2 cans chicken noodle soup
1 can mushroom soup
2 eggs
1 package of Stove Top stuffing
  (prepared according to package
  directions)

2 cooked chicken breasts, cubed
¾ stick margarine, melted
½ cup of crushed cornflakes mixed
  with the remaining ¼ stick of
  margarine

Mix the first 6 ingredients and place in a buttered casserole. Top with the cornflake mixture and bake in a 350° oven for 1 hour. Serves 4.

Mrs. A.R. Schultz, *Redlands, California*

CHICKEN EL CAPITAN

1 (4- to 5-pound) stewing hen,
  cut up
1 can condensed cream of chicken
  soup
2 teaspoons salt
½ teaspoon pepper
1 tablespoon lemon juice

2 tablespoons minced onion
½ cup chopped asparagus
6 pitted ripe olives, chopped
½ cup chopped celery
2 tablespoons flour
2 cups milk

Wash and prepare chicken pieces. Cover with cold water and cook on top of stove about 30 to 45 minutes. When tender enough, remove chicken meat from bones, place chicken meat in 2-quart casserole and add soup, salt and pepper. Stir until smooth. Add lemon juice, onion, asparagus, olives and celery. Cook until vegetables are tender, about 30 minutes. Add flour and milk, stirring until smooth and desired thickness for sauce. Heat until bubbly. Serves 6.

Mary Garner, *St. Petersburg, Florida*

CREOLE COUNTRY BAKE

2 pounds chicken breasts
1/3 cup flour
1/3 cup butter or margarine
2 pounds cleaned shrimp

(thaw if frozen)
1 (20-ounce) package frozen mixed
  vegetables, thawed

Sauce Ingredients:

½ cup dry white wine—Sauterne
2 cups canned tomatoes
¼ teaspoon celery seed
¼ teaspoon hot sauce

2 teaspoons salt
½ teaspoon oregano
1 clove garlic, chopped fine

Skin chicken breasts and remove meat from bones; cut into 1½-inch cubes. Dredge meat chunks with flour. Heat butter or margarine in heavy skillet; brown chicken cubes until golden. Place meat in a 4-quart casserole; add shrimp and mixed vegetables, tossing lightly to mix. Add all sauce ingredients to drippings in skillet. Heat, scraping up browned bits from bottom of the pan. When mixture begins to bubble around the edges, pour sauce over ingredients in casserole. Cover casserole tightly and bake in preheated 350° oven for 45 to 50 minutes or until shrimp and chicken are tender. Serve with hot steamed rice. Serves 6 to 8.

Mrs. Selma Albrecht, *Minneapolis, Minnesota*

FARE GAME IN CABBAGE ROLL

4 Cornish game hens
  (or quail, partridge or squab)
4 cups shredded cabbage
4 small carrots, thinly sliced
4 slices bacon, cut in 1-inch pieces,
  crisply fried and drained
2 tablespoons butter or margarine,

melted
¼ teaspoon caraway seed
16 cabbage leaves
1 cup chicken broth
½ teaspoon crushed tarragon leaves
¼ teaspoon thyme

Preheat oven to 350°. Sprinkle birds inside and out with salt and pepper to suit taste. Combine next 5 ingredients; spoon a fourth into each cavity of birds. Wrap each bird in 4 cabbage leaves; secure with string. Place birds in deep casserole; add remaining ingredients and cover. Bake 45 to 60 minutes or until tender. Remove string and cabbage leaves. Serve with pan juices. Makes 4 servings.

Mrs. Lucille Bredy, *Homedale, Idaho*

MOZZARELLA CHICKEN AND LINGUINE CASSEROLE

3 gloves crushed garlic
1 tablespoon salad oil
1 to 2 pounds boneless chicken
1 pound linguine
16 ounces tomato sauce

¼ cup hot water
4 ounces sliced, drained
  mushrooms
Salt and pepper
4 ounces mozzarella cheese

Brown garlic in hot oil. Cook chicken 3 minutes on each side in oil. Cook linguine. Wash and drain it. Mix tomato sauce, hot water and mushrooms in a bowl. Salt and pepper to taste. Add the following to casserole dish: 1/3 sauce mixture, drained linguine, 1/3 sauce mixture, chicken, sauce mixture, mozzarella cheese. Bake in oven 20 to 25 minutes at 325°. Serves 6.

Rosalyn Segal, *Cambridge, Massachusetts*

THOROUGHLY MODERN CHICKEN LIVERS

2 pounds chicken livers
2 cups mushroom caps (large)
1 pineapple, peeled, cored,
  cut in half, each half to be cut
  in 16 wedges
1 cup chicken bouillon

2 tablespoons soy sauce
2 tablespoons salad oil
2 tablespoons lemon juice
½ teaspoon garlic powder
1 tablespoon sugar

Slice mushroom caps and chicken livers in half. Alternately lay chicken livers, mushroom caps and pineapple wedges on bottom of 2-quart oven-proof casserole dish. Combine chicken bouillon, soy sauce, salad oil, lemon juice, garlic powder and sugar. Pour over each layer of chicken, mushrooms and pineapple. Bake at 350° for 10 to 12 minutes. Serves 4.

Ensign Richard O'Brien, *Detroit, Michigan*

TIJUANA POLENTA

1 cup yellow cornmeal
1 cup cold water
4 chicken bouillon cubes
3 cups hot water
Butter or margarine to grease
  casserole

2 cups cold cooked chicken, cubed
1 (6-ounce) bottle hot taco sauce
3 cups hot half-and-half
½ pound Monterey Jack cheese,
  shredded

Stir the cornmeal into the cold water. Dissolve the bouillon cubes in the hot water and add the wet cornmeal. Cook, stirring constantly, until it draws away from the side of the pan. Butter a deep casserole or baking pan. Spread the polenta (cooked cornmeal) in the casserole. Sprinkle in the cold chicken cubes; pour on the sauce, then the cream. Lastly, sprinkle the cheese over all. Bake at 350° about 45 minutes, or until the cheese is melted and slightly brown. Use as a main dish. Serves 6.

Avis M. Alishouse, *Akron, Colorado*

"How did you enjoy your dinner, sir?"

CHICK-'N-CHILADAS

1 clove garlic, minced
2 tablespoons salad oil
1 (12-ounce) can tomatoes
  (1½ cups)
2 cups chopped onion
2 (4-ounce) cans mild green chilis,
  seeded and chopped
1 teaspoon garlic salt

½ teaspoon oregano
½ cup water
3 cups bite-size cooked chicken
2 cups grated Monterey Jack cheese
2 cups sour cream
1/3 cup shortening
1 package corn tortillas (15)

51

Cook garlic in salad oil until tender. Add tomatoes, onion, green chilis, garlic salt, oregano and ½ cup water. Cook over low heat until thickened. Combine chicken, cheese and sour cream; mix. Heat shortening. Dip tortillas just enough to make limp; drain. Fill tortillas with chicken mixture; roll up. Place open side down in baking dish. Spoon tomato mixture over top. Bake at 325° for 15 minutes or until hot through. Makes 15.

Joel Allard, *San Antonio, Texas*

CORNISH CASSEROLE

4 Cornish hens
2 cups bread crumbs
4 teaspoons dried salad herbs
½ teaspoon salt
¼ teaspoon pepper
1½ cups Sauterne wine

½ pint sour cream
1 (4-ounce) can mushroom bits
  and pieces, drained
1 (16-ounce) can boiled onions,
  drained
½ cup melted butter

Cut each hen in half and wipe dry. Combine bread crumbs, herbs, salt and pepper. Dip hens into wine and then coat with bread crumb mix. Place on wax paper. Combine wine, sour cream and remaining crumb mixture. Grease a 2- to 3-quart baking dish. Spoon crumb mixture into dish and spread around. Cover with mushrooms and onions. Place hens on top of ingredients and pour melted butter over all. Bake at 350° for 60 to 70 minutes or until hens are tender. Serves 4.

Mrs. Marilyn Uhl, *Clyde, Ohio*

BREASTS OF CHICKEN VICHYSSOISE

3 whole broiler-fryer
  chicken breasts, halved
½ teaspoon salt
½ cup pancake mix
½ teaspoon garlic salt

¼ cup margarine, melted
1 (13-ounce) can vichyssoise soup
1 tablespoon freeze-dried chives
¼ cup Sauterne wine

Sprinkle chicken breasts with salt. Put pancake mix and garlic salt into a small plastic bag and shake chicken pieces in it to coat. Melt the margarine in a casserole or baking dish large enough to hold chicken in a single layer, and roll the skin side of the chicken in it to coat; then turn pieces skin side up. Bake at 425° until chicken is lightly browned. Mix together soup, chives and wine and pour over chicken. Cover and bake at 350° for about 35 minutes, or until chicken is fork tender. Serves 3 to 6.

Georgia Dotson, *Washington, D.C.*

CHICKEN PETIT

1 large onion
1 clove garlic
3 tablespoons cooking oil
4 cooked chicken breasts,
    each in quarters
1 cup white rice

1 cup water
1 (15-ounce) can dark red kidney
    beans
½ packet of taco seasoning
2 ounces cream of coconut

Sauté onion and 1 sliced garlic clove in cooking oil. Quickly stir-fry chicken in 12-inch skillet; brown lightly. Remove chicken to platter. Add to remaining onion and garlic in skillet 1 cup rice, 1 cup water and can of kidney beans plus taco seasoning. Cover tightly and cook over low heat for approximately 20 minutes. After 10 minutes you may need additional small amount of water (or white wine). When rice is almost ready, add diced chicken and coconut cream to skillet. Cover and cook additional 10 minutes. Serve piping hot with green salad and corn bread. Serves 6.

Mrs. Marianne J. Whitney, *New City, New York*

CHICKEN SUPERB

1 plump fryer, cut into pieces,
    or 5 plump chicken breasts
1 teaspoon salt
4 tablespoons butter
1½ cups seasoned poultry stuffing
1 (10-ounce) can condensed
    cream of mushroom soup

½ cup sliced mushrooms
½ cup sliced, pitted black olives
1 small jar sliced pimientos
½ cup chicken broth
1 (16-ounce) can French-style
    green beans

Place chicken pieces in small saucepan. Cover with water; add salt and 2 tablespoons butter. Simmer until meat is tender. Remove from heat; cut from bones and chop into large cubes. Place in 1½-quart casserole. Add 2/3 cup of stuffing, mushroom soup, mushrooms, olives, and pimientos. Pour chicken broth over mixture and toss lightly. Add beans and toss again, mixing ingredients well. Sprinkle remaining stuffing over top. Place thin pats of remaining butter over top of stuffing. Sprinkle liberally with water. Bake in 350° oven for 30 minutes, or until casserole begins to bubble. Garnish with parsley. Serves 6 to 8.

Susan Gibson Rainey, *Weldon, North Carolina*

NANA'S CHICKEN

1 (2¼- to 3¼-pound)
    quartered chicken
¼ cup flour
½ teaspoon salt
¼ teaspoon pepper
1 teaspoon paprika

¼ cup butter
1 cup cream of
    chicken soup
1 (3- or 4-ounce) can sliced,
    undrained mushrooms
1 tablespoon sherry

Combine flour, salt, pepper and paprika. Place in bag with chicken and shake to coat. Melt butter in shallow casserole. Add chicken (skin-side down). Bake in 400° oven for 30 minutes. Turn chicken. Combine and heat chicken soup, mushrooms and sherry. Pour over chicken and bake 15 to 30 minutes longer, or until tender. Yield: 4 servings.

Mrs. June Eberbach, *Indianapolis, Indiana*

FISH
The Ones That Didn't Get Away

SEAFOOD WITH A
SOUTHERN ACCENT
By George Rector

Southern seafood traditions will bear a good deal of investigating all right. New England and Louisiana have had plenty of play from itinerant epicures, but there is a long stretch of seashore and imaginative cookery in between. Maryland terrapin, for instance, is adequately famous, but few outsiders have ever experienced what a Carolina cook can do with a "slider"—the local name for ordinary turtle—and I never yet met anybody who had ever heard of, let alone experimented with, the Florida cracker's habit of eating the weird animals which inhabit conch shells. We don't even have to move outside Charleston to find another rib-sticking version of an easily available shellfish. Did you ever have a Carolina shrimp pie?

It isn't a pie at all, being totally innocent of crust, but there's never any point in being pedantic. Fresh shrimp, boiled and shucked, is the best possible beginning, but good canned shrimp will do all right. Two pounds will work out to feed four people to the danger point. If the shrimps are big, cut them in two. Then chop up a small onion and fry it light brown in two tablespoons of butter in a frying pan along with a chopped-up green pepper. Crumble three slices of stale white bread into an ordinary-sized can of tomatoes, mix in the shrimps, all pink and innocent, season them discreetly with pepper and salt and two tablespoons of chili sauce, and then introduce the whole into the frying pan, to be cooked slowly along with the onion for twenty minutes. Three hard-cooked eggs pretty well chopped up join the party at this point, and then everything is poured into a greased baking dish, covered with fine dry bread crumbs, dotted with butter for a richener and softener. Fifteen minutes in a moderate oven will brown the crumbs and produce a magnificent swamp of mingled this and that underneath. It's as rich as the mud in a Sea Island rice plantation, and illustrates the why of the local proverb that Charleston lives on tourists in the winter and shrimps in the summer. With minor variations for stepping the liquid content either up or down, the same layout will do equally well for oysters, crab meat, lobster meat, scallops, and so forth.

HOW TO MAKE A
DOWN-EAST LOBSTER STEW
By Samuel T. Williamson

Boil two one-pound lobsters, preferably female, for fifteen minutes. Slit the lobsters open on a flat pan so as to save the juice. Remove tomalley, any coral roe and all meat, including that from the big claws. Squeeze juice from each small claw. Put meat, juice, tomalley and roe in a pan with one-third cup of melted butter. Stir so that each piece is buttered, cover and let stand for about four hours. Heat a quart and a half of light cream in a double boiler to just below the scalding point, then add buttered lobster meat and juice, a quarter teaspoon of sodium glutamate, one teaspoon Maggi liquid flavoring, and, if extra coloring is wanted, a quarter teaspoon of paprika. If necessary, salt to taste, although in most cases the butter and salty juice should be sufficient. When the mixture is cool, put in refrigerator for at least twenty-four hours. Reheat before serving, adding a couple of tablespoons of sherry if desired. Serves six.

OUTDOOR OYSTER ROAST
By Roy Andries de Groot

This requires a large, flat, open, iron pan, balanced over the fire. (I use a Spanish paella, 18 inches across.) Since "roasting" is very quick, first prepare all ingredients. Scrub and wash 3 dozen oysters, or more. Melt, in smallish iron pan, ½ pound butter and keep lukewarm. Coarsely grate ½ cup shelled pecans. Get large open pan spitting hot. Quickly lay on oysters, hollow shell downward. Cover at once with soaking wet burlap sacking. This involves much hissing and steam. Heat butter until it starts sizzling, add grated pecans and stir until darkish brown, being careful not to let them burn. Then add, in one measure, 2 teaspoons tarragon wine vinegar. Sauce will froth violently. Stir once and remove from fire. After about 4 or 5 minutes, lift edge of burlap covering and, with tongs, remove each oyster that has opened sufficiently for a knife to be inserted. Discard flat top shell and serve oysters, with pecan sauce spooned over each.

CLAMBAKE

Buy sweet and white baking potatoes, a few pounds of yellow onions, 2 or 3 ears of corn and 1 small lobster per person. At the beach, immediately organize hunting forces for razor and surf clams, cherrystones, mussels, bay scallops and crabs. Start surf casting for fish. Above the high-water mark dig a trench 2 feet deep, 3 feet wide and 6 feet long. Line the trench with smooth rocks, fill with dry wood and start the fire about 3½ hours before you wish to eat. To clean clams and mussels, scrub and soak in a bucket of sea water to which have been added several handfuls of flour. Wash potatoes, husk corn and wrap each in foil. Clean lobsters and crabs. Cut cleaned fish into chunks, sandwich between onion slices and foil-wrap. After about 2½ hours when the fire dies down to a white-hot and smokeless bed, cover it with a 6-inch blanket of wet rockweed covered with sackcloth soaked in sea water. Vary and spread assorted food interspersed with onions on the cloth in an even layer. Cover with more wet sackcloth, another 6-inch blanket of wet rockweed and over all place a heavy canvas tarpaulin weighted with stones to seal in the steam. Allow about 1 hour for the cooking. Then unroll the tarpaulin from one end and take out only enough food for the first serving. Serve with melted butter in dipping bowls.

PAN-FRIED TROUT WITH EGGS

Allow ¾ pound trout per serving. Clean (leaving on heads and tails), wash, dry, and lightly coat with cornmeal. Break 8 eggs into bowl, add 1 table-spoon finely cut chives and beat lightly. Melt 5 ounces butter in frying pan and put in trout. Brown on both sides for about 10 minutes, then add salt and pepper. Remove fish to a warm dish. Melt another 5 ounces butter and gently stir in ¾ pint heavy cream. Stir continually until sauce has boiled down to the consistency of light cream. Pour half over fish. Give eggs a final beat, then slosh into pan and scramble over gentle heat. Spoon eggs alongside fish and serve garnished with watercress.

OYSTERS LONGCHAMPS AND OYSTER STEW
By George Rector

It was probably my pride in handling oysters with loving care that helped reconcile me to our fancy oyster dishes at the old place—oysters Long-champs, for instance. It's a fine thing to do with bulk oysters in the home. That remark back there about oysters out of a paper bucket was not intended as a slur on anything or anybody but the soulless restaurateur who tries to fake half-shell service, you understand.

A big frying pan is the first field of action for oysters Longchamps. Melt a couple of tablespoons of butter in it and cook in the butter for a few minutes a couple of small white onions minced fine and a half cup of chopped mushrooms. Then thicken that with a couple of tablespoonfuls of flour by patient degrees to avoid lumps. When the mixture reaches a boil, toss in two tablespoons of sherry, a half teaspoon of salt and a few grains of cayenne—all of which makes a very pretty background for an oyster's rich subtleties. Enter the oysters, a full pint of them, plus a tablespoon of chopped parsley—step down the heat before the oysters are put in. They cook in the mixture for just one minute and then the whole business is poured into a shallow casserole, covered with buttered bread crumbs and baked brown in a moderate oven. In the face of that bland creamy delicious-ness, it's hard to maintain that oysters should never be cooked. The same holds good for old-fashioned oyster dressing for roast chicken and roast turkey.

If we must cook oysters, however, I can be blinded and backed into an oyster stew without much trouble. The proper way of making an oyster stew is a sort of elementary education in the cooking of oysters in general.

Don't let an unworthy hankering after richness at all costs trick you into making one of those all-cream stews—hot cream is a fine thing for coffee, as they serve it in Vienna, but for any other purpose, it's always sickly rich. The prescription here is two parts of milk to one of cream—not even half and half. Eight oysters to a portion is adequately generous, to be planted in a saucepan with a quarter cup of the oyster liquor, a dash of cayenne, a pinch of salt and, if you fancy the effect, a generous pinch of celery salt. Bring that to a quick boil and give it just a minute of boiling. Then skim the top and put in the milk-and-cream mixture, which should be hot, but not have been allowed to boil. Turn up the fire and stir a little and, just as it reaches a boil again, throw in a tablespoon of butter. Paprika sprinkles prettily over the top, and the oyster crackers, which should of course be served with the stew, are to be floated and pursued by the spoon, no matter what the book of etiquette says.

SCRAMBLED CLAMS AND EGGPLANT EN CASSEROLE

1 eggplant (about 6 inches long)
½ teaspoon salt
1 (6-ounce) can minced clams
1 cup milk
2 tablespoons minced onion
2 tablespoons butter or margarine
1½ tablespoons flour
2 tablespoons chopped parsley
½ cup boiled mushrooms
1/8 teaspoon garlic powder
1 tablespoon Worcestershire sauce
½ cup soft bread crumbs

Cut peeled eggplant into cubes and boil in small amount of salted water. Drain clams, and add to eggplant. Combine milk and clam liquid. Sauté minced onion in 1 tablespoon butter. Add flour, milk, and clam liquid to saucepan and when sauce boils, add parsley, mushrooms, garlic powder, Worcestershire sauce, clams and eggplant. Bake in greased 1½-quart casserole at 325° for 35 minutes. Sprinkle top with bread crumbs and remaining butter. Serves 4.

Jean S. Bailey, *Saratoga, California*

SHORE AND COUNTRY CLAM PIE

4 (6½-ounce) cans minced sea clams
1 pound fresh mushrooms
3 tablespoons margarine or butter
4 or 5 dashes of pepper
1 teaspoon Worcestershire sauce
1 cup clam liquid
1 cup sour cream
2 tablespoons flour
Pastry for 2-crust 9-inch pie
3 tablespoons clam liquid for pie top

Drain clams, SAVE all liquid. Clean and coarse-chop mushrooms to same size as clam pieces. In 10- or 12-inch covered frying pan, cook chopped mushrooms in margarine. Add pepper and Worcestershire sauce. Remove cover, and cook away most of juice. Reduce heat. In separate pan, boil 1 cup clam liquid down to ½ cup. Add concentrated clam liquid to mushrooms. (Total liquid should appear to be a generous ½ cup when pan is tipped away from mushrooms.) Add sour cream to mushrooms. Add flour to clams and mix. Add floured clams to mushrooms. Stir until thickened and remove from heat. Spoon clam-mushroom filling into pie shell. Cover with well-slashed top crust. Sprinkle the 3 tablespoons clam juice over top crust of unbaked pie. Bake in preheated 450° oven for 10 to 15 minutes. Reduce heat to 400° and bake 30 minutes longer or until pie is golden brown and bubbly. Serves 6.

Mrs. William H. Walsh, *Bay Village, Ohio*

CHANNEL CAT, "SHOW-ME" STYLE

2 channel catfish (1 to 2
  pounds each)
Salt
Pepper
Garlic powder
2 lemons (1 for each fish)
Oregano
Paprika
1 tablespoon butter (per fish)

Place fish on aluminum foil. Sprinkle generously with salt, pepper and garlic powder on each side. Grate the rind of one lemon on each fish. Then squeeze the juice of one lemon on each fish. Add a pinch of oregano and dust on both sides with paprika. Dot with butter. Seal aluminum foil with a drugstore wrap so juices do not leak out. Bake in a 350° oven for 45 minutes to one hour, depending on the size of the fish. Serves 4.

Mrs. Gay Schroer, *St. Peters, Missouri*

COD FISH CASSEROLE

1 package frozen codfish
1 teaspoon seasoned salt
6 servings instant mashed potatoes
½ pound salt pork, diced
1 tablespoon butter
1 medium green pepper, sliced
1 small onion, diced
½ cup celery, sliced
1 can cream of celery soup
  (undiluted)
8 ounces fresh mushrooms, sliced
1 package (8-ounce) cooked
  salad shrimp

Season codfish with salt. Wrap in foil and bake 30 minutes at 350°. Drain excess juice and flake. Set aside. Prepare instant mashed potatoes, making them stiff. Set aside. Fry salt pork which has been diced, until crisp. Drain off grease. Add butter, green papper, onion and celery and cook until onion is clear using medium to low heat. Add celery soup, mushrooms and shrimp. Line 12-inch oval casserole with mashed potatoes. Place fish and shrimp mixture in center. Bake in 400° oven for 15 to 20 minutes (until piping hot). Serve garnished with alternate slices of fresh tomatoes and green peppers. Serves 4 to 6.

Mrs. Cletus A. Bille, *Huron, Ohio*

FISH "BATES" CASSEROLE

2 stalks celery
1 to 2 medium onions
2 pounds fresh or frozen fish fillets
  (cod, flounder, or fillets of your
  choice)
Basic recipe for white sauce (butter,
  flour, milk and seasonings)
½ cup dry white sherry wine
  (optional)
Juice of ½ lemon
Paprika
2 to 3 tablespoons Parmesan cheese
Salt and pepper
½ cup prepared bread stuffing mix
3 tablespoons slivered almonds

Line greased oblong shallow baking dish with diced celery and onions. Use enough to cover bottom of baking dish. Place fillets on top of celery and onions. Spoon white sauce mixture over fillets. If wine is used, add to white sauce. Sprinkle with lemon juice, paprika and Parmesan cheese. Season with salt and pepper. Sprinkle with bread stuffing and almonds. Bake at 350° for 30 to 35 minutes or until fish flakes easily. Serves 6.

Mrs. James C. Bates, *Chamblee, Georgia*

THREE-MINUTE TUNA-SPINACH CASSEROLE

1 (7-ounce) can tuna
1 (10-ounce) package frozen
  chopped spinach, thawed
1/3 cup fine dry bread crumbs
3 tablespoons herb seasoned
  stuffing
1 tablespoon lemon juice
¼ teaspoon salt
½ cup mayonnaise
3 tablespoons Parmesan
  cheese, grated

Combine all ingredients in casserole. Sprinkle with additional cheese. Bake at 350° in preheated oven for 20 to 25 minutes. Serve plain or over cooked rice. Serves 4 to 6.

Mrs. Michael Gutshall, *Totowa, New Jersey*

DOWN EAST FISH CHOWDER

¼ pound salt pork, diced
2 medium onions, sliced or diced
1 small whole onion
4 cups raw potatoes, cut in small
    pieces
1 cup or more of water
2 to 3 pounds haddock fillets

1 teaspoon salt
¼ teaspoon black pepper
Pinch of thyme
1 quart of whole milk
1 small can evaporated milk
1 to 3 tablespoons butter

Fry diced salt pork slowly in large kettle until crisp. Add diced onions and
cook slowly until yellowed, not brown. Add potatoes and enough water so
that potatoes are covered. Bring to a boil. Place fish (whole pieces) on top of
potatoes. Add small, whole, peeled onion and seasonings. Cook slowly until
potatoes are tender and fish is cooked through. Do not break up fish. Pour in
both kinds of milk and heat through thoroughly. Do not boil. Chowder is
best when cooked and left to stand (in refrigerator) for an hour or so.
Reheat. Add butter and remove whole onion. Serve with crackers and pickles
(pilot crackers and sour cucumber pickles are best). Serves 6.
Mrs. A.C. Archibald, *Eastport, Maine*

SEAFOOD CASSEROLE SUPREME

4 cups cooked brown rice
1 stick butter (¼ pound)
4 large mushrooms, sliced thin
3 large tomatoes, peeled and cut
    in wedges
¼ cup grated onion or
    1 tablespoon dried minced onion
2 cups cooked lobster or crab meat
    or 2 cans of either, rinsed
    and drained
½ teaspoon salt

2 or 3 dashes ground pepper
1 can water chestnuts, sliced
¼ cup slivered almonds
1 teaspoon monosodium glutamate
¼ teaspoon bitters
1 cup heavy cream
2 tablespoons minced parsley or
    1 tablespoon dried parsley
½ cup brandy
¼ pound cooked baby shrimp

Melt butter in large skillet. Add mushrooms; stir and cook for 5 minutes. Stir
in tomatoes and onions. Cook for another 5 minutes. Add lobster (or crab),
salt, pepper, water chestnuts, slivered almonds, monosodium glutamate and
bitters. Stir and cook for 3 minutes. Stir in cream and cook until it bubbles.
Add parsley and brandy and remove from heat. Line a 2-quart greased
casserole with the cooked rice. Turn in the lobster or crab mixture. Top with
the baby shrimp. Bake at 350° for 20 minutes. Serves 8.
Mel Wylie, *Richmond, California*

SCALLOPED OYSTERS

1 medium onion, chopped
½ cup chopped celery
1 clove garlic, chopped
¼ cup butter or margarine
2 cups toasted bread crumbs
1 quart oysters

1 teaspoon salt
1 teaspoon pepper
2 hard-cooked eggs, sliced
1 tablespoon Worcestershire sauce
1 pint milk

Cook onion, celery and garlic in small amount of butter until slightly brown; remove from pan. In baking dish, place a layer of bread crumbs, oysters, onion, celery, and garlic. Sprinkle salt and pepper over contents. Make a second layer of all ingredients, and top entire dish with sliced eggs. Add Worcestershire sauce to milk, and pour milk over entire dish. Place in oven at 325° for half hour, or until juice and milk are absorbed. Serves 10.

Mrs. Russell O. Behrens, *Apalachicola, Florida*

PERCH PIQUANT

2 (1-pound) boxes frozen perch
  (or similar fish)
2 large potatoes, peeled, cooked
  and sliced ¼ inch thick
½ pint sour cream

3 tablespoons prepared horseradish
½ cup mayonnaise
2 tablespoons pickle relish
1 teaspoon minced parsley
Salt and pepper to taste

Preheat oven to 350°. Lightly grease a shallow 2-quart casserole. Place fish and potatoes in casserole and dot sparingly with butter. Bake for 20 minutes. Mix sour cream, horseradish, mayonnaise, pickle relish, parsley, salt and pepper together and pour over fish and potatoes. Bake an additional 10 minutes. Serve while sauce is still bubbling. Serves 8.

Mrs. Beryl D. Ames, *New Orleans, Louisiana*

AHOY CASSEROLE

1 (8-ounce) package egg noodles
3 tablespoons butter or margarine
3 tablespoons flour
1½ cups milk
1 (11-ounce) can cream
  mushroom soup
1 (10-ounce) package frozen peas
1 cup grated cheese

½ teaspoon salt
¼ teaspoon pepper
1½ pounds scallops, fresh or frozen
  (thawed)
1 cup fresh mushrooms, sliced
¼ cup diced celery
2 tablespoons butter or margarine

Cook noodles as directed on package and drain. Melt 3 tablespoons butter in saucepan, stir in flour; add milk gradually, stirring constantly. After milk comes to a boil, blend in undiluted soup, frozen peas, ½ cup cheese and seasonings. Set aside. Sauté scallops, mushrooms and celery in 2 tablespoons butter. Drain and add to cheese sauce. Combine this mixture with noodles. Pour into greased casserole and top with remaining cheese. Bake at 400° for about 25 minutes. Serves 6 to 8.

Mary N. Walker, *Harbor City, California*

SHRIMP OR FISH CREOLE

2½ pounds shrimp (cooked) or fish
  (fresh or frozen tuna, etc.)
2 medium onions, choppsed
1 cup green pepper, finely chopped
1½ cups celery, cut in large pieces
¼ cup bacon drippings or oil
3 cans condensed tomato soup
  (10¾ ounces each)
1 tablespoon vinegar

1/8 teaspoon garlic powder
1 bay leaf
4 teaspoons chili powder
3 dashes Tabasco sauce
2 teaspoon salt
Dash Worcestershire sauce
Dash black pepper
½ to ¾ cup white wine

61

Sauté onion, green pepper and celery in oil until tender. Add remaining ingredients except fish; simmer 30 minutes. Add shrimp or fish and simmer for 10 to 15 minutes. Serve over hot rice. Serves 10.

David Savidge, *Fair Oaks, California*

DANISH SHRIMP SALAD

3 pounds shrimp, shelled
  and deveined
1 tablespoon shrimp spice
¾ cup mayonnaise
½ cup dairy sour cream
2 tablespoons minced onions
3 tablespoons lemon juice
2 to 3 tablespoons chopped

fresh dill
2 teaspoons salt
¼ teaspoon pepper
3 to 4 drops liquid hot
  pepper seasoning
Greens (romaine or Boston lettuce),
  washed

Cook the shrimp in water to cover with the shrimp spice, 5 to 8 minutes. Cool shrimp in the broth. Mix together mayonnaise, sour cream, onion, lemon juice, dill, salt, pepper and pepper seasoning. Drain shrimp and place in bowl; add dressing and mix well. Chill several hours. To serve, arrange shrimp on bed of greens. Serves 6.

Bess Slagle, *St. Peters, Missouri*

"What's for dinner?"

PARTY SHRIMP

2 pounds large shrimp
1 tablespoon lemon juice
3 tablespoons salad oil
¾ cup raw rice
2 tablespoons margarine
¼ cup minced green peppers
¼ cup minced onions

1 teaspoon salt
1/8 teaspoon pepper
1 can condensed tomato soup
1 cup heavy cream
½ cup sherry
½ cup slivered almonds

Cook shrimp in boiling salted water for 5 minutes. Place in 2-quart casserole. Sprinkle with lemon juice, oil. Meanwhile cook rice as package directs. Mix shrimp and rice and chill. Sauté peppers and onions in butter. Mix all ingredients in recipe together, with the exception of the almonds. Bake at 350° for 55 minutes. Top with slivered almonds. Serves 6.

Kay Conrad, *Wayland, Massachusetts*

SWEET-SOUR SHRIMP

1 medium onion, quartered
1 cup celery sliced diagonally
2 tablespoons salad oil
2/3 cup firmly packed brown sugar
2 tablespoons cornstarch
½ teaspoon salt
1/8 teaspoon ginger
1/3 cup vinegar

3 tablespoons soy sauce
1 (6-ounce) can pineapple juice
1¼ cups water
2 cups cubed pineapple
1 pound cooked shrimp
1 green pepper cut into
  1-inch pieces

Sauté onion and celery in hot oil until clear but not brown. Dissolve sugar, cornstarch, salt and ginger in vinegar and soy sauce. Add this mixture plus pineapple juice and water to the vegetables. Cook, stirring constantly until thickened. Add pineapple, shrimp and green pepper. Cover and cook for about 5 minutes. Serve over hot rice. Serves 4 to 6.

Helene Drown, *Rolling Hills, California*

SOLE AND CRAB

1 pint sour cream (2 cups)
3 egg yolks
3 tablespoons lemon juice
  (or white wine)

Salt and pepper
2 pounds filet of sole
1 or 2 packages (6-ounce) frozen crab

Mix sour cream, egg yolks, lemon juice, salt and pepper. Cover bottom of 9-by-13-inch baking dish with thin layer of sour cream mixture. Place layer of sole on sauce, season with salt and pepper. Cover with layer of crab, then second layer of sole. Cover with rest of sour cream mixture. Bake at 350° about 30 minutes or until sole flakes easily. Serves 6.

Mrs. C. N. Christensen, Indiana State Symphony Society, *Indianapolis, Indiana*

BREAD
In Time of Knead

SOUTHERN CORNBREAD
By Mary Alice Sharpe

Cornbread, like the polenta of northern Italy, is hearty, nutritious, cheap. In Italy, the cornmeal is poured slowly into salted boiling water until the water is saturated and a kind of wet cake is made which is served as a base for meatless stews and tomato sauces, and then fried the next morning with cheese for breakfast. In the South, the bread is cooked in the oven rather than on top of the stove and here the principle of overcook is deadly. It should be crusty on the outside of the pan and almost mushy in the center. And it should be eaten so hot butter doesn't stand a chance. Burnt fingers and a smile should be the only memory.

1½ cups white cornmeal
½ cup self-rising flour
2 tablespoons sugar

½ stick butter
2 eggs, slightly beaten
1½ cups buttermilk

Mix cornmeal, flour and sugar. Mix butter, eggs and buttermilk and stir into dry mixture. Bake in greased pan about 20 minutes in preheated 400 to 450° oven.

A piece of cornbread with a bowl of vegetable soup makes an unpretentious winter lunch, with stick-to-the-ribs-rather-than-some-other-area vitality.

HONEY BREAD

Homemade bread baked with honey instead of sugar will remain moist longer. The following recipe is for a fruit loaf that makes an excellent gift or a morning snack with coffee.

1¼ cups sifted all-purpose flour
1 teaspoon salt
½ teaspoon baking soda
2 teaspoons baking powder
1 cup whole wheat flour
2/3 cup honey

1 cup buttermilk
3 tablespoons oil or shortening
2 eggs, well beaten
½ cup raisins or chopped dates
1 cup finely chopped
    walnuts or pecans

Sift the flour again with the salt, soda and baking powder. Add the whole wheat flour. Separately, mix the honey, buttermilk and oil with the beaten eggs. Stir in the dry ingredients. Do not over-stir. Fold in the nuts and the dates or raisins. Spoon the batter into a greased 9x5x3-inch loaf pan. Bake for 50 to 60 minutes in a 325° (moderate) oven.

POPOVERS

Popovers are as light as milkweed blowing in the wind. They're easy to make and their mystery is in the two oven speeds (though there's no reason to tell anybody that).

2 eggs
1 cup milk
1 cup sifted all-purpose flour

½ teaspoon salt
1 tablespoon salad oil

Mix eggs in bowl with milk, flour and salt. Beat 1½ minutes with electric beater. Add salad oil and beat for ½ minute more. Don't overbeat. Fill 6 to 8 well-greased custard cups or a muffin pan about half full. Bake at 475° for 15 minutes. Reduce heat to 350° and bake 25 to 30 minutes, until browned. Before removing from the oven, prick each popover with a fork to let the steam out. You can stuff these with filling—meat, or cheese sauce, or a mushroom, parsley and almond mixture. By themselves, with butter or margarine, they're unforgettable.

ORANGE-DATE-NUT BREAD

The closer bread is to cake, the better. So say some. Children won't argue. And parents might not if the cake is an orange date nut loaf, full of natural ingredients, yet sweet enough to tempt little teeth away from cavity-making, jaw-breaking candies.

1 package pitted dates
   cut into small pieces
   (about 8 ounces)
2 tablespoons shortening
1 tablespoon grated or shredded
   orange peel
½ cup fresh orange juice
1 egg, beaten

2 cups sifted
   all-purpose flour
1/3 cup sugar
1 teaspoon soda
1 teaspoon baking powder
½ teaspoon salt
½ cup chopped pecans

Put the dates and shortening in a large bowl and pour ½ cup of boiling water over them. When this has cooled, add the orange juice and peeling. Stir in the egg. Sift together flour, baking powder, soda, salt, and sugar. Add to the mixture, stirring until just blended. Add the pecans. Pour into a greased, floured loaf pan, about 8 by 4 inches. Bake at 325° for about an hour. Before turning out of pan, cool for about 10 minutes. This may be stored in foil in the refrigerator.

WAFFLES A LA JOHNSON
By Nunally Johnson

Two cupfuls of flour are mixed in a sifter with two teaspoonfuls of baking powder, a half teaspoonful of baking soda and a pinch of salt. Beat this lovely conglomeration into a batter with milk, using the latter as needed for a fairly thick consistency. Add four tablespoonfuls of melted lard. Toss in an egg and continue to beat until the iron is good and hot.

At the end of five minutes one of the handsomest waffles you ever saw will emerge from this iron and, served with butter, will make another man out of you.

CINNAMON, RAISIN LOAF

1 package active dry yeast
¼ cup warm water
½ cup lukewarm milk
1 tablespoon sugar
1 teaspoon salt
1 egg
1 tablespoon margarine

1 tablespoon ground ginger
2 teaspoons grated lemon rind
2/3 cup raisins
2 2/3 to 3 cups unbleached flour
3 tablespoons margarine, melted
Cinnamon
Brown sugar

Dissolve yeast in water in large bowl, adding a pinch of sugar to prove yeast. Stir milk, sugar, salt, egg, margarine, ginger, lemon rind and half the flour into yeast mixture. Mix until smooth. Add raisins and enough flour to make handling easy. Turn onto floured board and knead in only as much of the remaining flour as will knead in easily. Place in greased bowl, turning so that top is also oiled. Cover and let rise until doubled.

Shape into 11-by-17-inch rectangle on very lightly floured board. Spread with melted margarine, shake on cinnamon and sprinkle lightly with brown sugar. Roll up and shape into loaf. Place in oiled pan and let rise, covered, until doubled. Before baking, brush top with melted margarine and sprinkle lightly with brown sugar. Bake at 425° for 25 to 30 minutes. If sugar becomes too brown, cover loaf with foil for remainder of cooking time. Yield: 1 loaf.

Mrs. Dee Stein, *Lincolnwood, Illinois*

THE SATURDAY EVENING POST

"Good morning to you, good morning to you, good morning dear sweetheart, good morning to you."

ARNO'S BREAD

2 packages dry yeast
1/3 cup lukewarm water
2 tablespoons sugar
12 cups unbleached all-purpose
   flour
2 cups milk
2 medium potatoes
   (peeled, boiled and mashed)
2 cups potato water
   (from potatoes above)

3 tablespoons melted shortening
1 tablespoon salt
1 cup pitted dates
½ cup dry apricots
½ cup pitted prunes
1 cup raisins
½ pound margarine, soft
1 cup brown sugar
1 tablespoon cinnamon
1 small jar honey

Dissolve yeast in warm water with 2 tablespoons sugar. Let stand a few minutes. Place 6 cups flour in large mixing bowl. Add yeast mixture, milk, mashed potatoes and potato water. Mix with spoon until batter is soft and bubbly. Cover with dish towel and let rise in warm place until doubled in bulk (about 1 hour).

Add remaining 6 cups of flour, melted shortening and salt. Chop dates, apricots and prunes and add to batter along with raisins. Place dough on floured board and knead for 10 minutes. Place in mixing bowl, cover and let rise again for 1 hour.

Punch down dough and divide into 4 equal parts. Roll each part into a 12-by-16-inch rectangle. Spread with soft margarine and sprinkle with mixture of brown sugar and cinnamon. Drip on honey in a crisscross pattern. Roll up dough, tuck in ends and place in greased bread pans. Cover pans with towel and let rise to top of pans (at least one hour). Bake in preheated 400° oven on middle rack 10 minutes. Reduce heat to 350° and bake 50 minutes longer. Remove bread from oven and turn out of pans onto cooling racks. Wait 20 minutes before cutting. Yield: 4 loaves.

A. R. and Polly Justman, *Fort Walton Beach, Florida*

NO-KNEAD
GRANOLA SWEET BREAD

1 quart skimmed milk
1½ cups shortening
3 tablespoons salt
6 eggs
1 cup sugar

3 packages active dry yeast
2 cups granola
2 cups raisins
Flour

Heat milk, shortening and salt on medium burner until shortening melts. Cool slightly. Beat eggs and sugar together in large bowl. Add milk and shortening mixture to eggs, then yeast, granola and raisins. Add flour until dough is slightly thicker than cake batter but thin enough to pour into well-greased bread pans. Fill pans to half full. Using warm setting on oven (not more than 150°), allow bread to rise in oven for 45 minutes. Raise temperature setting to 275° and bake slowly for another 45 minutes or until done. Glaze with powdered sugar thinned with hot water. Cool before slicing. Yield: 5 loaves.

Fran Gorton, *Spokane, Washington*

CONVERTIBLE EVERY DAY WHITE BREAD

9 to 10 cups all-purpose flour, sifted
3 tablespoons sugar
1 tablespoon salt
2 cups very hot water

2 cups cold water
3 packages dry yeast
½ cup vegetable shortening
 or cooking oil

Use glass bread pans or equally heavy material. Place all flour in large bowl. With wooden spoon, press flour up around sides of bowl, leaving a hole or depression in middle of flour.

In a smaller bowl, stir together the sugar, 3 tablespoons flour (taken from large bowl) and salt. Add very hot water and stir smooth. Add cold water and stir smooth. Then add the 3 packages of yeast. Stir, cover and keep warm for about 15 to 20 minutes, until mixture is light and bubbly. Stir and then dump yeast mixture (all at once) into the depression of flour in large bowl. Stirring slowly from bottom, add flour until a soft batter is made. Beat this until it seems smooth, being careful not to use too much flour at this stage. Cover and keep warm for 15 to 20 minutes. Then stir slowly from bottom, adding a bit of flour constantly until you can use your hands to knead all remaining flour, and dough becomes soft and spongy. Place on board and continue kneading until dough does not stick to your hands, about 5 minutes. Grease large bowl and put dough back in bowl. Grease dough and cover. Keep in warm place until doubled in bulk.

Punch down and knead again until soft. Grease and let rise again in bowl until doubled. Always knead on floured board. Punch down again and knead for a few minutes before forming into 3 loaves. Place in well-greased pans and "bathe" loaves with melted shortening. Let rise until doubled, keeping warm. Handle carefully while placing in a preheated oven of 425°. Bake for 30 or 35 minutes. Check after first 15 minutes. If it seems a bit hot, turn back to 375° or 400°. When done, remove from pans and cool on rack. These loaves may be frozen and kept for an indefinite time in freezer. Yield: 3 loaves.

Mrs. Tod S. Chearonn, *Londonville, Ohio*

GRANDMA VOELKER'S COFFEE CAKE

1 cake yeast
1 cup lukewarm water
½ cup lard
1 cup boiling water
1 cup cold water

½ cup sugar
2 to 3 eggs, beaten
1½ teaspoons salt
9 cups flour
 (approximate)

Soak yeast in 1 cup lukewarm water and set aside. Melt lard in 1 cup boiling water. Add cold water, sugar, eggs, salt and yeast to lard mixture. Stir in about 4 cups of flour and beat 3 minutes (as for cake). Work in the remaining flour and keep beating until you have a soft dough. Place in greased bowl and let rise until doubled in bulk. (May be regrigerated overnight, or longer.) Divide dough and place in four 8-inch or 9-inch round cake pans. Brush with melted butter or margarine and sprinkle with a mixture of sugar and cinnamon. Let rise again until doubled. Bake in 350° to 375° oven for 20 to 30 minutes. Yield: 4 coffee cakes.

Mrs. Adolph Voelker, *Tell City, Indiana*

ALMOND ROSE ROLLS

1 package active dry yeast
¼ cup lukewarm water
1/8 cup margarine
1/8 cup vegetable shortening
¼ cup sugar
1 teaspoon salt
1 tablespoon grated lime rind
½ cup scalded milk
½ cup ice water

1 egg, slightly beaten
4 cups presifted all-purpose flour
1/3 cup squeeze liquid margarine
3/4 cup firmly packed
  light brown sugar
2 tablespoons instantized flour
1 teaspoon almond flavoring
1 teaspoon rose extract
Cream

Dissolve yeast in lukewarm water. Combine margarine, shortening, sugar, salt, grated lime rind and scalded milk. Add ice water; cool to lukewarm. Blend in egg and the dissolved yeast. Add flour gradually, mixing well after each addition. Cover and let rise in warm place 45 to 60 minutes.

Combine squeeze liquid margarine, brown sugar, instantized flour, almond and rose extracts and mix well. Reserve as filling for rolls.

Roll dough into two 12-by-10-inch rectangles. Spread with almond rose filling. Roll as for jelly roll and cut into ½ inch slices. Arrange slices on greased baking sheet. Flatten to ¼-inch thickness. Place a blanched almond and preserved rose petals (if available) in center of each roll. Let rise 30 to 45 minutes. Brush tops of rolls lightly with cream. Bake in preheated 400° oven 12 to 15 minutes. Remove immediately from baking sheet. Yield: 2½ dozen.

Mrs. Helen Mize, *High Point*, *North Carolina*

BUTTERSCOTCH PARTY ROLLS

1 cup evaporated milk
1 cup brown sugar
½ cup butter
1 tablespoon vanilla
4 eggs
2 teaspoons salt

2 packages active dry yeast
½ cup lukewarm water
6 cups white flour
1 cup chopped nuts
2 cups confectioners' sugar

Combine evaporated milk and brown sugar in a saucepan and cook for 5 minutes after mixture has started to boil, stirring constantly. Take off stove and stir in butter and vanilla. Reserve ½ cup of this butterscotch sauce for the filling and frosting. Break eggs into a large mixing bowl and beat well. Add salt, lukewarm butterscotch sauce, and yeast that has been dissolved in the lukewarm water. Add 3 cups flour. Mix together using low speed, then beat at medium speed for 3 minutes. Stir in the remaining flour and half the nuts. Scrape bowl down, cover, and let rise until double in bulk. To the ½ cup reserved butterscotch sauce stir in 2 cups sifted confectioners' sugar.

When the dough is doubled in size, punch down and roll out to an 18-by-24-inch rectangle. Spread half the filling on the dough. Roll up as for a jelly roll, starting with the 24-inch side. Cut in 36 equal pieces. Put in greased muffin tins and top each roll with an equal amount of the remaining filling and nuts. Let rise until double in size. Bake at 375° for 20 minutes, or until golden brown. Yield: 36 rolls.

Marilee Jean Johnson, *Robbinsdale*, *Minnesota*

FRUIT MUFFINS

1 cake compressed yeast	1 teaspoon salt
¼ cup lukewarm water	1 rounded tablespoon shortening
½ cup old-fashioned oatmeal	2 cups boiling water
½ cup yellow cornmeal	5 cups white flour
½ cup All Bran	Cooked prunes
½ cup brown sugar	

Dissolve yeast in lukewarm water. Mix together oatmeal, cornmeal, All Bran, brown sugar, salt and shortening in bowl. Pour on boiling water and let stand until lukewarm. Add yeast mixture and beat a few minutes with spoon. Add 5 cups white flour and knead into soft ball.

Place in greased bowl and let rise until doubled in bulk. Spoon into large muffin pans, filling half full. Make deep hole in center of each muffin and place cooked prune deep in hole. Lightly spread muffin dough with butter and let rise again until doubled. Bake in 350° oven approximately 25 minutes or until golden brown on top. Remove from pans, spread tops with butter and sprinkle with wheat germ.

Mary E. Ralph, *Forsyth, Missouri*

SOUR CREAM NUT-FILLED ROLLS

4 cups sifted flour	dry yeast
¼ cup sugar	2 tablespoons sugar
1½ teaspoons salt	½ cup milk
1 cup (2 sticks) margarine	1 cup sour cream
2 yeast cakes or packages of	2 beaten eggs

Cut the margarine into dry ingredients in large bowl, as for pie crust. Make a "well" in center of mixture. Dissolve yeast and sugar in milk. Place in "well" with sour cream and eggs. Stir all ingredients together, using a large spoon to mix, forming a soft dough. Cover with a damp cloth or merely sift a little flour over the top of dough and place bowl of dough in refrigerator to rise overnight. The next morning, roll out half of dough at a time on well-floured board, forming a circle. Cut 12 pie-shaped wedges from each circle. Put a spoonful of nut filling at wide end of each wedge. Roll up, sealing ends as you start by pulling ends of dough up over the nut mixture, then rolling toward point of dough. Let rise in 2 greased 9-by-12-by-2-inch pans, or use two jelly-roll pans, if preferred. When rolls have doubled in size, bake at 350° for 20 to 25 minutes. Soon after taking from the oven, drizzle top with glaze.

Nut Filling:

¾ cup (1 stick) margarine	½ cup sugar
2 cups walnuts, ground	½ teaspoon cinnamon (optional)

Melt margarine in saucepan and add remaining ingredients.

Glaze:
¾ cup confectioners' sugar
1½ tablespoons water
½ teaspoon vanilla

Stir these 3 ingredients together in cup or bowl and drip over the rolls while they are still very warm from the oven.

Joyce H. Orcutt, *Punta Gorda, Florida*

DESSERTS
Executive Sweet

CREPES SUZETTES
By George Rector

*I suppose that the famous crêpes Suzette are the culminating
outburst of what the continent of Europe can do with a pancake. They do
call for quite an array of liqueur bottles, but that's not so much of a handi-
cap for the American cook as it was a short time ago, so here goes. Follow
my lead and you'll have a stranglehold on one of the most eminent dishes in
the world, and one that really deserves its reputation.*

*You want fairly substantial cakes here, so the eggs take a back seat. The
formula for the batter is half a cup of flour, a tablespoon of sugar and a
quarter teaspoon of salt, into which go half a cup of milk and one egg, to be
stirred coonily until the batter is smooth. Get down the little frying pan—a
little more than five inches is the right diameter—butter it well and, when it's
hot, pour in just enough batter to cover the bottom when you turn it this
way and that. Brown each cake nicely on both sides and stack them in a
warm place while you fix the sauce—a process which will fill the kitchen
with the odors of paradise, although not the teetotal Mohammedan kind.*

*Beforehand you've rubbed eight lumps of sugar on the rinds of a lemon
and an orange until the sugar is full of the oils—not so difficult as it sounds,
although it takes time. Now you can break out the chafing dish that came
with the wedding presents and melt a tablespoon of butter in it, adding four
lumps of sugar to melt with the butter. Then in go a couple of tablespoons
of rum or brandy, ditto of curaçao or Grand Marnier, ditto of benedictine.
While that mixture of good things is getting good and hot, you fold four of
your pancakes in quarters and then, when the sauce is hot as blazes, drop
them in and sort of flop and fiddle with them—toss is the professional
word—until they absorb all the sauce. You'll probably be dizzy from the
smell, but carry on—repeat the sauce, toss the rest of the pancakes—the
above recipe ought to make eight—and then you can sit down and discover
what a swell cook you are.*

SUITE TOOTH
By Mary Alice Sharpe

*To really set the world on fire—or the reverse, which seems to be more
what's wanted these days—serve this with hand-cranked honey ice cream.*

*In a saucepan, mix 1 quart milk, 1 quart heavy cream, 1¾ cups honey.
Heat until lukewarm. (Be careful not to scorch.) Chill. Add 1 tablespoon of
vanilla. Beat six egg whites until stiff. Using the same beater, beat the egg
yolks until thick. Fold into the chilled mixture. Fill chilled freezer container
2/3 full with mixture, adding milk if necessary. Cover tightly, set in freezer
tub and follow directions for right amounts of cracked ice and ice cream
freezer salt. When mixture is frozen, remove dasher. Pack down ice cream.
Replace cover. Return to freezer tub. Set in ice until ready to serve. Makes 1
gallon. To make chocolate, melt 2 cups of chocolate chips in the combination of warm milk and cream.*

Since children will *eat candy, you might try chocolate-nut squares made
by melting a 6-ounce package of semisweet chocolate pieces in 3 tablespoons
of honey and 1 teaspoon of vanilla over very low heat; stir just until the
chocolate is smooth. Add a cup of coarsely chopped pecans or walnuts and
¼ teaspoon of salt. Pat candy into a buttered pan. When cool, cut into
squares.*

CAN'T WAIT APPLE CAKE

4 cups apples, diced	1½ teaspoons soda
½ cup cooking oil	½ teaspoon salt
2 cups sugar	1 teaspoon cinnamon
2 eggs, well beaten	1 teaspoon vanilla
2 cups flour	1 cup chopped walnuts

Combine apples, oil and sugar. Add beaten eggs. Sift together flour, soda, salt and cinnamon and add to batter. Stir in vanilla and nuts. Bake in greased 9-by-13-inch pan in 375° oven for about 45 minutes.

Lillian Freedman, *Van Nuys, California*

AUNT BERTHA SANBORN'S BLUEBERRY CAKE

1 3/4 cups flour	¼ cup shortening or butter
2 tablespoons baking powder	1 egg, beaten
Pinch salt	3/4 cup milk
1 cup sugar	1 cup or more floured berries

Sift together flour, baking powder and salt and set aside. Cream together sugar and shortening. Add egg and milk and beat well. Add sifted dry ingredients. Fold floured berries into the batter before the dry ingredients are completely moist and put in greased and lightly floured 9-by-5-inch loaf pan. Bake in preheated 350° oven 40 to 45 minutes or until top is golden brown. Serves 8.

Miss Lynne Ellen Zalesak, *Harwich Port, Massachusetts*

"Now, that's what I call a rum cake."

MAPLE BLUEBERRY CAKE
WITH LEMON GLAZE

¼ cup shortening
½ cup maple syrup
½ cup brown sugar
3/4 cup sour cream
2 eggs, beaten
3/4 cup blueberries, drained

2 cups flour
1 teaspoon ginger
1 teaspoon baking soda
¼ teaspoon salt
½ cup drained blueberry juice

Heat shortening, syrup, and sugar together in a saucepan. Add sour cream, beaten eggs, and blueberries. Sift dry ingredients, and add to batter. Mix well, and pour in greased 10-inch spring-form pan, or 10-inch bundt pan. Bake in 350° oven for 30 minutes, or until inserted knife comes out dry. After cake cools, pour reserved blueberry juice over the cake (this allows for the cake to become extra moist, before applying the lemon glaze).

Lemon Glaze:

1 tablespoon milk
2 tablespoons lemon juice
¾ cup confectioners' sugar

Gradually blend milk and lemon juice into confectioners' sugar and pour over cake before serving, let glaze set; then slice cake. Serves 10 to 12.
Mrs. Martha Swanson, *Killingworth, Connecticut*

HOLIDAY APPLE CAKE

3 cups chopped peeled baking apples
3/4 cup sugar
3/4 cup golden raisins
1/3 cup chopped almonds
3 tablespoons flour
1 teaspoon cinnamon
2½ cups unsifted flour
2 teaspoons baking powder

1½ teaspoons salt
2 eggs
1/3 cup oil
1/3 cup water
1/3 cup sugar
1½ teaspoons vanilla
Confectioners' sugar frosting

Combine chopped apples, 3/4 cup sugar, raisins, chopped nuts, 3 tablespoons flour and cinnamon. Set aside. Blend the flour, baking powder and salt. Beat together eggs, oil, water, 1/3 cup sugar and vanilla. Gradually stir in flour mixture until completely blended. Turn batter out onto well-floured board; with floured hands shape batter into ball and divide into 3 equal pieces. Roll out one piece to make a 9-inch square. Place it in an oiled 9-inch square baking pan. Cover with half of the apple mixture. Roll out the second piece just as the first piece and place over the apple layer; then cover with remaining apple mixture. Roll out third piece of dough also to 9-inch square and place over second apple layer to form top crust. Make several slits in it to allow the steam to escape. Bake in 350° oven 60 to 70 minutes. While warm frost with confectioners' sugar frosting. Frosting: Mix 1 cup confectioners' sugar with 2 tablespoons milk or water and ¼ teaspoon vanilla extract. Spread on warm cake. Serves 9.
Mrs. E. Duncan, *New Britain, Connecticut*

CARIN' ABOUTCHA CARROT CAKE

2 cups flour
2 teaspoons baking powder
1 teaspoon salt
1½ teaspoons soda
2 teaspoons cinnamon
2 cups sugar

1½ cups oil
4 eggs
2 cups grated carrots
1 (8½-ounce) can crushed pineapple
½ cup chopped nuts

Combine flour, baking powder, salt, soda and cinnamon. Add sugar, oil and eggs. Mix well. Add carrots, drained pineapple and nuts. Bake in 9-by-13-inch greased and floured pan at 350° for 35 to 40 minutes.

Frosting: (Optional)

½ cup butter
1 (8-ounce) package cream cheese
1 teaspoon vanilla

1 pound powdered sugar
Milk

Cream butter, cream cheese and vanilla. Add powdered sugar. If too thick, add milk to spreading consistency. Serves 12.

Lee Craig Douglas, *Los Angeles, California*

AUNT DOROTHY'S CHEESECAKE

13 graham crackers
3 tablespoons butter
1 pound cream cheese

1 cup sugar
3 eggs
1 teaspoon vanilla

Topping

1 pint sour cream
1 tablespoon sugar
½ teaspoon vanilla

Crush graham crackers; combine with butter and line an 8-by-12-inch or an 8-by-8-inch baking dish. Blend cream cheese, sugar, eggs and vanilla. Pour mixture in lining and bake 25 to 35 minutes in 350° preheated oven. Mix sour cream with 1 tablespoon sugar and ½ teaspoon vanilla. Spread this topping on cake after it has cooled. Place in oven at 300° for 5 minutes. Refrigerate overnight.

Mrs. Harry S. Gill, *South Yarmouth, Massachusetts*

CREAM CAKE

4 eggs, separated
1½ cups sugar
½ pint heavy cream

1 teaspoon vanilla
1¾ cups (self-rising)
  cake flour

Beat egg yolks until lemon colored. Add sugar and beat until well combined. Add cream and vanilla and blend at low speed. Add cake flour and mix thoroughly. Beat egg whites until stiff and fold into batter. Pour into greased 9-inch or 10-inch tube pan. Bake in 350° oven for approximately 1 hour.

Mrs. Donald S. Law, *Bradenton, Florida*

FROZEN MINT JULEP PIE

1 1/3 cups crushed zwieback or
    chocolate wafer crumbs
2 tablespoons sugar
¼ cup melted butter
1 envelope unflavored gelatin
½ cup sugar

1/8 teaspoon salt
3 eggs, separated
1 cup light cream
¼ cup bourbon
2 tablespoons mint-flavored jelly
1 cup heavy cream, whipped

Combine crumbs, 2 tablespoons sugar and melted butter. Butter a 10-inch pie plate and press crumbs firmly into the bottom and against sides of pan. Chill.

Combine gelatin, ¼ cup sugar, and salt in medium saucepan. Beat egg yolks lightly and add with light cream and bourbon to gelatin mixture. Cook over low heat, stirring constantly until custard coats the spoon. Stir in mint jelly. Chill until mixture begins to thicken. Beat egg whites to soft peaks. Gradually beat in remaining ¼ cup sugar; beat until meringue is stiff. Fold meringue and whipped cream into the thickened custard. Turn into crumb crust. Place in freezer until firm. To serve: remove to refrigerator shelf 2 hours before cutting. Garnish with sprigs of fresh mint. Makes 8 to 10 servings.

Bess Slagle, *St. Peters, Missouri*

CHOICE PUMPKIN PIE

1 8-inch pie crust
1 tablespoon butter
1 cup rich milk, scalded
2 large eggs, beaten slightly
2/3 cup white sugar

¼ teaspoon salt
¼ teaspoon ginger
1/3 teaspoon mace
½ teaspoon cinnamon
1 cup light golden pumpkin

Add butter to scalded milk. Mix beaten eggs with sugar. Add salt, ginger, mace and cinnamon to pumpkin and add to egg mixture. Gradually add milk, beating gently just until mixed (not foamy). Pour into unbaked pie crust and bake in preheated 450° oven about 10 to 12 minutes to set crust. Then lower heat to 400° for about 5 minutes. As crust begins to turn a delicate brown on edges, lower heat to about 300° (filling must never start to bubble; if it should, you may have to lower heat to about 275°). Bake until a knife blade inserted in the center of the pie comes out clean. If baked properly, the entire crust should be a light golden brown on the bottom. Serve with butterscotch whipped cream below.

Butterscotch Sauce

1¼ cups brown sugar
2/3 cup dark corn syrup
4 tablespoons butter
3/4 cup thin cream

1 pint heavy cream, whipped
1 teaspoon vanilla
1 teaspoon rum flavoring

Mix brown sugar, syrup and butter in pan and bring to a boil, stirring constantly until syrup forms a very soft ball in cold water. Remove from heat and immediately pour in 3/4 cup thin cream. Beat cream into the syrup until thoroughly mixed. Pour into jars, leaving a 2-inch space at the top for mixing the sauce each time before it is served. Cover; refrigerate. This sauce keeps indefinitely under refrigeration. For a double recipe of the pie, whip 1 pint of cream until just stiff. Fold in ½ cup of the butterscotch sauce; add 1 teaspoon vanilla and 1 teaspoon rum flavoring. Serve on top of each slice of pie.

Crust for Pumpkin Pie

3 cups flour
½ teaspoon salt
1 cup lard

1/3 cup vinegar
1/3 cup cold water

Mix flour with salt. Cut in lard until like fine meal. Mix vinegar and cold water and add to flour mixture. Mix until dough will leave the bowl in a clean ball. Wrap in plastic wrap and put in plastic bag. Seal tightly and refrigerate. Makes 2 medium-size double crust pies. Remove from refrigerator an hour or two before using.

Ruth G. Gleason, *Helena, Montana*

RAISIN-BLACK WALNUT PIE

1 unbaked 8-inch pie shell
4 eggs, beaten
½ cup brown sugar, packed
½ cup white sugar

¼ cup soft butter or margarine
1½ cups light corn syrup
1 cup black walnuts
1 cup chopped raisins

Combine eggs, sugar, butter and beat until thick and fluffy. Add syrup and beat well. Fold in nutmeats and raisins. Stir gently. Turn into unbaked pie shell and bake in 375° preheated oven for 40 to 50 minutes or until center is firm. Serve plain or topped with ice cream or whipped cream. Serves 6.
Mrs. Lyle H. Camp, *Fullerton, California*

78

EGGNOG PIE

1 baked 9-inch pastry shell
1½ teaspoons unflavored gelatin
2 tablespoons cold water
3 egg yolks
2/3 cup sugar
1/8 teaspoon salt

1 teaspoon vanilla
2 tablespoons milk
3 egg whites
½ cup heavy cream, whipped
2 to 4 tablespoons rum (optional)
1 teaspoon nutmeg

Soak gelatin in cold water. Beat egg yolks, add 1/3 cup of sugar, salt, vanilla, and milk. Cook over very low heat until thickened. Add gelatin to hot custard mixture. Stir until completely dissolved. Beat egg whites until stiff but not dry; gradually beat in other 1/3 cup of sugar. Fold the custard mixture into the egg whites. Set aside to cool. Fold in whipped cream and rum. Pour into baked pastry shell. Sprinkle top with nutmeg and place in refrigerator until firm. Serves 6 to 8.
Mrs. Frank C. Volpert, *Peru, Indiana*

GRAND FINALE PIE

1 baked 9-inch pastry shell
2 egg whites
1 cup sugar
2 tablespoons water
¼ teaspoon cream of tartar
¼ teaspoon salt

½ cup chocolate chips
1 cup coconut
1 cup chopped nuts
1 teaspoon vanilla
2 cups whipped cream
   or whipped topping

Combine in the top of a double boiler the first five ingredients. Beat with an electric mixer over boiling water for 5 minutes until the mixture stands in stiff peaks. Remove from hot water; add chocolate chips. Let stand about 10 minutes to melt. Fold coconut, nuts and vanilla into the cooked mixture. Cool, then fold in whipped cream. Gently pile into baked pastry shell. Refrigerate for an hour or longer. Serves 6 to 8.
Marleen Carol Johnson, *Robbinsdale, Minnesota*

AFTER DINNER COCKTAIL PIE

Vanilla Wafer Crumb Crust

1½ cups crushed vanilla wafers
1/3 cup melted butter or margarine

Mix vanilla wafer crumbs and melted butter well. Press mixture into bottom and around sides of a 9-inch pie plate. Bake in preheated 375° oven for 8 minutes. Cool.

Cocktail Chiffon Filling

2¾ teaspoons unflavored gelatin
  (little less than 1 package)
¼ cup cold water
¼ cup egg yolks (about 4 large)
5/8 cup sugar
¼ teaspoon salt

1/3 cup fresh lime juice
3 drops green food coloring
1/3 cup light rum
5/8 cup egg whites at room
  temperature (about 4 large)
¼ cup sugar

Soften gelatin in cold water. Beat egg yolks with 5/8 cup sugar and salt until light in top of double boiler. Add lime juice gradually. Cook over boiling water, stirring constantly, until mixture thickens slightly—about 3 to 4 minutes. Do not over cook! Remove from heat. Add softened gelatin and stir in thoroughly. Add food coloring and rum. Chill in refrigerator until mixture thickens—20 to 25 minutes. Beat egg whites until foamy throughout; gradually add remaining ¼ cup sugar and continue to beat until they hold shape in distinct folds. Gently fold the cooled lime-rum mixture into the egg whites. Pour into cooled Vanilla Wafer Crust and chill.

Whipped Cream Topping

1 cup heavy cream
2 tablespoons sugar
½ teaspoon vanilla extract

Combine heavy cream, sugar, and vanilla. Whip until soft peaks form. Spread on pie and decorate with finely grated lime rind.

  Donald L. Herman, *Yardley, Pennsylvania*

HELEN'S LEMON PIE

1 baked 8-inch pie shell
1½ cups sugar
3 tablespoons cornstarch
1 tablespoon flour
Pinch of salt

Grated rind and juice of
  1½ lemons
1½ cups water
3 eggs, separated
3 teaspoons sugar

Combine sugar, cornstarch, flour and salt. Add grated lemon rind and juice, water and egg yolks. Cook until thick in double boiler and pour into baked pie shell. Beat egg whites. Gradually add 3 teaspoons sugar and beat until snowy white and stiff. Spread on top of pie. Bake at 350° for 15 minutes to brown. Serves 6.

Mrs. Helen L. Mayo, *Benton, Illinois*

GOLDEN NUGGET DISCOVERY PIE

Pastry:

1¼ cups all-purpose flour
½ teaspoon salt
½ cup shortening

3 tablespoons instant cocoa
3 tablespoons boiling water

Filling:

1/3 cup sugar
1 (8-ounce) package cream cheese
2 tablespoons milk
2 unbeaten eggs

1 tablespoon grated orange rind
1 teaspoon vanilla
½ cup (2 medium) orange sections,
   cut into small pieces

Prepare pastry: Combine the flour and salt. Measure the shortening, instant cocoa and water into mixing bowl; mix well. Add dry ingredients all at once. Stir quickly until mixture holds together. Form into a ball. Flatten to ½-inch thickness. Roll out between lightly floured waxed paper to a circle 1½ inches larger than an inverted 8-inch pie pan. Fit loosely into pan; prick with fork. Fold edge to form rim; flute. Bake at 425° for 12 to 15 minutes.

Prepare orange cheese filling: Cream the sugar and cream cheese with the milk. Add eggs, one at a time, beating well after each. Blend in orange rind and vanilla. Fold in orange sections. Pour into baked shell. Bake at 350° for 20 to 25 minutes, until center is almost firm. Chill. If desired, top with Orange Whipped Cream and sprinkle with chopped toasted almonds about 1 hour before serving. Chill. Serves 6 to 8.

Orange Whipped Cream: Beat 1 cup whipping cream until thick. Stir in 2 tablespoons sugar and 2 tablespoons grated orange rind.

Mrs. Harold Johnston *Anaheim, California*

HARVEY WALLBANGER PIE

22 chocolate wafers rolled fine
4 tablespoons melted butter

Mix wafers and butter together. Pat into a 9-inch greased pie pan covering bottom and sides. Bake 8 minutes. Cool.

22 marshmallows
3/4 cup orange juice
1 tablespoon Cointreau

3 tablespoons Galliano
½ teaspoon grated orange rind
1 pint whipped cream

Melt marshmallows with orange juice in top of double boiler over boiling water. Cool. Add Galliano, Cointreau, and grated orange rind. Refrigerate until slightly thickened. Fold in half of whipped cream. Pour into crust. Refrigerate until firm. Garnish with remaining whipped cream.

Marjorie V. Anderson, *Mount Zion, Illinois*

BRANDIED CHERRY
BUTTER BALLS

Cookie Dough

2/3 cup granulated white sugar
½ teaspoon double-acting
  baking powder
¼ teaspoon salt
½ cup butter or

margarine (softened)
1 large unbeaten egg
1 teaspoon imitation brandy extract
1¾ cups pre-sifted all-purpose flour

Brandied Cherry Filling

30 maraschino cherries
  (drained on paper toweling)
1 tablespoon pure honey

1 teaspoon imitation brandy extract
3 tablespoons walnuts, chopped

Glaze

1 cup unsifted confectioners' sugar
1 tablespoon light corn syrup
2 tablespoons maraschino cherry juice

(heated until hot)
½ teaspoon imitation brandy extract

Prepare brandied cherry filling by placing cherries close together on wax paper. Combine honey and brandy and brush tops of cherries with this combination using a pastry brush. Sprinkle cherries with walnuts. Set aside.

Make cookie dough by combining all ingredients except flour in a large mixing bowl and beat at low speed for 1 minute. Gradually add the flour at low speed until a stiff dough forms (about 1 minute). Form dough into a large ball. Pinch small balls of dough (1 well-rounded teaspoonful) from prepared dough; flatten with fingers in palm of hand to about 1/8-inch thickness. Place 1 brandied cherry with honey and nuts on it in center of dough. Roll to form a ball. Repeat with remaining dough and cherries. Place each ball on an ungreased cookie sheet about 2 inches apart and bake on second and third oven racks from bottom of preheated 350° oven for 12 to 15 minutes, until cookies are delicately golden color.

When cookies are cool, make glaze and spread about ½ teaspoonful on top and sides of each cookie using the inside of teaspoon to spread glaze. Place on wax paper until glaze sets. Yield: 2½ dozen.

Mrs. Gloria Dutrumble, *Uncasville, Connecticut*

HONEY BARS

½ cup shortening
½ cup sugar
½ cup honey
1 egg, well beaten
2/3 cup sifted flour
½ teaspoon baking soda

½ teaspoon baking powder
¼ teaspoon salt
1 cup quick-cooking rolled oats
1 cup flaked coconut
1 teaspoon vanilla
½ cup chopped nuts

Cream shortening, sugar and honey until light and fluffy. Add egg and blend. Sift flour with soda, baking powder and salt; add to creamed mixture. Add oats, coconut, vanilla and nuts. Spread in greased 10½-by-15-inch pan; bake in 350° oven for 20 to 25 minutes. When cool, cut into bars. Yield: 36 bars.

Madelyn E. Jones, *Waterbury, Connecticut*

BUTTERSCOTCH COOKIES

½ cup margarine or butter
1½ cups light brown sugar,
   packed in cup
2 eggs
2½ cups all-purpose flour
½ teaspoon double-action

   baking powder
1 teaspoon soda
½ teaspoon salt
1 cup sour cream
1 teaspoon vanilla
½ cup nuts (optional)

Cream margarine and sugar. Add eggs and beat. Sift flour, baking powder, soda and salt together and add alternately to batter with the sour cream to which vanilla has been added. Stir in nuts and chill until dough is firm. Drop by teaspoons 2 inches apart on lightly greased baking sheet. Bake 10 to 15 minutes in moderate hot oven (about 400°.)

Brown Butter Icing

1/3 cup butter
1½ cups sifted confectioners' sugar

1 teaspoon vanilla
1 to 2 tablespoons hot water

Melt butter over low heat until golden brown. Blend in confectioners' sugar and vanilla. Stir in slowly 1 to 2 tablespoons hot water until of consistency to spread.

Kathleen Wagner, *Peru, Indiana*

82

"Would you mind repeating that recipe—without the arsenic?"

ALMOND CUSTARD

1 cup almonds, grated or ground
3 eggs
¼ cup sugar
1/8 teaspoon salt
2 cups milk, scalded
1 teaspoon almond flavoring

Sprinkle bottoms of 5 custard cups with half of the almonds and press down
Beat eggs until light. Add sugar and salt. Stir scalded milk into egg mixture.
Add almond flavoring and pour into cups. Sprinkle the remaining almonds
on top. Bake in 350° oven 40 to 45 minutes. Serves 5.

Mrs. Deveaux M. Ackley, *Jackson, Mississippi*

CRESCENT APPLE DESSERT

1 package refrigerated crescent rolls
4 tablespoons soft butter
1/8 cup cinnamon-sugar mix
2 cups warm applesauce
1½ teaspoons cinnamon
½ cup sour cream
   (or sweet whipped cream)

Open rolls, attach 2 triangles, making a square. Place on cookie sheet. Repeat
with other roll. Butter tops and sprinkle with cinnamon-sugar mix. Bake in
350° oven for 10 minutes. Split and butter bottoms. Alternate pastry and
applesauce (flavored with cinnamon). End with sugared top. Spread with
sour cream or sweet whipped cream. Serve warm. Cut servings with a knife
and serve with a spoon. Serves 4.

Mrs. Carl L. Johnson, *Pompton Plains, New Jersey*

APPLE-RAISIN-NUT PUDDING

2 cups chopped tart apples
½ cup raisins
1 cup chopped nut meats,
   preferably pecans
1 cup sugar
¼ cup vegetable shortening
1 egg, large
1 cup flour
1 teaspoon baking powder
1 teaspoon soda
1 teaspoon cinnamon
¼ teaspoon nutmeg
¼ teaspoon salt

Topping

2 tablespoons melted butter
5 tablespoons brown sugar
2 tablespoons cream

Wash, quarter and core unpeeled apples. Run apples through food chopper
and measure. Run raisins and nut meats through food chopper. Cream sugar
and shortening; add egg and beat until waxy. Sift dry ingredients into
creamed mixture; batter will be stiff, the only liquid being the chopped
apples. Add chopped apples, raisins and nuts to batter. Beat until well
mixed. Pour into 9-by-13-inch shallow pan (greased). Bake about 40 minutes
in a 350° oven. Before removing from oven prepare a mixture of butter,
sugar and cream and pour over hot cake. Place under broiler until lightly
browned. Serve plain or with whipped cream. Serves 12.

Mrs. Artia Chambers, *Skiatook, Oklahoma*

INSTANT MOCHA CREAM LOG

1 cup heavy cream
1 cup cold milk
2 teaspoons instant coffee
1 (4½-ounce) package instant

chocolate pudding
1 cup chopped nuts
1 (6-inch) bakery jelly roll

Pour cream and milk into a deep mixing bowl. Add instant coffee and pudding. Beat until well mixed, about 1 minute. Fold in nuts. Gently unroll jelly roll and spread with half of pudding mixture. Roll up and frost with remaining pudding mixture. Freeze until firm. Slice into 6 servings.
Mrs. Olga Jason, *New Bedford, Massachusetts*

ELEGANT MAI TAI MOUSSE

18 ladyfingers, split
2 envelopes unflavored gelatin
½ cup pineapple juice
   (from crushed drained pineapple)
5 egg yolks
¾ cup sugar
¼ teaspoon salt
1 cup milk, scalded
1/3 cup lime juice

1/3 cup white rum
1 (#211) can crushed pineapple,
   well drained
5 egg whites
½ cup sugar
1 cup heavy cream, whipped
¼ cup chopped macadamia nuts
   or walnuts

Line sides and bottom of 9-inch spring pan with split ladyfingers. Soften gelatin in pineapple juice. Beat egg yolks in top of double boiler. Stir in sugar and salt. Blend in milk, cook over boiling water, stirring for 5 minutes or until thickened. Blend in gelatin-pineapple mixture, lime juice and rum. Add well-drained pineapple. Chill until thickened but not set. Beat egg whites, adding sugar. Fold pineapple custard and whipped cream into egg whites. Pour into lined pan. Chill several hours or overnight. To serve, remove pan rim. Sprinkle with nuts. Serves 12.

ORANGE BABA DESSERT

1 (13¾-ounce) package hot roll mix
¾ cup warm water
2 eggs
2 tablespoons melted butter

2 tablespoons sugar
1½ teaspoons grated orange rind
1 tablespoon brandy (or
   2 teaspoons vanilla)

In large mixing bowl, combine warm water with yeast (from hot roll mix). Stir until dissolved. Stir in eggs, melted butter, sugar, orange rind, and brandy. Add flour a little at a time and beat well, until batter resembles cake batter. Butter a 9-inch torte pan; half fill, spooning into pan. Cover and let rise until double in size (about 30 to 45 minutes). Preheat oven to 375°. Bake 20 to 30 minutes, or until brown. (If browning too fast, cover with brown paper.) Turn baba out on a serving dish and baste with hot syrup until all syrup is absorbed. Garnish with sliced almonds. Serves 6.

Orange Baba Syrup

Bring to a boil 1 cup sugar and 1 cup water. Add 1 tablespoon butter and one 6-ounce can frozen orange juice concentrate.
Mrs. Joe Hrvatin, *Spokane, Washington*

INTERNATIONAL SPECIALTIES

The World in Your Hand

BALLOTINE DE DINDE
By Ruth M. Malone

One of the world's experts on bringing exciting new ideas to family dining is Ruth M. Malone, author of The Dogpatch Cook Book, Where to Eat in the Ozarks, *the* Holiday Inn International Cook Book, *and articles beyond mention for national magazines, among them* The Saturday Evening Post. *It is from her recipes in the* Post, *specializing in international flavor, that the following are selected. The peripatetic lady really knows whereof she speaks, worldwide.*

10- to 12-pound turkey
3 black truffles
  (1 small can)
½ cup shelled and
  skinned pistachio
  nuts
6-ounce piece of
  cooked ham
6-ounce piece of
  cooked smoked
  tongue
1 cup dry port
  wine or cognac
Pepper and salt
½ pound butter

¾ pound veal and ¾
  pound pork ground
  together very finely
3 eggs
2 onions, chopped
1 clove garlic
2 teaspoons salt
Dash of pepper
Pinch of allspice
½ teaspoon ground
  thyme
Needle, white
  thread
Butcher's twine

The day before: put out all your ingredients. Dice the truffles, shell pistachio nuts, cut ham and tongue into finger-shaped pieces. Put pork and veal mixture into a large mixing bowl. Add lightly beaten eggs, thyme, allspice, salt, pepper, crushed clove of garlic, ¾ cup of port or cognac. Mix till light. Gently saute the onion in a quarter pound of butter. Take almost 10 minutes to do this, cooking onions so gently that they only yellow and do not brown. Add onions and butter to the bowl. Mix thoroughly. This is the stuffing. Put boned turkey flat on the table, skin side down. Season the meat side (inside) with pepper and remaining wine. Spread a layer of stuffing inside the turkey. Then sprinkle pistachio nuts, truffles, ham and tongue over it. Repeat both steps twice. Sew up turkey. Tie in 4 places as you would a rolled roast, making sure stuffing does not go to the ends. Salt, pepper and brush the skin with melted butter. Store in refrigerator until four hours before dinner. Christmas Day: Roast turkey breast side up in a 350-degree oven, allowing 20 minutes per pound. Keep basting top and sides to insure even browning. Serve with natural pan gravy. Serves 8 to 10 easily. If you wish to serve a wine with the dinner, Chassagne Montrachet 1959 is recommended. It is a mildly sweet white wine that will suit most palates.
(Note: The pate maison used for stuffing the ballotine makes a delicious stuffing for a turkey that has all its bones.)

MERINGUE GLACEE

A memorable dessert that is light enough to follow a Christmas dinner is suggested. You may also use peach ice cream and peach slices, or other combinations.

1 cup sifted
  granulated sugar
4 egg whites
Pinch of salt
¼ teaspoon cream
  of tartar

almond extract
1 quart strawberries
1 quart ice cream
1 cup red
  currant jelly
2 tablespoons cognac

Cover cookie sheet with greased, unglazed brown paper. Beat egg whites until foamy. Add salt, and cream of tartar and continue beating until peaks form. Add sugar very slowly, beating until sugar is dissolved. Add the vanilla. Drop by mounded teaspoonful onto brown paper. Bake in 250-degree oven for 1½ hours. At the end of the time, turn off oven, open door and allow meringues to cool in the oven. Leave on paper until ready to use. Christmas Day: Hull the strawberries. Melt the currant jelly and cognac over a low fire. Put ice cream on the dish, surround it with strawberries. Pour warm sauce on the berries and top with meringues.

RED SNAPPER A LA VERACRUZANA
(Huachinango a la Veracruzana)

1 2½-pound red snapper
2½ cups chopped tomatoes
2 onions, chopped
3 green peppers, chopped
3 cloves garlic, crushed
1 bunch parsley,
  chopped fine
2 chili peppers,
  chopped fine
  (small elongated
  green chili)

1/3 cup finely chopped
  green olives
1/3 cup capers
4 tablespoons vinegar
8 jalapeño peppers
  (cut in half,
  fried and cut in strips)
1 pint oil
1 teaspoon oregano
Salt and pepper
¼ pint dry sherry

Cut red snapper into 6-ounce fillets. Saute the tomatoes in a skillet, adding onions, then green peppers, garlic, parsley and chili peppers. Then add chopped olives, capers, vinegar and jalapeño strips. Blend in oil. Season with oregano, salt and pepper. Simmer slowly until all is tender and thickened. Add sherry during last part of cooking.

    In a separate skillet, heat a little oil and add well-washed red snapper fillets. Cover fish with sauce. Cover and cook over low heat 20 minutes. Keep fish from sticking with wide spatula. Serve with rice. Serves 4 to 6.

AUNT ELIZA'S BID FOR FAME
By Sophie Kerr

In my Scotch-Irish family there was one aunt who married among the Pennsylvania Dutch, and it was she who, ever-blessed, imparted the recipe for making the local form of peach pie. It is as follows: Line a pie pan with the raw crust and fill it with halves of very ripe yellow peaches, hollow side up. Lay the peaches close together, sprinkle heavily with granulated sugar, then pour in enough thick sour cream to cover the peach halves, and sprinkle on more sugar if needed. Then put on your crisscross strips, pinch them well at the edges, and slide this concoction into the oven for a slow, careful baking. If you want to add two or three kernels taken from cracked peach stones, you'll have a subtle bitter-almond flavor—indeed, a few peach kernels add chic to any peach pie, whether made a la Aunt Aliza or not.

IRELAND'S GIFT TO APPETITES
By George Rector

If it's a short-term trip, you can get the ingredients ready before you start, and pack them in a large pot and two saucepans. You'll want to scrape six medium-sized carrots, peel four potatoes, dice two green peppers into inch cubes, cut up half a cup of leeks and half a cup of celery crosswise, lay in a dozen small white onions and a cup of canned tomato pulp. Also you pack along a mixture of of a teaspoon of mixed mustard, and a tablespoon each of Worcestershire sauce, A-1 sauce and tomato ketchup. That begins to sound good already to me. Also—this is the business end—three pounds chuck of lamb, a pound of breast of lamb and a pound chuck of beef, all cut into two-inch cubes and with as much fat as possible trimmed off the lamb. It sounds like food for a regiment, I know, but don't try to get more than six grown people into one stew if you serve it outdoors after waiting for it to cook.

Simmer your beef for an hour. Then start the lamb in a separate pan and simmer both for another half hour, skimming the fat off the lamb water all the time. Then lamb and beef go into the big pot, along with the liquid, plus the potatoes and carrots quartered, the green peppers, the onions, leeks and celery. Let them all coop up harmoniously for half an hour. Ten minutes before that, put in the tomato pulp and the seasoning, and take the pot off the fire—but keep it right next door, so she'll stay plenty hot. At Dinty Moore's they garnish the end product with a sprinkling of peas and a tablespoon of chopped parsley, but it's a roaring, ranting fine dish without that extra wrinkle and well worth the two hours of nursing it calls for. Let the rest of the party go off and chase butterflies or listen to the echo; you stick around and startle your and their palates with this stew of stews.

JEWISH COOKING
By Sylvia Schur

"Eat a little something," that familiar, age-old Jewish welcome, is an almost unnecessary invitation. In the presence of good Jewish cooking, it is nearly impossible to stop eating. "And it isn't just the food itself," explains one young matron. "It's partly the mood and the memories. I remember that as a child in our New York neighborhood, with the aromas of gefilte fish, roast chicken and yeast cake coming from every house, I couldn't get home fast enough. It was the same every Friday. And the baking of challah, that wonderful Sabbath bread, has as much religious fervor as cooking skill. Even now such smells seem to me like Peace and Love and Warmth. You know what I mean. If Betty Crocker could put those smells up in box mixes, we could end juvenile delinquency."

Jewish cooking today is an amalgam of contributions, picked up by generations of merchants and migrants who wandered the countries of the earth. In the melting-pot processes of the big city these culinary contributions have simmered down to a tasty heritage known as "New York-style Jewish cooking." In the more than three centuries since the first Jewish pioneer group arrived in New Amsterdam, this influence has spread till most cities in the United States today can enjoy its specialties.

GEFILTE FISH

3 pounds carp	2 eggs
2 pounds whitefish	¼ cup water
1 pound yellow pike	Salt, white pepper
3 onions	1 tablespoon cracker meal
Salt, whole peppercorns	2 carrots, scraped

Have fish dealer fillet fish, reserving heads and bones for stock. Salt fillets and refrigerate. Cover heads, bones, two peeled onions, salt and peppercorns with 1 quart water; bring to boil, simmer 20 minutes. Meanwhile put fish fillets and 1 onion through grinder with fine blade. Place in wooden chopping bowl. Add eggs, lightly beaten with water, salt, pepper and cracker meal. Chop mixture till light and well blended. Moisten hands with cold water and shape into loose balls. Slip into boiling stock with a spoon, add water if necessary to cover and simmer 1½ hours. Add carrots and cook another half hour until fish balls are white and about twice original size. Lift fish balls out with slotted spoon. Remove carrots, slice and set aside. Strain stock and pour half over fish. Pour remainder into jar; refrigerate to set. Serve cold, garnishing the fish with sliced carrot and chilled stock. Serves about 12.

SWEET AND SOUR POT ROAST

6 pounds beef
2 large onions, sliced
1 clove minced garlic
¾ cup of water or stock
2 bay leaves
2 tablespoons lemon juice

or vinegar
1 tablespoon brown
  sugar
3 tablespoons ketchup
½ cup raisins
Salt

Brown meat in hot fat on all sides, using heavy pot. Add onions and garlic, cook till brown. Add water or stock and bay leaves; cover and simmer one hour. Add lemon juice and brown sugar. Cover and simmer another hour. Add ketchup, raisins and salt. Cover and cook ½ hour. Serve hot with potato pancakes, noodles or brown rice. Serves 6 to 8 persons.

NOODLE FRUIT CAPON STUFFING

½ pound broad noodles, cooked
4 tablespoons fat (preferably
  chicken fat)
1 medium onion, minced
Liver and gizzards, chopped
1 tablespoon salt
1 teaspoon paprika

¼ teaspoon pepper
¼ teaspoon ginger
2 tablespoons minced parsley
1 cup minced apples
1 cup prunes, stewed and cut
Grated rind of 1 orange
1 beaten egg

Cook noodles, drain, rinse with cold water and drain well. Toss with one tablespoon of fat. Heat remaining fat, add onions, liver, gizzards, seasonings and parsley; brown. Stir in apples, prunes and grated rind. Add mixture to noodles in a large bowl, toss. Stir in beaten egg. Pack stuffing loosely in cavity of 6- to 8-pound capon, truss. Rub outside of capon with oil, place breast up in shallow roasting pan and bake in 350° oven for two to two and a half hours, basting with oil from time to time.

SABBATH CHOLENT

3 to 4 pounds of beef
1 pound dried Lima beans
3 large onions, sliced
¼ cup chicken fat
Salt, pepper and paprika

1 small clove garlic
½ pound barley
2 tablespoons flour
Boiling water to cover

For the meat use flanken or brisket. Soak beans overnight; then drain. Using heavy-duty pot, brown onions in hot fat, remove. Rub meat generously with salt, pepper, paprika, and garlic. Brown well in hot fat. Add all ingredients; sprinkle lightly with flour. Add boiling water to cover. Cover tightly and bring to boil. Taste, adjust salt, pepper. To finish cooking, place covered pot in 250° oven overnight and until noon next day or cook in 350i oven for 3 to 4 hours. Serves 10 to 12.

RICH NOODLE PUDDING

½ pound medium egg noodles
3 tablespoons butter
1 package (8 ounces) cream cheese
½ pound cottage cheese
½ cup sour cream
3 eggs, separated
½ teaspoon salt

½ cup sugar
1 teaspoon cinnamon
1 cup sliced peeled apples
¼ cup broken walnut meats
1 teaspoon grated lemon rind
½ cup white raisins

Cook noodles in boiling, salted water. Drain. Toss with butter in large bowl. Break up cream cheese with fork, add cottage cheese and sour cream and beat until light. Add egg yolks, beat well. Pour over noodles in bowl. Add remaining ingredients, except egg whites, and mix well. Beat egg whites stiff, fold in. Pour into greased casserole. Bake in 350° oven about 45 minutes, or until browned. Serves 6.

DANISH-AMERICAN WINNER
By Robert W. Wells

Mrs. Beck's Honskekod suppe *(chicken soup) with meat balls and dumplings:*

Soup:

One 3- to 4-pound chicken
2 teaspoons salt
1 soup wisp (celery leaves and

parsley tied together)
1 small onion
2 or 3 small whole carrots

Meatballs:

1 pound ground pork
1 cup milk
1 medium-sized onion
½ teaspoon pepper

1/3 cup flour (or bread crumbs)
1 egg
1 teaspoon salt

Dumplings:

1 cup boiling water
½ cup butter
1 cup flour

4 eggs
½ teaspoon salt

Cut up chicken. Place in boiling water. Add wisp, onion, carrots, salt. Water should just cover chicken. Simmer until done.

To make meatballs, stir milk into ground pork, adding grated onion, flour or bread crumbs, egg, salt, pepper. Mix thoroughly. Form into balls. Boil until done in salt water.

Dumplings: Melt butter in boiling water. Add flour and beat until smooth. Cool, then add eggs, one at a time, and beat well. Add salt. Use teaspoon to drop dumpling mix into hot but not boiling salt water. Bring to boil, agitating water gently so dumplings will turn over. Boil about two minutes.

Put several dumplings and meat balls into each dish. Slice carrots and put a few slices into each dish. Remove chicken from soup and serve it separately. Remove wisp, which may be thrown away or eaten by the cook. Pour soup on top of dumplings and meatballs. Garnish with sprinkled parsley. Serves 6 to 8.

VONDERFUL NICE
By Bill Wolf

Picnics bring out the cat in Dutch women. They contrive to sample rival cooks' products, conceal their own recipes and try to acquire those of other women. A confirmed taster will try everything on the long tables, then say to a select group of friends: "That potato salad made by Sadie Habecker, it's vonderful nice, of course, but"—she will pause judiciously—"it don't seem to have zaktly the right amount of bacon drippin's. Do you spose she uses celery salt as vell as celery?"

Everything really did taste "vonderful nice"—Dutch cold pressed chicken, cold ham, beef, pork, cold fried chicken, pickled and deviled eggs, an amazing variety of cakes and pies, and always the Dutch potato salad. There are many variations. This is the way I know it best:

Boil and cube eight potatoes or cut them in thick half slices. Add diced celery, four chopped hard-boiled eggs, at least one onion chopped fine—even more skilled cooks scrape the juice from the onion over the potatoes. Now for the dressing: Fry eight slices of bacon cut into small pieces. In a separate bowl, mix a half cup of water, same amount of vinegar, a half teaspoon of salt, quarter teaspoon each of dry mustard and black pepper, two well-beaten eggs. Stir and add to hot bacon and fat.

After this mixture thickened on the stove, it was poured over the cold ingredients, everything was stirred slightly and set aside to cool. A somewhat similar sour dressing, minus the mustard and plus some butter, cream and sugar, is poured hot over dandelions in the spring for greens, or on lettuce leaves.

SHOOFLY PIE

Then there are the pies, such as the famous shoofly, which are really cakes in a pastry shell. Addicts of the shoofly—the name is probably a corruption of chouflour, *since the finished pie somewhat resembles a cauliflower—are sharply divided into Wets and Drys, although both camps would probably agree that the molasses that goes into a shoofly is the most important factor. With many perfectionist cooks, the bottled variety will not do; real barrel molasses is a necessity. In any case, ¾ cup of baking molasses is mixed with a well-beaten egg yolk and ¾ cup of boiling water in which 2 teaspoons of baking soda have been dissolved. In another bowl, ¾ cup of flour is sifted with ½ cup of brown sugar; 1/8 teaspoon each of nutmeg, ginger and cloves; ½ teaspoon of cinnamon and ¼ teaspoon of salt, and worked into 2 tablespoons of shortening to form crumbs. A pie dish is lined with pastry, and alternate layers of the liquid and the crumb mixture are added, topping with the latter. It is baked at 450 degrees until the edges are brown, then the oven is reduced to 350 degrees, and the shoofly is baked until firm. For a "wetter" shoofly—one with a stickier bottom—more molasses is added.*

Also characteristically Pennsylvania Dutch are milk pies. As the name implies, milk or buttermilk is poured into a crust, a bit of sugar and butter are added with 2 teaspoonfuls of flour and a dash of cinnamon and nutmeg, and the whole baked in a hot oven. All laws of cookery would indicate that the only result would be an inedible mess and an oven in need of immediate cleaning, but strangely enough a delicate custard emerges.

KUGEL
(Potato Casserole)

10 medium potatoes
1 small onion
1 teaspoon salt

Generous amount of garlic powder
¼ cup flour
2 tablespoons chicken fat

Chop potatoes and onions in blender. (Do one or two potatoes at a time, adding a little water each time. Then strain all.) Add all remaining ingredients: place in casserole and dot mixture with chicken fat. Bake, uncovered, for 1 hour at 400°. Cover casserole and bake a second hour at 350°. Serves 6.

Jennifer Gould, *Brighton, Massachusetts*

CHICKEN AND PORK MECHADA
(Philippine)

1 young chicken
  cut into regular pieces
1 pound lean pork, cubed
1 onion, diced
½ cup shortening
Salt and pepper
1 (15½-ounce) can tomato sauce

1 (8-ounce) can tomato paste
3 potatoes, quartered
3 carrots, quartered
½ red pepper, sliced
½ green pepper, sliced
1 can sweet peas
Rice

Sauté chicken, pork and onions in shortening in 6-quart Dutch oven. Season with salt and pepper. Add tomato sauce and tomato paste. Simmer for 10 minutes. Add potatoes, carrots and red and green peppers, and cook for 30 minutes or until meat is tender. Add sweet peas and simmer another 5 minutes. Serve with boiled rice, if desired. Serves 6.

Remy J. Garcia, *Peru, Indiana*

CAMARON REBOSADO
(Philippine Fried Shrimp)

1 pound shrimp
1 tablespoon salt
2 eggs
3 tablespoons flour

1 tablespoon cornstarch
1 teaspoon baking powder
Fat for frying

Sprinkle shrimp with salt and let stand for 1 hour. Beat eggs; add flour, cornstarch and baking powder. Mix thoroughly. Dip shrimp one at a time into batter and fry in deep fat.

Carmen Wilhelm, *Centreville, Virginia*

AUTHENTIC SPANISH BEAN SOUP

¾ pound garbanzos (chick-peas)
1 teaspoon salt
  (for soaking garbanzos)
1 beef bone
1 ham bone
1½ quarts water

4 ounces whole bacon
1 onion
½ pound potatoes
1 pinch saffron
1 tablespoon salt
1 chorizo (Spanish sausage)

Soak garbanzos overnight with one teaspoon salt in water to cover. Before cooking, drain salted water and put garbanzos, beef bone and ham bone in 1½ quarts water. Cook 45 minutes over slow fire. Fry bacon and finely chopped onion. Place in pan, adding potatoes, saffron and salt. When potatoes are almost done, add chorizo cut in thin slices. Simmer 20 to 25 minutes. Serves 6.

Shirley Martin, *Tampa, Florida*

LATVIAN MIDSUMMER CHEESE

½ gallon fresh milk
5 pounds dry cottage cheese
1 stick butter or margarine

4 eggs
1 teaspoon salt
2 tablespoons caraway seeds

In a large kettle pour milk. Add dry cottage cheese and stir until it begins to boil. Turn off heat. Place cheesecloth in a large bowl. Add the boiled mixture. Take the corners of the cheesecloth to the top, let the liquid drip out, then squeeze cheesecloth as dry as possible. Place dry cheese in a bowl with the butter or margarine, eggs, salt and caraway seeds. With wooden spoon stir until it is well mixed and the cheese is solid in one piece.

Irma Henkels, *Indianapolis, Indiana*

SERINA KAKER
(Norwegian Cookie)

1¾ sticks butter or margarine
1 1/8 cups sugar
2 eggs, separated
2¼ cups flour, sifted

1½ teaspoons baking powder
1 teaspoon vanilla
50 almonds, chopped

Cream butter and sugar. Add 2 egg yolks and one egg white and mix well. Sift flour and baking powder together and add to batter. Add vanilla and form small round balls about one inch in diameter. Place on lightly greased cookie sheet and press down with bottom of glass. Brush with other egg white and sprinkle with almonds. Bake in 350° oven until very light golden. Do not let brown. Yield: 4 dozen.

Mrs. William Wesely, *Wayne, New Jersey*

HUNGARIAN KALACS

2 fresh yeast cakes
1 cup lukewarm water
4 tablespoons sugar
½ cup butter, melted

4½ cups flour
2 egg yolks
1 teaspoon salt

Filling:

½ cup milk
1½ pounds ground walnuts
½ cup sugar

1 tablespoon butter
1 teaspoon lemon juice

Crumble yeast and add water and sugar. Let stand 5 minutes. Mix melted butter and flour as for pie crust. Make a well and add egg yolks, salt and yeast mixture. Stir until smooth and dough leaves sides of bowl. Divide into 4 pieces and roll out as thin as possible; spread with filling. Place on greased pan and brush with egg white, very gently. Let stand in warm place for 1 hour. Bake at 350° for 30 minutes or until light brown. Cover with damp cloth as soon as it comes from the oven. Keep covered about 10 minutes to make a nice crust.

Directions for filling: Heat milk; add walnuts and stir. Add sugar, butter and lemon juice. Cool before spreading on dough.

Helen Horvath, *Fort Lauderdale, Florida*

"I'm afraid that's going to break the spell."